Leadership Development

Leadership Development

A Guide for HR and Training Professionals

Rosemary Ryan

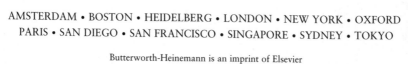

AMSTERDAM • BOSTON • HEIDELBERG • LONDON • NEW YORK • OXFORD
PARIS • SAN DIEGO • SAN FRANCISCO • SINGAPORE • SYDNEY • TOKYO

Butterworth-Heinemann is an imprint of Elsevier

Butterworth-Heinemann is an imprint of Elsevier
Linacre House, Jordan Hill, Oxford OX2 8DP, UK
30 Corporate Drive, Suite 400, Burlington, MA 01803, USA

First edition 2008

Notice
No responsibility is assumed by the publisher for any injury and/or damage to persons
or property as a matter of products liability, negligence or otherwise, or from any use or
operation of any methods, products, instructions or ideas contained in the material
herein.

British Library Cataloguing in Publication Data
A catalogue record for this book is available from the British Library

Library of Congress Cataloging-in-Publication Data
A catalog record for this book is available from the Library of Congress

ISBN: 978-0-7506-8193-3

For information on all Butterworth-Heinemann publications
visit our web site at books.elsevier.com

Printed and bound in Hungary
07 08 09 10   10 9 8 7 6 5 4 3 2 1

Contents

List of Figures

List of Tables

Acknowledgements

I would like to thank a number of people for their support during the writing of this book.

Firstly, I would like to thank the companies and individuals with whom I have worked over the years, for giving me the opportunity to see different cultures and working environments at first hand. They have provided the experiences that have created the content of this book. Particular thanks to the individuals who contributed to the interviews for this publication.

I would like to thank Robert Adam, my business partner at Represent Limited, for his unfailing support and willingness to work with me, making our work both fun and meaningful.

I would like to thank Frank Dick OBE for his inspiring belief that we can achieve whatever we set out to do in life. I thank him for introducing me to the world of coaching and for his great views on life in general.

Particular appreciation goes to my brother Neil for his hours of editing and supportive feedback throughout the writing of this book.

Above all, I would like to thank my husband Chris, Sean and Charlotte for their willingness to try out endless leadership development exercises and their encouragement for this latest project. Without them, none of this would be worthwhile.

This book is dedicated to my parents Pamela and John for everything they taught me.

Rosemary KC Ryan
www.represent.co.uk

Introduction

This book is designed to be a practical guide to Leadership Development. It describes the characteristics of effective leadership. It explains the different skills that are needed by leaders at different levels. The book provides tips and techniques for leadership development specialists to enable them to fully understand and carry out their roles and responsibilities. It provides guidelines for developing coaching, training and consulting skills. Most importantly, there are a number of reflection points to test and challenge your current working practice.

This book is based on my personal experiences of working with teams and individuals in many different walks of life. The guidelines and techniques outlined are purely my personal view of what constitutes best practice. I hope this guide supports you in your own personal development and gives you new ideas for the development of leaders in your company.

Many current business publications focus either on a complex succession of leadership models or purely on top line leadership development strategy. It is all too easy to keep these two subjects separate, and it is rare to find a book that brings both these themes together. We will draw together some of the most useful thinking on leadership and link it to practical strategies for developing these skills in our leaders and managers. We will address the question of how to develop leaders within different types of organizations. We will examine the factors that influence leadership in different organizations and we will outline different approaches to leadership development that can apply within organizations.

Many companies continue to deliver leadership development activities that are neither innovative nor helpful in developing leaders for the future. The challenge in the arena of learning and development is to create an innovative and effective approach to developing leaders for the next generation.

Effective leadership does not come naturally to many people. Despite the numerous books on the subject, there seems to be a lack of translation from concept to reality. There is a tacit belief that once a person is given the title of 'Manager' or 'Leader', the individual will magically transform into a role model of best practice. As we know, this is frequently not the case.

Many who work in the field of leadership development will have seen the effects of this belief. People are promoted, because they are good at doing their job, into a role where they have had little or no training. They are then expected to act as leaders, developing and coaching their teams to achieve constantly changing expectations. Often there is then a dip in their motivation as they realize the difficulties and challenges of creating high performance all around them. This leads to a lack of achievement, less confidence and the start of a downward spiral of performance.

This book will pull together the various facets that learning and development managers need to address if they are to provide practical leadership development, which enables leaders to focus on their three responsibilities of:

(a) achieving their personal objectives,

(b) developing their people to deliver great performance,

(c) creating the environment for others to succeed.

We shall look at four main areas:

(1) What good leadership looks like in practice in different types of organizations?

(2) Tips and techniques for introducing a variety of leadership development activities.

(3) The role of HR and learning and development managers in creating and implementing leadership development activities that work for their organization.

(4) The skills and attributes required by HR and learning and development managers to deliver their role effectively.

We shall also assess the views of leaders from a variety of organizations to look at the different approaches to leadership development across diverse business sectors.

Throughout the chapters there will be different checklists to assist you in using the ideas and techniques in a practical way that fit with the needs of your company.

We shall use case studies from different companies to show the various approaches that can be taken. There is no one right approach. It depends on where your organization's strengths are in terms of leadership aptitude and the challenges that are faced.

1 What is effective leadership?

This chapter looks at the following topics:

The difference between leadership and management

Different leadership styles

The leadership styles

Entrepreneurial leaders

Multi-cultural leadership

Different levels of leaders

Management is doing things right; leadership is doing the right things.
                                                    – Peter F. Drucker

The difference between leadership and management

Many current textbooks deal with leadership as though there is one set of defining characteristics. Our experience, from interviewing leaders for this book, has shown that this is certainly not the case. The requirements of senior leaders and board-level executives are clearly different from the attributes required by the middle managers who are expected to implement the strategy that has been agreed by the Board. In addition, aspiring leaders such as graduate trainees need to demonstrate different traits and characteristics. All these groups need to demonstrate leadership competence but at different levels and in different ways. There is no single recipe for leadership.

However, let us start by making the distinction between leadership and management, if only to ensure that we are using a shared language throughout the rest of this book.

The model shown in Table 1.1 is adapted from the model by John Kotter of Harvard Business School in his article 'What leaders really do' written for *Harvard Business Review* in 1990. Taking the main headings from the Kotter model, the main differences have been detailed in the following context.

Direction – vision and strategic thinking

Leaders need to have far-sightedness, the ability to look far into the future with regard to their company, team or department. They need to have external antennae, assessing the market changes, environmental forces and competitor activities.

Table 1.1 Model of leadership versus management

	Management	Leadership
Direction	Planning and budgeting	Creating a vision and strategy
	Keeping an eye on the bottom line	Keeping an eye on the horizon
Alignment	Organizing and staffing	Creating shared culture and values
	Directing and controlling	Helping others grow
	Creating boundaries	Reduce boundaries
Relationships	Focus on task – produce/sell goods and services	Focus on people – inspiring and motivating followers
	Based on a position of power	Based on personal power
	Acting as boss	Acting as coach, facilitator, persuader
Personal qualities	Organizational skills	Strategic view
	Problem solving	Open mind
	Telling	Asking
	Conformity	Innovation
Outcomes	Maintains stability	Creates change, often radical change

Even more challenging than simply having far-sightedness, they need 'double vision' – the ability to look into the future and at the day-to-day situation at the same time. They need to be looking at the future, with one eye on the current position and be able mentally to conduct a constant gap analysis of the situation.

Leaders need to be able to define this vision in a way that people can buy into and want to follow. This is a competence in itself. Many leaders have a much focussed vision, but seem to have overlooked the fact regarding people's need to share it. One law firm conducted a staff survey on a yearly basis where they asked people as to how clearly they understood the vision of the firm. Only 20 per cent of the people agreed that there was a clearly communicated vision. Not surprisingly, there was also a lack of focus on achieving the targets and financial goals of the firm. This was simply because most people did not even have this on their radar screen. They were very clear about the need to provide excellent client service and to develop their professional expertise, but when they were asked what the strategy was for the next three years, there was a distinct lack of clarity. This simple example shows the value of effective direction. Leadership time spent on communication has clear financial benefits. How much time do your leaders spend on communication of strategy? This does not mean the once-a-year conference; it means how much time is spent on a monthly and weekly basis.

While leaders need to focus on vision and strategy, managers are more concerned with implementing the vision and strategy, and translating them into tangible plans and projects. They need clear organizational skills, planning skills and the ability to take limited resource and make it go further – a challenging requirement at any time.

They are required to achieve short-term goals, but efficiently and quickly. Their focus is more on the day-to-day objectives and one of the greatest challenges when developing leaders is exactly this. They are not used to thinking broadly, looking at the external market and seeing what is happening in the wider frame. They are purely focussed on delivering the short-term objectives, which ultimately achieve the overall business plan.

Alignment

Leaders need to be concerned with the overall alignment of vision, goals, values and culture. This means that they should be spending time on

- defining the company values
- creating a shared culture of behaviours
- creating an organization structure that fits in with the needs of the future
- identifying key skills and attributes required for the future

Managers should be

- working towards alignment within their own work teams
- communicating the values and should be making them a reality
- resourcing and recruiting people with the right skills for the future
- ensuring that people develop skills needed in their current job

Relationships

Leaders need to be highly influential, both externally and internally. One of the key differences in terms of relationship management is that senior leaders spend more time influencing and persuading others with whom they have no positional authority. They work with key stakeholders rather than with reporting teams and they need to have well-developed skills in this area.

Managers are more concerned with supporting and training their team members on a regular basis in order to achieve day-to-day objectives. Obviously, there will be differences depending on the levels of management and the size and/or culture of the organization.

Personal qualities

So, do leaders and managers need different interpersonal skills? Many of the personal skills are what bind the two groups together.

Many of the skills apply to both managers and leaders (see Figure 1.1). The interpersonal skills unite these two groups of behaviours. The difference between the behaviours of leaders and managers is in the context in which these skills are utilized. Effective leaders need to use some management skills and effective managers need to use some leadership skills.

However, one of the most significant issues is that managers and potential leaders are often not given the opportunity to put some of these leadership characteristics

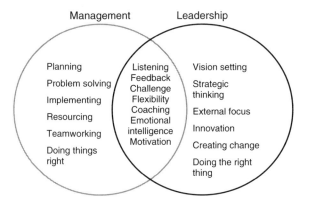

Figure 1.1 Personal skills

into practice. Not surprisingly, therefore, they do not get much practice and then find it difficult when they need to use these skills on a regular basis.

Outcomes

The key difference here is that leaders are focussed on creating change in order to meet the moving market conditions. Their focus is on advances and change. Manager's primary focus is on maintaining stability during these periods of change.

Reflection point

Consider the leadership and management activities you currently provide for your people.

How much focus do you set on leadership development?

How much focus is there on junior management development?

How much focus is there on professional and technical skills development?

How clear are your people in distinguishing leadership from management behaviours?

When did you last review the topics covered in your leadership development programmes?

What topics do you need to be covering more of/less of in light of the Kotter model?

In summary, owing to the difference in the skills required, one can start to see the need for different types of leadership development depending on the seniority of the individuals and also on the size and type of organisation in which they are employed.

So, what does a good leader look like in practice?

Many people think that effective leaders have great charisma. What do we mean by charisma? If it means the ability to persuade people that they want to follow you then charisma is important. It does not mean that the leader needs to be larger than life and twice as loud. Leaders need a set of skills that persuade people to want to work with them. Leaders set the emotional standard. They are watched and listened to more than other people and their behaviour has a higher influence on the behaviour of others. They need to be self-aware and aware of the needs of the people around them. Leadership is a 'contact sport'. Charismatic leaders have the ability to inspire people to want to raise their game and to perform better. They cannot do this by e-mail; they do it by human interaction and warmth and by the ability to listen and learn from others. They need to be coachable as well as coaches of others.

Charismatic leaders are responsible for creating an environment where others can perform to their best.

In practical terms, how do leaders go about this? One of the key responsibilities of leadership teams is to define a shared understanding of the culture required to meet the agreed vision. By culture, we mean 'the way things are done round here'. Leadership teams need to spend time debating what culture is required and how to communicate that desired culture to everyone within the company.

For a good leader – one with integrity and intelligence, charisma makes the whole job a lot easier. No matter the size of the team, leaders must energise their people. Leaders have to persuade their people to take them as leaders.
– Jack Welch

Case study

The Board of a successful construction company worked with us to help them develop their effectiveness as a leadership team. At the end of the workshop, they came up with a 'Code of Conduct' for how they wanted to be seen by their people. They effectively translated the concept of charisma into some specific behaviours and actions.

Code of Conduct:

(1) More effective delegation

(2) Celebrate achievement

(3) Challenge ideas more

(4) Demonstrate visible ownership of the business

(5) Improve profile of senior team

(6) Be more inspirational

(7) More innovative

(8) More personal leadership

At the end of the workshop, there was some debate about how to communicate this to the rest of the staff who would no doubt be wondering what their senior team had been doing for two days.

Rather than sending an e-mail to everyone, they decided to start practising these behaviours with each other and with their teams over the next four weeks. They agreed to review their behaviour against this code of conduct at the end of each meeting. They would then ask their people if they had seen a difference.

Four weeks later, they analysed the response. People had indeed seen a significant difference and, even more; the Directors realized that their people were starting to behave differently. They were more challenging on issues and seeing less personal criticism; decisions were being made without days of discussion and the whole pace of business was picking up. This simple example shows the power of leaders setting the climate for others to follow.

Six months later, the Board continued to review their progress against these behaviours and continued the work to develop the culture they wanted to achieve, using some simple behavioural measures as a temperature gauge.

Good leadership relies on leaders taking time out to review their personal effectiveness and style. Effective leadership teams make a conscious decision to behave in certain ways in order to create the culture they desire.

Different leadership styles

Great leaders demonstrate a range of behaviours and attributes that can be collectively known as leadership style. There is lot of research done on different leadership styles; in this chapter, we shall look into only some of the most recent researches on this subject.

Daniel Goleman, the author of *Emotional Intelligence*, conducted research on nearly 4000 executives to identify the effect of different leadership styles on the overall performance of a company. He identified six main styles that had an effect on financial returns.

The styles are as follows:

- Coercive – 'do what I tell you'
- Visionary – 'come with me'
- Affiliative – 'people come first'

- Democratic – 'what do you think'
- Pace setting – 'do it better and faster'
- Coaching – 'try this'

Four of the six styles were shown to have a positive effect on the climate for performance: visionary, affiliative, coaching and democratic. The coercive style had short-term benefits, and pace setting quickly resulted in people's motivation dipping and lower results being gained.

- Visionary – leader states the end game but gives people plenty of leeway to devise their own means
- Affiliative – develops relationships and encourages sharing
- Coaching – raises performance and develops people for the future
- Democratic – builds buy-in and consensus

Visionary style

The visionary style works on the basis of moving people towards a shared picture of success. Leaders with this style build allegiance with their people towards a shared dream and therefore inspire them to follow the journey to get there. Think of athletes who look forward four years to the next Olympics. Together with their coaches they live a shared dream of the gold medal and then work backwards to plan the training schedule. In a business context, this style works best when there is a need for a change of direction or when the business is starting off.

What do leaders do to demonstrate this style?

- Share their ideas for the future
- Think long-term and beyond the current problem-set
- Communicate at all levels to get buy in
- Eloquently articulate a vision that people can understand and want to buy into
- Tell stories to build a rich picture of what is needed
- Talk about future and not about past
- Act as a role model for how they would like others to behave
- Set the pace rather than allow the pace to be set

Examples of this style of leadership would include Richard Branson – How many other people could persuade people to buy a seat on a rocket into space at 200 000 dollars per ticket?

Coaching style

This style of leadership helps people to improve their performance by building their long-term capabilities. The coaching style focuses on people's skills and develops them to improve their performance on a day-by-day basis. It builds motivation by tapping into what the individual values are i.e. increased personal skill level while also building value for the organization.

There are many organizations in which this style is clearly observed and valued. These organizations are recognized for their skills in developing people and for revenue generation. Coaching style of leadership takes time but has lasting benefits.

What do leaders do to demonstrate this style?

- Listen to the needs of their people
- Work at the pace of the individuals being coached rather than impose their own pace
- Demonstrate active listening and empathy
- Ask tough questions to make the individual think for themselves
- Challenge people to do things differently
- Help people to set clear development goals
- Give frequent feedback
- Give regular praise and recognition

Affiliative style

The affiliative style builds motivation by creating harmony and by bringing people together in a collaborative way. Affiliative leaders value time with their people and are open about their own emotions. They put emphasis on personal relationships above task completion and strive to keep people happy and in harmony with each other. This style can have greater benefits in forging close teamwork; but when used alone can often fail to highlight weaknesses or poor performance. This style is used most effectively with the visionary style. People are clear on the shared goals and are valued for their individual contribution to a greater extent. Affiliative leaders build tremendous loyalty and are comfortable with giving praise and recognition. They believe that the people who feel good about themselves perform better. They need also to temper this with the other styles to ensure that they highlight issues when they arise and that they focus on honest conversations and developing even better performance.

Within a very successful skin care products company that was founded about 10 years ago, the two women founders shared a strong visionary style, constantly expanding the vision of what was possible. The successful factor was that one of the founders also had a highly developed affiliative style which made people want to do their best for her. She cared about the 200 or more employees, knew them all personally and spent time socializing with them. The company had monthly social events. During these events, all the employees were given samples of the new products and for every Christmas, a carol service and a party were conducted, boosting social morale. It may be asked, what impact this has on the bottom line? But when sales exceeded all targets and plans, during Christmas, one particular year, everyone turned out on their own to pack and wrap the products and ensured that they got out of the door in time.

What do leaders do to demonstrate this style?

- Give frequent praise and recognition
- Spend time on personal conversations
- Get to know what makes people tick
- Collaborate rather than compete
- Focus on the person rather than the task

Successful affiliative leaders mix this style with the other styles to ensure that they keep standards high and do not tolerate average performance.

Democratic style

Leaders with democratic style build commitment by participation and by valuing people input. They believe that everyone has a view and that it should be heard. They have high empathy and do not judge ideas too quickly. This style is useful when there is a need to create consensus among widely differing views. Democratic leaders are skilled at healing rifts in groups and at resolving conflict. This style is of high importance with many mergers and acquisitions when people are coming from very different starting points. Again, this style works well with visionary leadership, because, when people have a shared goal, they find it easier to agree.

This style is similar to partnerships in professional services and also small niche consultancies where people are working together with strong, shared beliefs and values. Characteristics of these knowledge-based companies include a lot of time spent on discussion and listening to different views. The disadvantage can be the amount of time it takes to get decisions made but there will be great buy in once the decision is made. This is obviously important in structures where all parties have an equal voice or ownership of the company. However, this style takes time owing to the amount of discussion and debate that is needed before actions are taken.

What do leaders do to demonstrate a democratic style?

- Listen
- Ask for others' views
- Mediate different views effectively
- Collaborate
- Influence skills
- Develop strong teamwork
- Allow themselves to be open to alternative suggestions

All of these four styles have been shown to have a positive effect on the climate for performance. Therefore, we need to focus on developing these specific competences in our leaders. Later in the book, we shall show how development programmes can integrate these different attributes and develop them in the most effective way.

These four styles are only a way of defining leadership styles. Another well-known concept of leadership styles was developed by Paul Hersey and Kenneth Blanchard in their book *Management of Organisational Behaviour*.

This model of leadership takes two axes – competence and commitment.

Competence is the level of skills possessed to do a particular task.

Commitment means the level of motivation for doing that task.

This leadership model works on the basis that you need to identify the leadership style based on the individuals' situation and tasks that need to be done.

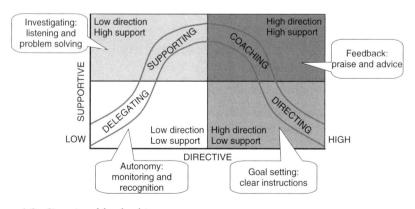

Figure 1.2 Situational leadership

For example, an IT manager may be required to fix a software problem for his manager. If he has the appropriate technical skills, he is likely to be in the delegation box – high competence and high commitment. If he was then asked to give a presentation to the Board on HR and resource allocation, he is more likely to have low competence and low commitment! The same person, but a very different situation.

The four basic leadership styles depends on the level of development of the individual and the task they are required to carry out (Figure 1.2).

- **Style 1: Directing** – The leader provides basic instructions and closely supervises the task. This style is for people who lack competence but are enthusiastic and committed. Often these people need direction and supervision just to get started.
- **Style 2: Coaching** – The leader continues to direct and closely supervises task accomplishment and also explains decisions, solicits suggestions and supports progress. This style is for people who have some competence but lack commitment. They need direction and supervision because they are relatively inexperienced. They also need support and praise to build their self-esteem and involvement in decision-making to restore their commitment.
- **Style 3: Supporting** – The leader facilitates and supports people's efforts towards task accomplishment and shares responsibility for decision-making. This style is for people who have competence but lack confidence or motivation. They do not need much direction because of their skills but support is necessary to bolster their confidence and motivation.
- **Style 4: Delegating** – The leader turns over responsibility for decision-making and problem-solving to his/her people. This style is for people who have both competence and commitment. They are able and willing to work on a project by themselves with little supervision or support.

If someone has low commitment and low competence they require a directive style of leadership.

If someone has high commitment but a low level of competence they require a coaching style of leadership.

If someone has low commitment and high competence they require a supportive style of leadership.

If someone has high commitment and high competence they require a delegating style of leadership.

The leadership styles

In summary, there are four major styles (Table 1.2) which may be used according to the person and the task.

So, leaders need to be flexible in their approach. They need to adjust their style to the needs of the individual and the different situations they find themselves in. Many leaders find one style they are comfortable with and then stick to it. They work from a default style and fail to adapt to the needs of the individual and the situation. Effective leaders flex their style and work in different ways according to the situation.

11

Table 1.2 Situational leadership

	The style	Appropriate situation
Directing	• Specific instructions • Close supervision	• When quick decisions needed • For inexperienced people
Coaching	• Provide encouragement • Ask for questions • Praise progress • Leader still makes final decision	• For people who are beginning to grow in confidence • If enthusiasm is waning
Supporting	• Less supervision • Ask opinions • Involve them in decision making • Staff carry out decisions they agree with	• More competent people • For those who have something to offer and want to contribute
Delegating	• Give them freedom to plan their work • Allow them to take decisions on their own • Give occasional feedback	• For top performers • For those ready to be self-sufficient

What are the benefits of finding a style that suits and sticking with it?

• Leader feels comfortable

• People know what to expect from the leader

• It sometimes works very well

• It comes naturally and therefore takes little time

The disadvantages

• It will only work with some people and some situations.

• The leaders will not get the best out of all the people

• Some people will become very de-motivated

• The leader will not develop

• The team will not develop

• Performance will suffer

• The business will not gain the best solution

Much of the work of learning and development managers is concerned with persuading people of the need to change their management style. Until they see the benefits of changing their approach, there will be little incentive to do so.

So, how do you persuade people of the need to change their leadership style?

• Give them verbal feedback on the effect their leadership behaviour has on you as an outside party.

• Provide a 360 feedback profile for them

- Ask what impact they think their style has on others
- Expose them to different individuals with a very different style and ask for their views
- Engage them in discussion about the different leadership approaches they could use to approach a situation they need to address
- Ask them to complete a leadership style questionnaire and review the findings with them

In addition to particular leadership styles, there are some core attributes that differentiate good leaders from the merely average.

Key attributes of a leader

T – Trust

R – Resilience

E – Positive energy

E – Empathy

Trust

Being trustworthy is without doubt the most important attribute that a leader needs. Leadership only happens when there are followers. You cannot be a leader if no one wants to follow you. Trust is a key requirement for this to happen.

> *Reflection point*
>
> Think of someone at work, whom you trust. What do they do that makes you trust them? Write them down.
>
>
> If they were filling in this detail, what characteristics would they list about you? Write them down.

Typical responses to this question are as follows:

- Being reliable
- Doing what they say they will do
- Being honest with me
- Being on the same side
- Putting my interests first
- Challenging me
- Shared values
- Good values
- Fair
- Consistent
- Support

Very simply, leaders need to engender trust with all those they come into contact with.

Resilience

It is the ability to keep going when the going gets tough. It is the ability to not give up when life seems hard. This attribute is based on having sufficient self-esteem not to take things personally when a decision turns against them. When the environment is hard, individuals need their leader to keep up the momentum and maintain the pace of effort in order to turn things round. The best leaders are those individuals who have extreme levels of patience and persistence. They are the first to come up with new ideas, to look on the positive side and to encourage others to keep going. They put time into raising the motivation of others rather than thinking about their own personal feelings. For them failure is not falling off the bike; it is not getting back on. These people do not enjoy the mistakes they make in life, but they do learn from them. They do not accept 'no' for an answer, they will find another way to meet their goals. This takes time and enormous personal effort which leads us to the next core attribute.

Energy

I have worked with some leaders who have high energy but mainly of the negative kind. These leaders complain about the market, criticize their competitors and take out their frustration on others. They are the 'half empty' brigade of leaders who feel they have the weight of the world on their shoulders. We are talking about leaders who have positive energy which creates a positive environment for those around them.

Energy is contagious. Leaders set the standard of behaviour wherever they are. In order to create a climate for success, they need to engender an atmosphere of high energy in order to achieve results. Think about many of the world's political leaders such as Tony Blair and Bill Clinton. Whatever our political views are, we cannot fault their ceaseless energy to follow their cause over years of constant pressures, set backs and energy sapping opposition. Similarly, Late Mo Mowlem, and others, who worked in Northern Ireland for over 10 years to negotiate and achieve a lasting peace. In sport, we see huge passion and energy expounded every weekend as schools, local and national football teams follow their dreams of success at whatever level they can aspire. They do not give up because they lose a match. If only business leaders demonstrated as much energy over their game of business as we see in sport, we would see a significant increase in performance.

Business leaders at every level need to show this positive energy. It is not enough to rely on the senior leaders to do this; leaders at every level will distinguish themselves by showing a passion and energy for what they are aiming to achieve.

Empathy

We said earlier that a leader needs followers. I have met some leaders who could be described as highly energetic with strong levels of resilience but without empathy; they fail to gain followership. Empathy means the capacity to see things from the other person's point of view. Empathy means being able to stand in other person's shoes and view their map of the world rather than your own. Empathetic leaders spend more time listening than talking, more time asking questions and more time engaging in relationship rather than task. In terms of Daniel Goldman's leadership styles, they use an affiliative and coaching style of leadership.

Reflection point

Which leaders in your organization demonstrate TREE strengths of Trust, Resilience, Energy and Empathy?

What benefits does the team/business gain from these attributes?

How would you rate yourself on these attributes?

T

R

E

E

What could you do to develop each of these attributes further?

We have spoken about characteristics of leadership, but what about the characteristics of good followership? Good leaders know when to stand on centre stage and when to move aside to let others to take the lead. Richard Branson is renowned for surrounding himself with strong teams. He recruits people who have skills and strengths that are both different and complimentary to his own. Branson knows when to trust his own judgement but is also a good follower of others when needed.

Good leaders benefit hugely from good followers. Think of a football team who all know the positions they each play and have a synergy from using each other to their best advantage. Perhaps, followership is a less popular concept now in the times of rapid turnover and change, more contract workers and consultants, and a growing sense of individualism within organizations. The concept of loyalty has been turned around by external competitive pressures with a resulting lessening of long-term loyalty from company to individual and vice versa.

Entrepreneurial leaders

Herb Kelleher, CEO of the fourth largest airline in the USA, is often referred to as one of the most adored entrepreneurs in the USA. Kelleher is renowned for his ability to run a highly successful business with an almost eccentric sense of fun. Under his leadership, the airline won many awards and had continuous profit for 29 years in spite of a worldwide industry slump. So what was the secret of his leadership style?

On many occasions, he flew on his own plane to find out what the experience was like for his customers. Remember TREE – the need for empathy. He had a passion for customer service and asked them how to improve the service. He also listened to his own people and consulted them in order to find out the best ways forward. He recognized when he could learn from others and went out of his way to gain their involvement and buy in. When he realized that some of his mechanics on late night shift could not attend a company BBQ, he organized a 2.00 am BBQ for them with himself and some of the senior staff acting as chefs.

In addition to his astute strategic ability, Kelleher also demonstrated high emotional intelligence and a resonance with the people who worked with him. He applied his positive energy and resilience to constantly looking for new avenues of revenue, changing the way the airline service worked, and always looking into the future rather than back to the past.

There are many books outlining the attributes of entrepreneurial leaders but I particularly like the extract below from *Kick Start Your Business* by Robert Craven.

Figure 1.3   The entrepreneur as surfer

Entrepreneurs have the same skills as really good surfers (Figure 1.3).

- *Be obsessive* – Go far from the beach and look for the really big waves.

- *Surfers look after their own fitness and equipment* – Look relaxed but do your homework – always be prepared for trouble.

- *Surfers are always looking for the next wave* – Scour ahead, read the currents, underflows, and tides of the beach, respond to minute changes and read the environment.

- *Good surfers catch the waves that other surfers miss* – They see opportunities where others see none. They act on those moments of opportunity.

- *Success and failure go hand in hand* – It takes practice to ride the big waves – start on the nursery beaches and then keep moving up – be willing to take the risk!

- *Good surfers make it look easy* – The more you practice, the easier it looks.

- *Fallbacks are a reality even for the best* – Harness your skills to capitalize on even the shortest of waves – the environment is not smooth so invest energy in being ready to fight another day.

- *Relative power* – Like most growing businesses, the surfer lacks power relative to the waves – use the power of the current to your own advantage – find out where the power lies and ride with it.

- *Flexibility and responsiveness* – The surfer taps hidden depths of physical and mental ability – you need to be able to react to whatever the climate throws at you – keep moving in order to ride the wave!

Source: Robert Craven, *Kick Start Your Business*, Virgin Business Press.

The people who are crazy enough to think they can change the world are the ones who do.

– Steve Jobs, CEO of Apple

Multi-cultural leadership

Now, there is a well-documented body of research that shows that the norms of the way business is done and the assumptions people make about how to work together do vary from one nation to another. This goes beyond simple national stereotypes and shows that the way we try to resolve the universal dilemmas of say balancing individual and group accountability will vary. In the UK (and more so in the USA), it is seen as 'right' for an individual to be held responsible for his/her own mistakes – whereas in Italy it is more likely that the workgroup would be expected to take responsibility. This simple example can still trip up many trans-national plans.

Geert Hosted who first looked at cultural differences across a sample of IBM employees some 25 years ago and identified a model of cultural difference did the pioneering work in this area. More recently, Fons Trompenaars and Charles Hampton Turner have developed a model based on a survey of 50 000 managers from 100 countries. They looked at national culture as expressed by the common assumptions that people use to help solve problems and they have analysed the data against seven cultural dimensions.

Based on Hofstede's work, there are five dimensions of cultural difference. They are:

(1) **Power distance (PD):** The attitude to hierarchy in the organization. A high power distance implies a high respect for hierarchy. Managers will appear more remote from staff than in cultures with a low power distance.

(2) **Uncertainty avoidance (UA):** The attitude to the predictability of the future. A culture with a high uncertainty avoidance rating has belief that the future

18

is predictable and controllable and so places a high reliance on plans and standards. A culture with a low UA rating looks on the future as a river with many twists and turns, and the job of the manager is to steer the best course, avoiding the rapids as they appear.

(3) **Individual–Collective (IC):** The balance between individual rights and freedoms and the loyalty and support of the group. An individualist culture believes in the primacy of the individual, whereas a collectivist culture puts responsibility to the group at the forefront.

(4) **Neutral–Emotional (NE):** The degree to which expressing emotion in business interactions is desirable or acceptable. This is sometimes described as a masculine or feminine culture, but my evidence is that differences in attitudes to emotion transcend the sexes.

(5) **Universalist–Particularist (UP)** The balance between a belief in the rule of absolute and universal truths and the need to take account of the context of a specific situation. A universalist culture will tend to believe that somewhere there is a 'scientific' or 'universal' answer to a business problem. A particularist will look first at the particular circumstances in front of them at that time.

As an example, Table 1.3 illustrates the differences between a head office USA and its Italian subsidiary.

So, if company with its head office at USA and operations in the UK, Sweden and Italy wanted to improve its sales strategy and performance throughout Europe, then the head office might suggest introducing a performance management system; negotiating with all sales managers to set tough objectives and sales targets with high individual bonuses if they are achieved.

This fits with the culture in USA, i.e. low power distance allows a sales manager to negotiate freely and openly with their boss, high uncertainty avoidance means a belief that the future sales plans are within the manager's control. The individualist and neutral combination means that individual bonuses would be an expected way of rewarding hitting the target. And of course the USA being a universalist culture means that it is likely that the head office will think that this approach is founded on 'scientific principles' and so will be applicable throughout the world.

However, this approach is less likely to fit in Italy. A high power distance makes it more difficult for sales mangers to negotiate on equal terms with their boss, low uncertainty avoidance implies a belief that the hitting of sales targets may have more to do with reacting to changes in external market factors than in new strategies and plans. If by chance a change in the market meant that one sales manager dramatically overachieved his/her target, then a collectivist and

Table 1.3 Difference in cultural leadership

	PD	UA	IC	NE	UP
USA	Low	High	Individualist	Neutral	Universalist
Italy	High	Low	Collectivist	Emotional	Particularist

19

emotional culture may see a bonus paid to an individual as both divisive and cold. And, of course, Italy being a particularist culture, they would expect their senior managers to understand why 'things are different here' and American methods do not work!

Leadership across national borders means dealing with such problems every day. Experimental data such as that produced by Trompenaars and others give a means of at least analysing the problem and also give some insights as to where the issues are likely to arise. Leaders of multi-cultural teams need to take these differences into account as much as they take into account the individual personality difference and individual capability.

Source: David Archer of Socia Ltd

Different levels of leaders

Not all leaders need the same skills. When we are invited into organizations, the client often talks about leadership development as if it was one group of individuals. In addition to personality type and cultural types, there is also a difference depending on the level of leaders within the company. The following categorization is over simplistic but can provide a means of separating the different levels of leader within a company.

(1) Potential leaders
(2) Middle managers
(3) Senior leaders

We expect different behaviours from these different groups and therefore the development programmes and approach need to be significantly different.

Potential leaders

This group includes graduate trainees or young, high-potential individuals in the first few years of their business experience. At this stage, we want to see the attributes of the keen, enquiring mind, ready to learn like a sponge and able to pick up on the experience of others. These individuals need to be actively seeking out development opportunities for themselves and taking the initiative to become involved in projects and new experiences. They need to be able to ask for help, ask for answers and not pretend that they know everything. Their greatest skill is humility and the ability to build up relationships quickly so people want to help and coach them to improve. These individuals have little to give in terms of experience but lots to give in terms of quick thinking, analytical judgement and a fresh approach to old business problems. Their interpersonal skills need to be of top quality as their technical skills are still developing.

Middle managers

These people have the toughest job of all. They are expected to be good managers but also demonstrate some of the leadership skills that we looked at earlier.

They also have the added difficulty of being in the middle of the leadership ladder, having to manage the expectations of their teams and also the expectations of the senior leaders. They need to constantly demonstrate the skills of double vision – keeping an eye on the day-to-day while also keeping an eye on the future. We expect these individuals to be able to plan and manage the day-to-day operational issues and also start to develop their strategic thinking and market awareness. We need them to be able to work effectively in their peer group teams, build and develop their own teams and also work effectively across different teams and departments within the company as a whole. They are also expected to be excellent client managers and develop good customer relationships! Not surprisingly, this group of managers tends to need the greatest support and development and yet have the least time to dedicate to it.

Senior leaders

Our experience of working with senior leaders is that they have often been promoted due to their technical competence, and their challenge is to delegate the day-to-day requirements to their teams. This should free them to focus on the issues of strategy and direction, communication, developing a performance culture and creating innovation and change. However, these people are often very comfortable doing the technical aspects of their job and do not relish giving this up to their teams. This may be because they like the technical aspects of their role or it may be because they do not feel confident to take on the new challenges of leadership that face them at this stage.

Additionally, these people tend not to feel so comfortable sharing their weaknesses with others in a group setting, as it is expected that they should have all the required skills by this stage. This is a common trap that organizations fall into. They recognize that their new and potential leaders need development. They actively look to develop their middle managers and then it stops. As the sponsors of training and development programmes within their company, they often feel uncomfortable acknowledging that they also need development in some of these areas. It is also a difficult situation for the Head of Development and Learning to tell his/her manager that they may benefit from such programmes. However, if they are to act as role models within the organization, they need to demonstrate their willingness to learn and change their own behaviour.

Reflection point

How much resource/budget/time is given to development of:

Potential leaders

Middle managers

Senior leaders

Is this the right balance?

How committed are your senior leaders to their own development?

What can you do to address the need for senior leaders to engage further in their own development?

How much time do your leaders spend on management versus leadership?

Is this the right balance at the different levels?

How do your leaders know they are doing a good job?

Leadership is the art of getting someone else to do something you want done because they want to do it.

– Anon

2 Creating and communicating a leadership development strategy

This chapter will look at the following topics:

Why do we need a leadership development strategy?

Creating a management development vision

From vision to strategy

Communication of the strategy to the organization

The role of HR and development in strategy implementation

Key questions to address

Why do we need a leadership development strategy?

In order for any business to succeed, it is vital that the individuals have the capability to deliver the objectives of the business plan. The market and external environment are changing at an ever-faster rate. Customer expectations are increasing year by year. The fitness of any organization to meet these challenges is directly linked to the skills and capabilities of the people they employ.

Many organizations spend a considerable amount of money on development but have no clear means of assessing whether it is bringing the results they want. This is often because they have no clear idea of what is that they are aiming to achieve in terms of either skills, knowledge or attitude. Time spent on discussing the long-term vision for leadership development and linking it to the business strategy is fundamental if HR and learning and development teams are going to play a key role in delivering business success.

We are asked to go into many organizations who feel they need a leadership development strategy, but have no real clarity about how to create one. The approach we take is fundamentally very simple, but very effective, based on three key principles:

(1) Think to the future

(2) Involve all the stakeholders

(3) Keep it simple

Reflection point

Analyse the current approach to leadership development in your company.

(1) What are the top five leadership principles required for success in your business?

(2) What does the Chief Executive/Board think are the top five leadership principles required for success?

(3) What does a good leader look like now and in the future?

(4) What is the difference between the two and why?

(5) What is the succession plan for the top 20–200 individuals in the organization?

(6) What are the current skills gaps at management and leadership level?

(7) How do you import new ideas and approaches into the organization?

(8) How clear are managers/leaders and what is expected from them in terms of skills, knowledge and attitude?

(9) How robust is your performance review process and recruitment process?

(10) What will differentiate your organization from competitors over the next three–five years?

(11) How well does your current approach to development meet these needs?

(12) What gaps are there in the current approach to development?

(13) What would you like to see in the development strategy for the company that is currently missing?

These are some of the initial questions we ask when talking to companies who recognize the need for a cohesive approach to development. Do not underestimate the value of raising these questions as they often start to engage the key people in the discussions you need them to have.

Creating a management development vision

If you are to develop a management development strategy that people buy into, they need to understand where they are aiming to get to – this is the purpose of the vision.

The starting point has to be the business plan for the next 3–5 years. There is no point in developing specialized IT skills if the long-term plan is to outsource IT. Likewise, if the long-term plan is to extend customer-facing relationships, then the customer service is going to figure more strongly in your plans. If international expansion is a high priority, this will also have a significant effect on the development strategy in terms of development planning and succession planning.

Figure 2.1 gives a simple three-stage template for creating a workable strategy. The first stage is to conduct a strategic analysis of the company, then formulate a strategy that will meet the vision and takes into account the influencing factors. Thirdly, the strategy needs to be broken down into tactics and plans with associated measures.

Analytical review

The starting point for the strategy is to identify the external and internal factors that will influence the leadership requirements of the organization.

Two useful models for phase 1 are as follows:

(1) PESTLE analysis
(2) SWOT analysis

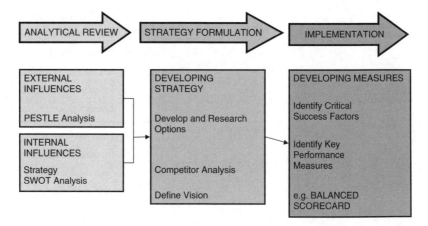

Figure 2.1 Strategy formulation model

PESTLE analysis

The PESTLE analysis is a simple way of examining all the external factors that may impact on the internal strategy of the company (Figure 2.2; Table 2.1). For example, the change in employment law in October 2007 regarding age discrimination influences the recruitment strategy. The change in immigration laws to include more countries in the EU has implications for resourcing and short-term labour.

Equally, changes in social mobility and lifestyle changes will impact on the degree to which people are prepared to move jobs across countries and take responsibilities for their own career development.

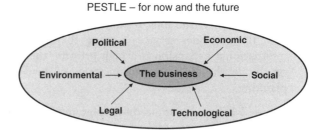

Figure 2.2   External influences

Table 2.1   PESTLE analysis

Political forces	• Government policy • Policy and influence • Lobby groups • Voting issues • Foreign trade regulations • Employment Law
Economic forces	• Business cycles • GNP trends • Interest rates • Money supply • Exchange rates • Inflation and unemployment • Energy price
Social forces	• Demographics • Income distribution • Social mobility • Lifestyle changes • Attitudes • Education level

Table 2.1 (Continued)

Technological forces	• Research spending • Focus of industry and government • New discoveries • Speed of technology transfer • Rates of obsolescence
Legal forces	• Changes in legislation • Changes in policing procedures
Environmental forces	• Environmental legislation • Greening of politics, consumers, etc. • Business environment • The 'feel good' factor

Complete a PESTLE analysis for your organization (Table 2.2), thinking about the different external influences which will impact on the organization in terms of leadership development.

Table 2.2 PESTLE template

Political forces	
Economic forces	
Social forces	
Technological forces	
Legal forces	
Environmental forces	

SWOT analysis

This is a simple way of looking at the internal strengths and weaknesses of the organization and then the external opportunities and threats which may affect it.

Again, complete the SWOT analysis (Table 2.3) for your organization and then identify the key factors that will influence the management development strategy for your organization.

This strategic analysis will highlight various factors that need to be taken into account when developing the key themes of your strategy.

We have seen organizations who wanted to take a short cut on this step, and not surprisingly, there is then less buy-in further down the journey, lack of willingness to find budget, and little take up of the development activities put in place. These are companies where HR and training teams are battling to get people to accept what they are doing. Equally, there are organizations that take this strategic analysis seriously and create strategies for leadership development that are both informed and linked to the demands of a changing external and internal environment.

Time spent on this diagnostic phase is important but cannot be done in isolation. The different views of people across the company are needed and the different stakeholders may well have different perceptions about effective leadership for the future looks like.

This diagnostic work can often take a fair time but the benefits are far reaching. In terms of numbers, we have worked with a High Street retail company of

Table 2.3 SWOT analysis

S Strengths	W Weaknesses
O Opportunities	T Threats

700 employees and included 100 people in either focus groups or one-to-one interviews. Many of the questions highlighted earlier can be used as a starting point for these one-to-one interviews or group discussions.

In a Building Society, of 1000 people, we saw 60 people at all levels of the organization from the Chief Executive to new graduates to gain their views on what skills and abilities they thought were required by leaders and managers over the next 3–5 years.

People-centred strategy

We often hear about top–down strategy or bottom–up strategy. Both these models assume that there is a source of expertise either at the top or at the bottom of the organization. The benefit of the approach taken above is that it takes different people with different views and exposes them to others in the organization. This results in a more emergent set of views that are built on different perspectives and different experiences. The resulting strategy is then a mix of different views, learning and reflection from within the organization and which reflects what is required for the future. Much of our learning around strategy formulation has centred on the importance of opening up discussion rather than over structuring the diagnostic phase. Free debate is a powerful way of discovering current cultural issues and identifying areas for change. This is not to say that there is no need for a process or a set of questions to start with. However, once the debate starts in the focus group or discussion, then the role of HR is to draw out the learning and challenge the breadth and depth of the discussion in order to distill the different views and thoughts.

This data then needs to be collated and drawn together into an overall view of the desired vision and blue print for what is required by the managers over the next 3–5 years. Generally, this vision is then defined and agreed by the senior managers and Board. It may take the form of a set of key definitions, key success criteria or a more-detailed set of behavioural competencies and behaviour definitions. Having a detailed multi-layer behavioural framework does not necessarily mean that you have a vision for people development in the company. A vision needs to have the following characteristics:

- Imaginable – conveys a picture of what the future will look like
- Desirable – appeals to the long-term interests of the employees, customers, shareholders and others who have a stake in the company
- Feasible – comprises realistic attainable goals
- Focussed – is clear enough to provide guidance in decision making
- Flexible – is general enough to allow alternative responses in the face of changing conditions
- Communicable – can be successfully communicated within five minutes

Source: John P Kotter, *Leading Change,* HBS Press.

Very often we start to compromise the vision before we have even defined it! Budgets, time and lack of resources, all conspire to make us think small. If we want to achieve a vision that meets the above characteristics, we need to go about it in a way that will give us the best chance of success.

One of the most powerful techniques for creating a vision is taken from the Neuro Linguistic Programming approach and is known as the Disney Visioning Technique. The Disney Corporation created such inspirational and spell-binding films such as Fantasia. Their creative approach was very structured and much focussed. They took their design teams through a three-stage process (Figure 2.3). Firstly, the design team put on a metaphorical 'dreamer' hat and spent time on brainstorming ideas and coming up with the ideal future picture.

The dreamer
Absolutely anything goes. No ideas are discounted or analysed at this stage. Individuals can be as wacky and creative as they like with no restrictions at this stage.

The realist
Once they have completely exhausted the story or ideas, then they are out of the 'realist' hat and start to sift through them, deciding if any are in any way realistic.

Could they be achieved? If not, is there a nugget of gold? The team agrees on what they are going to retain as a possible vision.

The critic
Only after the first two stages, the team are asked to put on the 'critics' hat and start to ask questions such as 'What about . . . What if . . . Have you thought about . . . ?'

What will the cynics say?

How much will it cost?

These questions are encouraged to challenge the vision and to ensure that it works in practice and is truly achievable. This is the final arbiter of whether a vision makes it through to the planning stage.

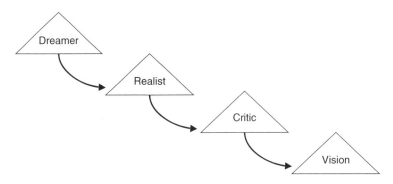

Figure 2.3 Disney strategy

We have been using this technique for many years with senior teams in strategy sessions. Explain the concept to everyone and then take the group through the three stages, giving enough time for each stage. Ask the group to create flipcharts at each stage and then the final stage is to agree what remains in the final strategy and plan.

From vision to strategy

The strategy is basically the journey you will take in order to reach your vision. Many HR departments claim to have a management development strategy but their managers have either never seen it or have no understanding of what it is. A clear strategy is one that:

- Should be capable of building wide involvement across the organization
- Should work from a vision of the future
- Should be capable of creating alignment between the business goals and what people actually do
- Should be action orientated and build on the inspiration and commitment of people

Source: Lynda Gratton, *Living Strategy*.

One company we worked with had a very clear vision and we worked with them to create a strategy to pull together the many different strands of development required at all levels.

The Specsavers Academy was launched in 2004 and pulls together the development pathways for senior leaders, middle managers and those aspiring to be managers. Importantly, it also pulls together the performance management process, recruitment practice and induction, all using a consistent set of behaviours and skill requirements.

Time was spent looking at what was already in place within the company. Various one day workshops were run to gain feedback on existing development programmes, the performance management process was in place and several senior managers already took advantage of one-to-one executive coaching. However, there was no overall plan and the different activities were often overlapping with each other with gaps in other areas. A day with the learning and development team highlighted these issues and together, a cohesive strategy was designed that met the needs of the company going forward. This strategy was the result of interviews with over a 100 staff at all levels, time spent with the HR team and analysis of current leadership development providers and policies and processes. This took about a two-month period but successfully gained buy-in from all levels of the organization. Directors, senior managers and team members had all been consulted on what was needed for the future strategy for the people development.

This was communicated in a simple visual to show the overall strategy for development and training for all staff within the company (Figure 2.4).

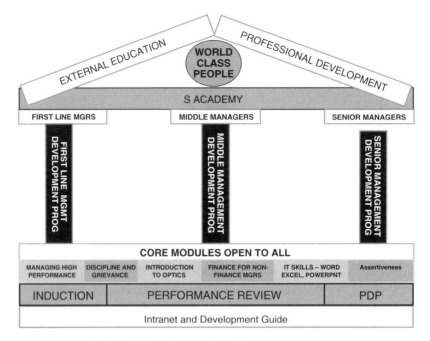

Figure 2.4 Example visual of learning and development strategy

What made this a successful strategy?

Firstly, the strategy was clearly defined and easy to remember – 'Developing world-class people.'

A visual portrayal of all the elements helped to anchor it in people's consciousness.

Secondly, a high proportion of people had been involved in the creation of the vision and strategy during the focus groups and interviews.

Thirdly, it was a cohesive strategy in which a consistent set of management and leadership behaviours were introduced as the backbone of the performance review process, the management development programmes and the one-to-one coaching that form part of the overall leadership strategy.

Obviously, each of the pillars of this strategy were broken down into detailed development programmes, customized induction programmes and tailored workshops for different groups of staff.

Communication of the strategy to the organization

Again, this will depend on the size and structure of the company. However, it is vital to plan the best way of communicating the overall picture or strategy to everyone, via the internal intranet, posters, team briefing and group briefings. Depending on the size of the HR and learning and development team, they may want to brief the different functions separately and work with them to identify what they need from the strategy in the short term and long term. This will involve assessing the development needs arising from the performance reviews, looking at any existing training needs analysis and most importantly, consulting with senior managers to agree how they can develop their people to achieve business success in the most effective way. Processes and templates are only part of the equation, the key value that the Development Manager brings is their ability to ask good questions, identify real needs and create flexible solutions that meet the needs of the individuals and the business.

The role of HR and development in strategy implementation

The strategy document is purely a road map for guiding actions and decisions along the way. Therefore, it does not need to be a 20-page manual or a 100-slide presentation. Its purpose is to guide the organization on how to develop their people to deliver the long-term business plan. The rules remain the same:

(1) Think to the future
(2) Involve all the stakeholders
(3) Keep it simple

In summary, the role of the learning and development team in the management development strategy can be seen as the following stages:

- Facilitating the creation of the vision
- Designing the strategy using data from diagnostic phase
- Gaining buy-in from the Board to the proposed strategy
- Communicating the strategy to the organization
- Implementing the plans to achieve the strategy
- Supporting managers in ongoing implementation

Key questions to address

(1) What is your current leadership development strategy?

(2) Who knows about it in the company?

(3) How does it influence development activity in the organization?

(4) What level of commitment do people have towards the strategy?

(5) How does it help you make decisions about resources and budget?

(6) How does it support the delivery of the business plan?

(7) How are you measuring progress and benefits?

(8) How well matched is your current leadership development strategy to the future business growth?

(9) What steps do you now need to take to improve your current leadership development strategy?

3   Team development

This chapter will look at the following topics:

Characteristics of effective teams

Step 1 – Understand that a team goes through a series of development stages to achieve high performance

Step 2 – Adapt your approach to their different stages of development

Step 3 – Creating a shared language for the roles that people prefer to play

Step 4 – Encourage diversity

Summary

Different working preferences

Learning points from this case study

The role of learning and development in team development

Key points

What makes an effective team-building event?

Design of the team intervention

Introduction exercises

Review of current team-working

Development of self-awareness

The role of learning and development managers in team building

A checklist of key questions for any team-building activity

Individual commitment to a group effort – that is what makes a team work, a company work, a society work, a civilization work.

– Vince Lombardi

Characteristics of effective teams

In this chapter, we will look at how to build and develop truly effective teams that can deliver results. Many of us inherit individuals who seem to work perfectly well in isolation, but fail to build a cohesive force for achieving results together.

Although our experiences may not be the same as just described, many of us see the necessary qualities in the individuals we manage, but still fail to bring out the best in them. Our challenge is to bring together the different skills, personalities and value sets to gain the momentum required to achieve greater performance from the team than we would gain from the same people working on their own.

There are many different types of teams and there is no single solution for all. However, there are some fundamental principles that will create the foundation for highly performing teams

The following list will provide a useful basis for any team discussion regarding team effectiveness.

- **A clear goal** – How clear are the team members on the overall vision and strategy for the team? Do they have a shared view on what is expected of them?
- **Clear measures of success** – Are the team members clear about what success looks like and how it should be measured? Are they individually and collectively measured based on results?
- **Shared commitment** – Do they all share an agreed commitment on what they are required to do?
- **Capable team members** – Do they have the appropriate skills and knowledge required to do the job?
- **Collaborative working** – How willing are people to help each other out and work with others to achieve a common goal?
- **Standards of excellence** – How do they set objectives and continually raise the standards?

Reflection point

Rate your team on a scale of 1 to 10 for each of the above criteria.

(1) What do they do well?

(2) What do they not do so well?

(3) What do they need to do differently, to improve their ratings on each criteria?

In order for teams to work effectively, the manager needs to pay attention to the following four steps:

Step 1: Understand that teams go through a lifecycle from forming to performing.

Step 2: Adapt the approach to meet the teams' needs at different stages of their development.

Step 3: Create a shared language to help the team understand what roles they would like to play and what roles they need to play in the team.

Step 4: Encourage different skills to flourish and recognize the benefit of diversity within the team.

Understanding the team's behaviour patterns and dynamics is essential if the team is to develop and perform. The skillful leader must do more than just focus on the task in hand; the leader needs to pay attention to the process of how the team is working and the feelings that are going on between individuals.

Figure 3.1 shows the different levels that operate in any team dynamics.

The 'content' is what the team is doing – its task.

The 'process' is how they are working together to achieve the task.

The 'relationships' are the emotions and interpersonal dynamics that affect the other two factors.

Many managers spend 90 per cent of their time on the task and forget the other two elements completely. Likewise, some managers feel that they are the counsellor of all and pay no attention to the process of getting the job done. The role of the manager is to pay attention to all three parts of the equation, as without any one component, the team can easily fall apart.

Content (i.e., the task)

Set clear objectives and parameters.

Clarify timescales and deliverables.

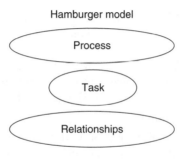

Figure 3.1 Process – task – relationships

Process

Agree on how the team will work together to achieve the task.

Allocate roles.

Agree on a plan.

Ensure that everyone is utilized to his or her best advantage.

Be flexible on changing the plan if the nature of the task changes.

Review progress and adapt if needed.

Relationships

Review on how people feel about working together.

Address any conflicts or issues.

Check out people's motivation levels.

Check whether everyone is included.

This process of process/task/feelings is a useful review mechanism for any team development you may be asked to undertake. This can either take the form of the group reviewing against each area themselves, or you may wish to give feedback on each of the three areas yourself.

In terms of setting some basic foundations for effective teams, let us consider the following steps.

Step 1 – Understand that a team goes through a series of development stages to achieve high performance

Twenty years ago, the psychologist Tuckman developed the ORMING principle, which demonstrated that teams go through a natural lifecycle. Leading teams involves understanding these different stages and taking time to allow the teams to go through the different phases, in order to achieve high performance at the end.

There are four main stages that a team will go through during its lifecycle (Figure 3.2).

1. **Forming**
   - Feelings not exposed or dealt with
   - No rocking the boat
   - Weaknesses covered up
   - Lack of clarity around expectations
   - Low involvement in planning and decision-making
   - Manager taking the lead and making most decisions
2. **Storming**
   - Experimentation with boundaries
   - More risky issues debated
   - Personal feelings raised

Stages in Team Development

Stage 4				Stage 1
	Mature closeness		*Testing/undeveloped*	
	Resourceful		Polite	
Performing	Flexible		Guarded	Forming
	Open		Watchful	
	Effective		Impersonal	
	Close and supportive			
	Getting organized/		*Infighting/experimenting*	
	consolidating		Controlling conflicts	
	Developing skills		Confronting people	
	Establishing procedures		Opting out	
Stage 3	Giving feedback		Difficulties	Stage 2
	Confronting issues		Feeling stuck	
Norming				Storming

Figure 3.2   Stages in team development

- More inward-looking
- Sometimes uncomfortable
- Establishing a pecking order
- Confrontation
- Disagreement

3. **Norming**
   - Agreed procedures
   - Clear expectations
   - Agreed ways of working
   - Established ground rules
   - Clear identities within the group
   - More systematic and intuitive

4. **Performing**
   - High flexibility
   - Maximum use of energy and ability
   - Needs of all members taken into account
   - Focus on development
   - Leadership shared depending on task
   - High achievement and delivery

So, what do you do to take your team through the different stages? In step 2, we will look at each of the four phases of team development.

Step 2 – Adapt your approach to their different stages of development

Forming – the undeveloped team

We have all joined a new team and experienced the feelings of discomfort and watchfulness while we wait to see how things work and how decisions will be made. At this stage, the team members will tend to be polite and courteous to each other, not wanting to share much personal information. They are looking very much to the leader to take control and manage the process.

- Demonstrate openness by example
- Encourage team members to discuss and share their views
- Listen to any individual's concerns and issues
- Provide solutions for any initial team problems
- Spend time as a group, both socially and informally
- Give maximum direction and support

Storming – the experimenting team

At this stage, people will start to find their own pecking order and the group will be looking to see who takes the lead and who follows. Disagreements may well occur as people start to feel more confident in their viewpoint and wish to assert themselves within the group. People will opt out if they feel that things are not going their way or that they will challenge the process and the approach being taken. Conflict and challenge are all part of the process of people getting to know each other well enough to work effectively later down the line. It is easy to try to cover up conflict and stop the disagreements that happen at this stage. However, it is only by allowing time for constructive disagreement and debate that people begin to understand the views of others and start to create some shared ways of working.

So, what do you do?

- Encourage greater openness between individuals
- Allow conflicts to surface rather than stopping them
- Involve the team in assessing their own performance
- Question decision-making and problem-solving methods being used
- Render high levels of support
- Encourage team members to air their issues with each other and come to their own solution

Norming – the consolidating team

By this point, the team will have created a clear role for themselves within the group and will be starting to agree to some formal or informal working norms. The distinct culture of the group will become more apparent and more focus will be on the task rather than on the process of how they work together. They are ready to start delivering the task…

So, what do you do?

- Clarify task objectives for the team and the individuals
- Regularly review performance and plan further improvements

- Develop the decision-making and problem-solving skills used by the team
- Encourage people to share their strengths and compensate for each other's weaknesses
- Celebrate successes
- Give moderate support

Performing – the mature team

By now, the team members are working at a high level of cohesion and they seem to know what part everyone plays. They may well be very defensive of each other against other teams and see themselves as the top of the bunch. They are delivering high-quality performance and seem to be needing your inputs less and less.

- They are clear about their objectives and stretch themselves.
- They define their job roles as needed without prompting.
- They continually build skills in questioning, listening and giving feedback.
- They support and trust each other.
- They confront issues face-to-face.
- They celebrate successful deadlines, key events and openly review mistakes and setbacks.
- They manage the entry and exit of colleagues easily.

So, what is your role now?

- Build bridges with other teams
- Allow leadership to change with the needs of the group
- Consider opportunities for further responsibilities
- Encourage informal communication
- Fight any insularity
- Expose team to external benchmarks and best practices
- Provide minimal direction and trust the team to perform independently
- Celebrate successes and show clear recognition for high performance

---

Reflection point

Think about the team that you are working with.

What stage of development have they reached? Forming/storming/norming/performing

---

What should you do to support them at this stage?

How do you begin to move them on to the next stage?

Step 3 – Creating a shared language for the roles that people prefer to play

Success can only be achieved when the team leaders and team members work together as one unit to achieve results. As the project manager or team leader, we have to develop the team to 'win the game'.

Using a sporting analogy, the game is the project or work function with its associated terms of reference. As the team leader or manager, our role is that of a coach and the team members are our team of world-class players. We may occasionally feel that they are more like the fourth division reserve team, but that is all part of the challenge.

The role of the manager is to coach the players through the game and ensure that they gain the best result possible.

Any successful relationship is dependent on the coach/manager establishing a relationship of trust in which the player is able to be honest in what he or she requires from that coach in order to achieve the highest potential. In addition, we all know that people are different and yet this seems to contradict the outdated management mantra 'I have to treat people the same to show that I am a fair manager'. The secret is in welcoming the diversity of players in our teams and exploiting those differences to the highest degree.

Earlier in this chapter, we looked at how teams develop over time with regard to how they work together. Obviously, their individual preferences will influence the roles they take on and this is where the use of team questionnaires is useful. There are many different personality and psychometric tests available in the market today.

Many successful organizations use the tried and tested Belbin Team-Type Questionnaire, designed by Meredith Belbin. This diagnostic instrument is easy to use and provides a great way of understanding the different roles played in the team.

The questionnaire is designed to highlight which roles people are most comfortable with in a team setting and which roles they should best avoid. According to the research of Meredith Belbin, all members of a team have two roles. Their first role is a functional role in terms of what they do, e.g. marketing or accountant or production engineer. The second role is much less obvious and yet equally valid. It is their role in terms of the process they use to achieve tasks and interact with other people in order to achieve the desired results. Meredith Belbin identified nine different temperament types in all as being the key to successful team working.

Briefly, the roles are tabulated in Table 3.1. So, how does knowing about your preferences for different team roles help create a better team?

Many of us know people who have been highly successful within a team and then go on to become far less successful when they move on. We have seen really great teams pulled down by the promotion of individuals out of the team. We have also seen teams that have produced far more than what the individuals could have produced on their own.

How often have we unconsciously recruited people into our project team who are similar to ourselves because it is often frustrating to work with people who approach things in a different way?

Although a 'shaper' or 'monitor–evaluator' or 'implementer' may be very different in their approach to the team in its achievement of objectives, all are equally valuable in the diversity of their contribution. If we have players who frequently fight to play in the same position, would it be helpful if they recognized another position that they could fall into when needed?

Table 3.1 Belbin team types

Plant	Creative, imaginative, unorthodox, solves difficult problems
Resource investigator	Extrovert, enthusiastic, communicative, explores opportunities, develops contacts
Co-coordinator	Mature, confident, good chairperson. Clarifies goals, promotes decision-making. Delegates well
Shaper	Challenging, dynamic, thrives on pressure. Drive and courage to overcome problems
Monitor–Evaluator	Sober, strategic and discerning. Sees all the options. Judges accurately
Team worker	Co-operative, mild, perceptive and diplomatic. Listens, builds, averts friction
Implementer	Disciplined, reliable, conservative and efficient. Turns ideas into practical actions
Completer	Painstaking, conscientious, anxious. Searches out errors and omissions. Delivers on time
Specialist	Single-minded, self-starting, dedicated. Provides knowledge and skills in rare supply

Source: Team Roles at Work by R. Meredith Belbin published by Butterworth-Heinemann/Elsevier (1993).

Using belbin, you can see when two people are fighting to play the same role. Using a secondary strength will often take the conflict out of the situation and allow the individuals to bring different strengths to the party. Increasing the self-awareness of the team by using a shared language is sometimes all that is needed to overcome these 'personality clashes'.

Alternatively, the manager needs to take account of the different team-type preferences when allocating people to new projects. There is no benefit in putting the creative, hard-driving decision-maker in charge of a low-key maintenance activity such as reviewing health and safety compliance when you have someone who is far happier working behind the scenes and who loves creating order and completing a job to the last detail.

Recently, we were working with a board team who had just completed their business plan for the year. Each Director then held an objective setting session with their team. The different departments split the tasks by who they felt was most suited to each activity rather than what they had always done before. The benefits were higher commitment to the overall strategy, greater understanding of everyone's part to play and the opportunity for development for individuals into new areas of responsibility. Surely, it is better to play to the strengths of a team as they develop rather than impose the same roles onto people year after year.

Step 4 – Encourage diversity

The managers can only achieve this buy-in if they truly understand the strengths of each team member. The role of the manager/coach is vital in identifying and growing the potential of each individual. They need to take time to find out how the player likes to play and what they need to help them move forward. The Belbin team profiles give the coach and the whole team a shared language to discuss their strategy for working together to achieve their objectives.

Summary

So, as the leader, what do we need to do when managing a team?

Identify what roles the individuals are best suited to play in any given project.

Develop an individual relationship with each player that maximizes their strengths.

Develop the agility of the team to play a number of different roles or positions when needed.

Develop personal flexibility to adapt your coaching style to the different needs of the different players.

Celebrate and encourage the diversity that leads to success.

The responsibility for achieving success lies with both the manager and the team members.

So, what does the whole team need to do?

Listen to each other and learn from each other

Communicate clearly and honestly with each other

Develop trust amongst individuals

Welcome diversity

Play to each other's strengths

Celebrate success as a team

The perfect team does not develop overnight or just because their names have been picked out of the hat. Building the team and keeping the team on target takes time, energy and constant coaching. The secret is to establish the value of each player within the team, work with him or her on their development, and create an environment of real teamwork that brings results.

Different working preferences

Teams are often made up of highly skilled individuals who fail to work effectively together. As we have seen from the belting work, individuals often prefer to play different roles in the team. However, there are many other diagnostic tools that can be used for looking at team dynamics.

One very useful instrument is the Insights Discovery Profile designed by Insights Learning and Development Ltd. The questionnaire can be completed online and is available in over 20 languages. This in-depth profile gives individuals an overview of their strengths and weaknesses, how they tend to interact and communicate with other people, and suggestions for their development. It also focuses on how to communicate with people who are of opposite types and gives ideas on how to manage the individual most effectively. This profile also provides a description of the team-role preference that the individual will be most comfortable with.

Again, this is a questionnaire that can be used at different stages of team development. With a team in the first stages of forming, it will be a useful way to get to know each other better. Likewise, in a team that is at the storming stage, this diagnosis may well help unpick some of the clashes and tensions between different team members.

It can also be used in a situation where two individuals are struggling to achieve a positive working relationship. In this case, they may complete the questionnaire individually and then the facilitator can run a session with the two people together, where they share their profiles and discuss areas of commonality and areas of difference.

Case study

Several years back, an HR Director was in the process of recruiting a new HR team. He was telling me how pleased he was that all four individuals he had selected seemed to share the same approach to current HR issues as he did. He explained how two of the women had been at the same university and how they all appeared to be fairly assertive and would be able to stand up to the fairly cynical workforce. It sounded like a great team in the making. Six months later, I met up with the Director and heard what had happened. For some reason, the team had not gelled at all and there had been great antagonism between two of them who were of the same age, same backgrounds and similar approach to life. He could not understand what had gone wrong.

'They spent all their time competing with each other rather than doing the job'.
'I thought I had recruited some great people, but they were hopeless'.

He had indeed recruited some great people but had taken no account of the fact that they needed to work closely with each other and that there is a huge difference between great individuals and great teams. He recruited great individuals and made the assumption that they would constitute a great team. Teams need effort and focussed support if they are to develop and work effectively.

We took the team away for a two-day workshop and together, they addressed the following areas:

Identified their strengths, both as individuals and as a team, using the Insights Discovery Profile.

Re-visited the distribution of objectives and re-assessed who was best suited to the different roles.

Allowed the team to voice their discontent with the ways of working and the relationships within the team.

Set some new groundrules for working together, having identified the shared values and the success criteria.

Six months later, the team looked back and realized that they had, by them, established a far stronger, collaborative style of working. Results are now improved and the atmosphere is currently far more positive for all concerned.

Learning points from this case study

Teams can achieve more than the sum of the individuals.

Attention needs to be given to three main areas – the process of how people work together, the content of the task in hand and the feelings of the individuals involved.

Teams develop on their ability to perform well. It does not happen by magic.

Individuals have different strengths and we need to know what they are.

Conflict is not always negative, sometimes it is needed to move the team on.

We can learn what we need to do differently by asking the team for feedback.

Recruit individuals for both their skills and their compatibility with the existing team.

The role of learning and development in team development

This is one of the areas where learning and development teams are often asked to help. There are three key steps that need to be followed in any team-development activity.

Diagnostics – Design – Delivery
Diagnostics to identify the objectives of the team-building activity.

This is the most important stage of any team development. It is all too easy to assume that we know what is required when managers ask for a team-building event. There are many reasons why a team-building event may be needed:

- A new team with members who do not know each other well.
- A team that has got stuck in the storming stage of its development.

47

- An existing team having changed roles and responsibilities.
- A high-performing team with members who want to celebrate success.
- An existing team that wants to review its strategy and plans for the year ahead.
- A team that wishes to develop an already successful strategy and ways of working.
- A team with a new leader, or new team members joining a well-established team.

These different scenarios, all require different types of team building, and it is the role of the learning and development manager to identify the objectives and desired outcomes of the team-building event. So, how to do this?

There are several methods for completing a team-development diagnostics:

Face-to-face interviews using a structured interview approach

Focus group with the whole team

Pre-event questionnaires, such as Belting or Insights Discovery Profile

The following questions can provide a useful template for one-to-one interviews or a group discussion. You may want to adapt the following questions to use with different teams, depending on what they have requested:

- What do you enjoy about working in this team?
- What do you not enjoy about working in this team?
- How well does the team perform when it comes to delivering results and right on time?
- How would your customers describe their experience of working with this team?
- How well does the team work together?
- What is your opinion on how the team communicates?
- What would you like to change about the team and the way it works?
- How are different views and opinions dealt with within the team?
- What would you like to gain from this team activity?
- What else do we need to know about how this team works as a unit and with other divisions of the company?

The results of these interview questions in terms of overall themes and views could be fed back to the group at the start of their event. This would then lead to an initial discussion about the key issues that are faced by the team.

The purpose of the team-diagnostic exercise is to identify the objectives for the team-building activity and to gain buy-in from the participants. The exercise is partly for the benefit of the learning and development manager to understand the needs of the team. It also serves the purpose of allowing individuals to voice their feelings and frustrations, which enable them to move forward more quickly when they get together. Knowing that other people share the frustrations can often be very helpful in getting the team to address the issues collectively and constructively.

Key points

- People will all have different perspectives on how the team operates.
- The manager will have different views as compared to the team members.
- Different people will want to achieve different outcomes from the event.

What makes an effective team-building event?

This depends on what the objectives are for the event. However, in my experience, truly effective team events manage to address two sets of objectives. They need to address key work-related issues for the team, as well as issues concerning team dynamics and team working. Team-building events are different from a team social event. There is a place for team socializing and this is very beneficial in maintaining team spirit and group morale. Team building is different in that it is a specifically designed intervention meant to develop the team in terms of what its members are doing and how they are working together.

Elements of a successful team-development event include the following:

- Clearly defined and written objectives
- A shared understanding and buy-in of the objectives
- Complied diagnostics with each of the participants and the leader
- Agreement on the roles and responsibilities of the leader/manager during the event
- A mixture of learning methodologies to suit different learning styles – input, discussion, activities, presentations
- A clear contract on what is expected from the facilitators
- An agreed set of specific and measurable actions at the end of the event
- A review held after the event to monitor progress
- Action and improvement in performance against the agreed measures

---

Reflection point

Think about the last team-building event you had organized or facilitated, and rate yourself on how well each of the above criteria were met.

What do you need to do differently next time?

Design of the team intervention

The design of the event will depend on what you are aiming to achieve. An effective team-development event should include at least some of the following topics:

Introductions and agreement on objectives

Review of current team-working

Identifying key issues to be addressed

Action plans for key improvement areas

Review of how people operate with each other

Increased self-awareness of impact of people's behaviour on each other

Personal action planning in relation to team working

Introduction exercises

People generally remember the start and finish of any team event most clearly. Any team event needs to start with a sharing of objectives and agreement on outcomes, roles and responsibilities for the event. There are various ways in which this can be achieved and I have listed a couple of them below:

In groups – Identify two ways in which you are similar and two ways in which you are different, and present this back to the main group. This exercise encourages people to share their personal knowledge about each other; useful when working with a team having members who are new to each other.

In groups – Create a Flipchart shield using a selection of 4–5 questions from the list below:

- What are your objectives for this event?
- What do you want/not want from the facilitator team?
- What worrying concerns do you have about this event?
- What would success look like for this event?
- What ground rules do we need to adopt for the event?
- What will you do to contribute to the success of this event?

All these questions will serve to kickstart the group focussing on what they want to achieve from their time together. You can choose several of these questions and split the groups into smaller units to work on this together as an introductory exercise. This is all part of the forming stage within the event. No matter how well people know each other, they need to spend time agreeing on what they want to achieve from their time together.

An alternative approach is to ask these questions in the diagnostic interviews and then present the complete set of responses back to the group. They can then discuss the responses and add any other still-outstanding objectives or issues.

The purpose of this introduction session is to focus people on what they need to achieve over their time together.

Review of current team-working

This can be done as a SWOT exercise, either individually or as a group, using four flipcharts around the room for people to go up and add their ideas to.

Discussion can them take place around how to exploit the strengths, overcome the weaknesses, maximize the opportunities and plan how to address the threats if needed.

With a team of 8–10 people, this discussion can take a couple of hours, or more if you have more people in the team.

The group can then identify the key areas they can influence and start to highlight the key areas to be addressed if they are to move forward.

Ideally, this exercise will then give you three to four key themes for the group to work on in terms of team improvement. These issues may be work-related such as increasing sales revenue or team dynamics-relates like improving sharing of best practice.

The team can then split into different working groups to come up with an action plan for each of the areas.

Alternatively, you may want to take a more creative approach to identifying the key issues facing the team by facilitating a now and future picture exercise.

The team creates a picture of how they see the team currently as a mode of transport. Encourage the team to think about the speed, colour, weight and size of their vehicle and identify who is driving it, where the people are and what the environment looks like for this vehicle. It may not be a typical vehicle; rather, it could be a mix of boat and car, space machine or a fleet of dinghies, all sailing in opposite directions.

Ask the group to explain their picture and identify the key strengths and weaknesses of the current situation.

The team members are then asked to create a future picture for one year from the present day. Create a model of transport that will describe how they would like the team to be working and what the future environment could look like for them.

Finally, the team members are asked to identify the key changes they need to make if they are to achieve their future picture.

This picture exercise can be used in a variety of ways. One team can create a picture of how they see the team internally, while another group can depict that exam from the perspective of customers or other stakeholders. This will also highlight the differences in perception and key issues from this point of view.

Development of self-awareness

The team-building event is an ideal opportunity to raise the awareness of the team in terms of how they operate as a group of individuals and how they work together.

Belbin team types are an ideal way of looking at team types for a group having relatively low awareness and little expertise of team dynamics.

Alternatively, with a more mature team or a team with people who are more advanced in their understanding of team working, you may want to consider using the Insights Discovery Profile.

Team exercises

Most team-building activities include one or more team exercises. The purpose of this is to engage the team in a working activity and then facilitate feedback on the behaviours and working styles that they demonstrate. This can then be used to add weight to some of the later discussions on how they work together.

There are many books around that list team exercises, and you will need to choose one that meets the needs of the team in terms of complexity, learning points that you wish to bring out and feasibility depending on the number of people you have involved.

Remember that people learn in different ways, and you need to design the event to encompass the different learning styles that people have:

Theorist – enjoys understanding theories and models – prefers well-proven ideas and case studies.

Reflector – likes to take time to think about what has happened and reflect on the group's thoughts and views.

Activist – enjoys new experiences and an opportunity to try new things.

Pragmatist – prefers practical examples and learning, which could be easily used back at work.

An effective team-building event needs to have elements of each of these learning approaches included.

Action planning – whole group

The output of the team event should be clearly understood and outlined with everyone, before the event finishes. One of the easiest ways to agree on actions is to use SMART and create a SMART objective for any of the actions to be taken forward.

- Specific
- Measurable
- Achievable
- Realistic
- Time bound

Again, the team should be working in groups on this and can then be asked to present their SMART plans back to the main group for comments and buy-in.

Action planning – individual

A tea event needs to work on two levels – the team objectives and the specific actions that individuals will take to develop their own performance in the team. Again, there are several approaches to this part of the event.

Individuals can be each asked to write up their own action plan using an agreed format:

- One thing I will stop doing
- One thing I will start to do
- On thing I will continue to do in this team

A more challenging approach is to ask people to give feedback to each other on what they would suggest they stop/start/continue. This will lead to a discussion between individuals about the behaviours they feel are useful to the team and the behaviours that they feel are not helpful. Individuals then choose the actions they feel that will gain the greatest benefit and that they feel they can take on willingly.

A team charter

Each person writes up his or her personal commitment to action on a flip chart and these are then printed up and circulated to the whole team. This encourages people to put their commitment into action because other people will be looking to see if they are making the changes they earlier signed up to.

A letter to yourself

Each person writes a letter to himself or herself, outlining the changes that they are looking to make. These letters are then held and sent to each individual a few weeks later, to act as a reminder of what they committed to do. They can then be shared at a review meeting.

All these techniques are simple ways of ensuring that people start to make changes in their behaviour after the event. The success of an event cannot be measured at the close of the event. It can only be measured a few weeks and months later when the team members review to see if they have achieved the improvement plans that they had set for themselves.

Common problems with teams

Often, the learning and development manager may be asked to come in and support a team with people who are not working effectively together. Some of the common issues are tabulated in Table 3.2.

This list can be divided into four different types of problem areas:

(1) Leadership
(2) Systems and processes

Table 3.2 Team issues

	Leadership	Systems and process	Skills and technical competence	Working relationship and interpersonal skills
Lack of competence	☐		☐	
Lack of confidence	☐		☐	☐
Poor interpersonal relationships	☐			☐
Confusion over roles and responsibilities	☐	☐		☐
Lack of trust between team members/leader	☐			☐
Lack of clear objectives	☐	☐		
Complacency	☐		☐	☐
Ineffective leadership	☐			
Too much internal competition	☐			☐
Too much group think	☐		☐	☐
Infighting	☐			☐
Low standards	☐	☐	☐	
Poor relationships with other teams	☐	☐		☐

(3) Interpersonal working relationships

(4) Skills and technical competence

As part of the diagnostics, it is important to highlight where the problems lie.

Not surprisingly, the success or failure of a team is directly related to the skills of the leader, and the interpersonal skills and team dynamics of all the individuals involved. Team problems are more often likely to be due to behaviour and team relationships. However, if the issues are mainly around technical skills and competence, then these issues need to be addressed separately.

The role of learning and development managers in team building

Experience of working with a wide variety of teams suggests that several factors need to be present in order to maximize the opportunity for improved performance through any team-building event:

Clear and agreed goals

The team must have a clear understanding of the vision and goals for the team. This should include the changes that need to occur, the expectations of individuals and the department as a whole, as also the methods of measuring progress towards the goals.

Support from senior management

This includes a willingness to accept feedback from the team, to make personal commitments to changes in behaviour or working methods, and the energy and drive to ensure that changes which the team agrees to are translated into action. Most team members want to see evidence of change from the top as a role model for the changes they may be asked to make themselves.

Involvement of the team

Decisions need to be agreed to and believed in. Although team members will inevitably have different views on the current situation, and possible solutions, it is important that people feel they have been listened to and have had a chance to voice and discuss their opinions.

The team needs to be engaged and involved if you are to gain their buy-in to the event and to gain their views on what the important issues are for them in terms of any development event.

Realistic expectations

People do not change their behaviour overnight, and a team is not developed in a day. The process of developing a team from its current state to that desired by the business will take several months, as also a lot of effort.

It is important for people to understand their own behaviour in order to start to understand the behaviour of others. You will be starting a process of change, which can then be continued by the team after the first event.

Direct linkage between work performance and team/individual behaviour

Many teams view their process – the way they work together to achieve their objectives – as being separate from what they do and the objectives that they achieve. Effective and high-performing teams recognize the fact that the two are clearly linked.

A checklist of key questions for any team-building activity

- What are the objectives of the proposed team-building activity?
- What issues are the team looking to resolve?
- What diagnostics have the team carried out already?
- How much time has been spent on team building before and what were the results?
- What would be the appropriate diagnostic questionnaires/interventions to use?
- How much time does the team want to commit to the team-building event?
- Over what timescale do they want to complete the team building?
- What activities are they looking to do and why?
- Should the team building be offsite and or residential?
- Who do they want to facilitate in the event – internal L&D or external consultants?
- How many people are involved/should be included in the team building?
- To what extent would they want to include team members in the design of the event?
- What would success look like for this event and how will they measure it?

4   'Change' leadership

This chapter will cover the following topics:

The change context

The role of the leader in managing change

The effect of change on individuals

Developing effective change leadership skills

An example change leadership workshop

The role of HR in supporting organizational change

The change context

The world is moving so fast these days that the man who says it can't be done is generally interrupted by someone doing it.

– Harry Emerson Fosdick

By any standards, the change that we see today in organizations is both faster and more radical than ever before. Significant changes are happening at a faster rate and the effect of these changes has created a new psychological contract between employees and their companies.

Thirty years ago, British Telecom was a state-owned monopoly. Twenty years ago, it was an organization that had no need for a sales team, no competitors and over 240 000 staff. Within 10 years, it had changed from a state monopoly to a privately-owned monolith trying to move more quickly than its processes and culture were ready for. Ten years on, with less than half the number of staff, it had lost whole chunks of its operation, slimmed down its operation and is now unrecognizable in terms of its culture, approach and speed of response. It has successfully made that transition. Examples like this are rare. Far too many organizations fail to make the transition either quickly enough or cleverly enough to successfully represent themselves in a changing world.

In addition, people have less loyalty to the companies they work for. There is no such thing as a job for life or a life-long career path. Companies need less people and those with constantly developing skill sets. Individuals get to work for a number of different companies; and these days, we see many more contract workers and freelance specialists moving in and out of companies, as and when needed.

This constantly changing environment is unlikely to slow down. Although we may think that there is a limit to the amount of downsizing, re-organizing and merger activity that can continue, there is no reason to suggest that it will not continue, as we appear to be smaller fishes in a larger global market.

Working with a global distribution company recently, there were 15 different nationalities at their leadership conference. The key topics were resourcing, succession planning and leadership development. This would seem fairly straightforward, apart from the fact that we had the added dimension of different pay conditions, different employment conditions and different levels of leadership capability. Eastern Europe had seen little leadership development in the past 20 years and was at a very different starting point than its Northern European counterpart. Pay conditions in China were significantly tougher than that in Europe. Succession planning policies had to take into account the need to move people across different cultures and give them a global skill set before promoting them to more senior positions.

In summary, there is an unprecedented degree of change that these leaders are expected to lead and to participate in is previously unimaginable.

This example is from a large global organization. The same also applies to smaller UK-based companies which are facing changes in all the following areas:

- Customer expectations
- Employee expectations
- Technology
- Financial constraints
- Legal and EU legislation
- Social conditions
- Environmental changes
- Global competition
- Changing skill sets
- Mobility of workforce
- Speed to market of new products

Reflection point

Look at the list above and highlight the key changes affecting your organization now.

In summary, we cannot ignore the need for leaders to be highly skilled in leading change through any of our organizations. My personal belief is that the concept of change managers is outdated. Many of the large organizations still have change management units. This is missing the point. All leaders without exception need to have these skills as part of their core competence. It is not a 'nice-to-do' activity undertaken by HR. It is a key part of any leader's role to lead change and to develop a change competence in their managers and teams. The role of Learning and Development is not to set up OD teams and Change Management Units but to develop these skills across the whole organization as a core set of skills at management and leadership levels.

The role of the leader in managing change

'Leading Change – Why Transformation Efforts Fail' by John P Kotter HBR was written in 1994, based on Kotter's own experience of working with many change initiatives within different organizations. Kotter talks about an eight-stage change framework and this framework is used within many successful change initiatives in a wide variety of organizations today. It also provides a useful template for leaders in terms of what they should be focussing on and what activities they should be undertaking at the different stages of a change initiative.

This links to the earlier discussion about the difference between leadership and management. Management is about a set of skills and processes that keep people and processes running smoothly and efficiently. Leadership is about defining the future, aligning people to that vision of the future and inspiring them to make it happen. Organizations that undergo successful change need to rely on leaders far more than we realize. Good managers will not create and implement change at the speed and scale that most organizations need if they are to stay in the game. Great leadership is required if organizations are to make the transitions that they need to make in the timescale they have open to them.

The Kotter eight-stage change framework

Figure 4.1 shows the Kotter eight-stage change framework and we will give a brief overview of what is required at each of the different stages.

Establishing a sense of urgency

Establishing a sense of urgency is crucial if people are going to commit to making significant changes to how they work and what they do.

> *when an organization is on a burning platform, the decision to make a major change is not just a good idea – it is a business imperative*
> — Daryl. R. Conner, 'Managing at the Speed of Change'

It is part of human nature that people will not change unless they see the benefits of doing so. Many organizations are full of people who feel very comfortable and do not see the need to change. They are complacent in their positions and this is the real enemy of a successful change.

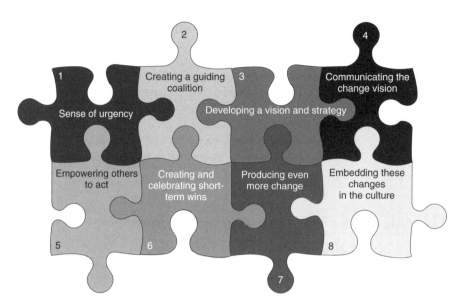

Figure 4.1   The Kotter eight-stage change framework

Characteristics of complacent employees

- Say yes and do nothing
- Achieve 50 per cent of what they could achieve
- Lack of initiative
- Low motivation
- Do what they need to do and no more
- Satisfy customers rather than delight them
- Influence others to take the same route
- Block new ideas and innovation

In order to start a journey of change and innovation, leaders need to instil a strong sense of urgency within a significant number of their people. Only having a mere 5 per cent of them feeling a sense of urgency is unlikely to create the momentum needed to move things forward. Leaders need to create this sense of urgency across all their teams. So, how do leaders do this?

Set higher standards: Complacency happens when people feel that they can easily achieve the targets and the goals that are set. I recently conducted a workshop in a marketing team and asked them as to how many people felt that they would reach their objectives and targets for the current year. Without fail, they all agreed that they would achieve this. They pointed out that they have had clear conversations with their senior leadership team to agree on reasonable targets and that there was no point in setting unrealistic goals. This may be true, but I did not see a sense of any urgency in them within the room. No one was concerned about not delivering and on top of this, there was a comfort level around their not having to do anything differently.

Setting higher standards has several benefits:

- It stretches people to achieve more.
- People feel more motivated when they are achieving more.
- It differentiates between poor performers, average performers and high performers.
- It sets the standard and therefore your standards of what 'good' looks like.

Reflection point

(1) How clear are my team members on what they are expected to achieve, both personally and as a team?

(2) How stretching are these goals?

(3) Who is performing well and who is not performing well?

(4) How much feedback am I giving them on their performance?

(5) When was the last time that I gave recognition to an individual for great performance?

(6) How much are the team members acting on the feedback that I am giving them?

(7) What are the implications for people if they do not develop their standards of performance?

(8) What am I doing to stretch the high achievers?

(9) What am I doing to develop the poor performers?

Provide more feedback on performance

Individuals will only start to gain a sense of urgency once they know how important it is to change. If they are unsure about what they are doing well and what they need to do differently, they will have little incentive to make changes. Leaders need to have clear, honest conversations with their people on how they view their performance and what constitutes 'good performance' in any particular field. These conversations need to be held regularly with a high degree of honesty and challenge. Many leaders work from the assumption that as they do not need any feedback from others, they do not have to give feedback to their team members either. If people are to perform well, they need to know how they are performing from the perspectives of their teams, colleagues, customers and leaders. It may not be easy to listen to, but if they are to develop their performance, they need to have data on which to measure themselves.

Case study

An MD of a multinational construction company came to talk to me about the issues that he was facing with his Board. Individually, they were all highly experienced leaders and had been in the business for many years. The MD was newly appointed and had taken the role after 5 years as a board member on the same board. The team had spent several days discussing the business goals and strategy for the next 2–3 years, and on paper everything was very clear. However, the MD was becoming frustrated that he could see no difference in how people were spending their time. Results were flat and the goals ahead were very challenging. He could see little prospect of the business plan being met if things continued in this vein.

When I asked him as to what conversation he had had with individuals on this subject, he suddenly went very quiet. At no time had he thought of having one-to-one conversations with individuals on their own personal objectives and focus. He had simply assumed that the team members were committed to the plan and therefore would make it happen. The team operated as a committee with a great deal of shared ownership, consensus and group discussion and buy-in. Decisions were only made when everyone had had their say and there was general agreement. This had lead to a lack of personal ownership and a lack of personal accountability when things went well or, more importantly, did not go well.

We agreed that he would sit down with each board member and agree to their improvement plan for their part of the business. During these sessions, several in the team admitted that they were not clear on what was expected of them personally; they felt that colleagues were getting involved in areas that were not part of their domain and that they were not truly accountable for delivery.

After having agreed on personal objectives with each of the board members and a stretching improvement plan for each area, the MD started to see a real difference in both the pace and the efficiency of how the board members were operating. He had successfully inculcated a real sense of urgency in each individual to deliver his or her part of the business plan. The team still has a sense of shared passion for the business, but they now have begun to possess a personal commitment to making it happen.

Creating a guiding coalition

Creating a close-leadership team with members who are all committed to the same goal is a key challenge for any leader. When you consider the scale of the changes that we are expecting leaders to achieve, they need to have support from a well-formed team with members who trust each other and have a shared objective. No one person can single-handedly develop, lead and implement the changes that people need to achieve today. Creating a guiding coalition does not mean putting together a committee of people who will come together each month, to slowly move forward on the action points from the last meeting.

A guiding coalition is a group of individuals who have a mixture of skills, experience, expertise and seniority, to create a powerful vehicle to drive change through the organization, quickly, willingly and with long-lasting effectiveness.

Do not

- Set up a team with members who cannot make decisions
- Have monthly meetings with standard agendas
- Ask the team to present its proposals to a higher decision-making authority
- Include people based on their title or job position
- Include someone from each department to make it fair

Do choose people who are

- Motivated
- Challenging
- Committed to a shared goal
- Having credibility in their work area
- Having expertise in the given field
- Having enough seniority to drive decisions
- Inspiring and engaging others to work with them

A guiding coalition is a diverse group of influential leaders who will drive a clear vision, and create momentum and space for their managers to deliver what is needed.

Developing a vision and strategy

Once there is a sense of urgency and a strong guiding coalition in place, the organization has to agree on its vision and strategy for changing the company.

Vision-setting is not a solo sport. The role of the leader is to involve people in the debate about what the future looks like and then to decide what the direction will be. The purpose of the vision is to motivate people to achieve something that may not be purely in their short-term interests. A vision is there to make decision-making easier. A vision serves to bring people together around a common cause.

What constitutes a good vision?

- It is imaginable
- It is desirable

- It is feasible
- It is focussed
- It is flexible
- It is communicable

The leader's role is to ensure that the vision fulfils these criteria; and they can only do this by spending time with people, engaging them in debate about what is possible and what is desirable.

Most organizations that have been in existence for more than a few years have a clear vision that has evolved and developed over the years. This is not the real challenge for many leaders. The real challenge is in communicating the vision and ensuring that people buy into it at every level within the organization.

Communicating the 'change' vision

We talked earlier about the need for leaders to demonstrate emotional intelligence rather than rely purely on their technical competence. This is often where even exceptionally bright and gifted leaders can fall. There is an assumption that once you have told people something once, then that is enough. Communication around the vision needs to happen regularly rather than on a once-a-year basis at the annual conference. Research conducted into communications in business highlighted that communication about the vision accounted for less than 1 per cent of total communication. When you consider the enormous quantum of messages e-mail and verbal communication carry each day, there has got to be a place for more discussion around the vision and what it means for people.

Communication about the vision also needs to be communicated via different channels. Team briefing and face-to-face meetings are the keys to enable people to air their views and discuss the vision and strategy. It also needs to form a part of written communication and play its part in company newsletters, quarterly updates and other in-house communications.

Discussion of the vision and strategy needs to happen at every level of the organization, not just in senior leadership forums. The skill of the leader is to adapt the message to a variety of different audiences and be able to gain buy-in at each level.

Reflection point

Analyse the communication skills of your leaders. Do they

- ☐ Regularly talk about the vision and strategy?
- ☐ Adapt their communication style to the needs of the audience?
- ☐ Include discussion of strategy at team meetings?
- ☐ Ask for views and ideas on the strategy?
- ☐ Relate operational activities to the long-term plan?
- ☐ Clearly communicate the vision both verbally and in written form?

☐ Engage and persuade others on the desirability and feasibility of the strategy?

☐ Inspire others to make it happen?

What do they do well?

What do they not do so well?

What do they need to do differently?

Empowering people to act

Kotter talks about this stage of the change process as removing the barriers and obstacles so that people can do a good job. Empowering is one of those words that engender a range of negative feelings in many people. However, by empowerment, one means a feeling of freedom to act in the best interests of the customer, or business.

Leaders cannot lead in isolation. They need people to implement the activities that will lead to achievement of the overall vision. So, how do good leaders empower others to act?

Case study

A large service organization had several hundred people employed in its call centre, in the early 1990s. Customer complaints were high, attrition rates in the call centre were over 100 per cent and there was a generally low morale and feeling of frustration in the centre. Staff were monitored on the time away from their desk, the time to answer calls and the number of calls answered per minute. This old-style approach to leadership had more in common with the theory of piece work than the enlightened high-technology environment that had been the dream of this particular multinational service organization.

Staff felt that they had no ability to make decisions, they had no freedom to act in the interests of the customers, and they felt untrusted and undervalued by the managers.

It took a new MD to decide to create a changed vision for the company and within a year, they had transformed the lives of these individuals, lowered attrition rates by 50 per cent and lowered the number of customer complaints dramatically. So, how did they do this?

First, they asked the staff what would make their work lives better.

Second, they took away the micro-monitoring mechanisms and created a new set of metrics that focussed on customer satisfaction rather than time to answer calls.

Most importantly, they listened to the concerns of the staff and gave them autonomy to take decisions about whether to reduce a bill, give a discount or remove a charge on their bill. Previously, a supervisor had been needed to make these financial decisions. Now the limits were lifted to allow all operators to take these decisions, based on agreed limits.

The benefits:

- Supervisors had more time to spend coaching rather than answering calls to customers who refaced to accept the answer of the operator.
- Customers were more satisfied with the service due to the fact that the operators took time to listen to them and acted on the conversation.
- Staff felt more valued and gained greater satisfaction from their work.
- Business results improved due to customer retention and minimal increase in costs due to discounting by operators.
- Operators developed their skills and increased the level of competence throughout the call centre.

This case study shows empowerment at its most practical. Individuals who feel that they are trusted to take decisions, do a good job. Great leaders provide the environment for their people to perform well. They allow their people space to do a good job and take responsibility for making a difference.

Reflection point

(1) What decisions do you currently make, which your team members could as well make?

(2) How much recognition do people gain for doing a good job?

(3) What do you do that makes the lives of your team members easier?

(4) What do you do that creates obstacles in their way?

Celebrating short-term wins

Most leaders understand the need for recognition and reward. Few leaders, however, provide these on a regular and consistent basis. Part of the key to this is ensuring that the company's performance-review process recognizes the skills and behaviours that make a difference, rather than re-enforcing old behaviours that actually act as obstacles to change. In addition, leaders need to be focussing on what people do well rather than constantly looking for what they do wrong. This is part of the pace-setting temptation. In an effort to raise standards, it is tempting to focus on the negatives and the problems rather than on the progress and the positive gains.

Recognition can take many forms:

- The public ceremony to recognize individuals and teams, offering prizes and gifts.
- The private one-to-one recognition by letter or through face-to-face interaction.
- The pat of the back when something goes well.
- The mentioning of good work at team meetings.
- Saying 'thank you' to individuals for continuing to do the day-to-day grind.
- Taking people out for lunch.
- Specific feedback on what the individual has done well.

Consolidating gains and producing more change

whenever you let up before the job is done, critical momentum can be lost and regression may follow

Throughout this book, the central message is around the need for leaders to provide positive recognition and support for their people. These final stages of the change framework are critical for long-term success. Recognition needs to be given, but there is also a need to provide continual motivation to maintain the pace and scale of change that is required. All too often, people celebrate the first year of a project and then find that the gains made in the second year are significantly lower. Creating a change journey is like running the marathon. The leaders and the teams need to pace themselves and realize that they are in for the long term rather than a short sprint. The responsibility is with leaders to set the pace and maintain motivation to keep the pace going till the chosen end-point is reached.

Embedding changes in the culture

This final stage of the change journey is around the need to create alignment between organizational policies and individual behaviour. If employees in a call centre need to be more empowered to make decisions for the customer, then the financial and commercial policies need to back this up. If the organization expects individuals to take initiative and be innovative, they need to support this with policies and procedures which encourage this rather than constrain it. Performance-review systems need to reward the behaviours that are needed for the future, not the past.

In order to assess the effectiveness of the change journey within an organization, there are several diagnostics that may be required. The short questionnaire below is a useful guide to ascertain where the leaders of the organization are succeeding and where they need to focus more of their energy and time.

The effect of change on individuals

It is often assumed that people react in similar ways to major changes in their lives. However, the key decide in how people react to change is whether they wanted the particular change to occur. There is great difference in leaving a job because you want to travel the world, and leaving the job because you have been made redundant. It is not the change itself that is the issue; instead, it is why the change is appending and how much control the individuals have over the effects of the change on themselves, personally.

Change can be seen as an enormously positive force:

- Exciting
- Energizing
- Motivating
- Innovative
- Chance to do new things
- Opportunity to learn more
- New challenges
- Freedom to try new ways of working
- Chance to work with different people

On the other hand, change can be seen as a highly negative force:

- A loss and ending
- Frustrating
- Demotivating
- Upsetting
- An end of good working practice
- Damaging to existing relationships
- Slowing down the speed of work

People need to have control over as much as possible during the changes in the organization. They need to be involved at each stage and have a say in how things will work in the future.

People like change – they don't like being changed . . .

Danger and opportunity – different experiences of change

Much of the organizational work around change comes originally from the world of grief counselling – and to some extent, all major organizational changes do involve an element of loss. It means people letting go of things they are used to, ways of working they are familiar with, and possible ending of work relationships they have established over the years.

Daryl Conner, in his book 'Managing at the Speed of Change', talks of the Chinese symbol for 'change' as being made up from two distinct ideograms – one representing 'danger' and the other 'opportunity' (Figure 4.2).

And from this, he develops a model of 'D' people and 'O' people.

Danger-oriented or 'D' type people see all change as full of dangers – they have probably suffered in previous organizational re-structuring. They may see themselves as victims of change and may look for conspiracy theories or others' personal agendas. Change causes major stress and their first reaction is to try and resist it.

Opportunity-oriented or 'O' type people see all change as opportunity – a chance to push forward new ideas and advance their own career. Change is exciting for them and they probably see life as a set of constantly shifting interconnected variables, which produce ever more opportunities and challenges.

The majority of people involved in leadership development – and the majority of people reading this book, are probably 'O' type people. They have got to where they are by seizing the organizational opportunities to make things happen. But, many of the people they have to influence from an organizational-change perspective are probably the 'D' type people – who view the whole programme from a quite different perspective.

People whose job role or life experience means that they are in charge of change – active participants in the process – often find it enlivening and stimulating; and so, tend to embrace it and welcome it.

Figure 4.2 Danger and opportunity

People whose job role or life experience means that change is imposed upon them – by someone high up the ranks, with no input from them – often find change threatening and stressful; and so, tend to ignore it or resist it.

Some people immediately want to calculate exactly what they will gain or lose, others want to know why past beliefs and 'sacred cows' have been done away with, and yet others are so keen and want to get really involved but also want to re-design the whole programme you would have probably spent months working on.

Similar differences occur in organizations too. A change strategy that works very well in one type of organization seems to fail completely in another – there are no universal answers. There seems to be some fundamental differences between different types of people and different types of organizational character, in the way we view the world and in how we react to major changes at work.

Mastering the change curve

The concept of the 'change' curve originally came from the world of grief counselling and was used to describe the emotional path that most people follow when faced with the overwhelming change of coping with the death of someone close to them.

- At first, there is a phase of *denial* – where people refuse to believe the reality of what they have been told. In organizational change, this can take many forms – from the shock and incomprehension often seen when telling people that they are being laid off as part of an organizational re-structuring – to the cynical 'I'll believe it when I see it', or 'if we keep our heads down, this idea will just go away like last year's'.

- Once over with the initial shock, people often enter a stage of *resistance*. People understand what you are trying to do, but want to make sure it either does not happen, or at least they are not seen to be supporting it. People often focus on the losses that they or others in their team may suffer, or it may be hidden and appear just as apathy which can make it all the more difficult to deal with.

- Some people never get out of this stage. They see themselves as losers from the change and if they cannot get their own way – they might just choose to leave. And for a proportion of the organization it is probably best that they do it sooner rather than later.

- In time, people start to turn around and enter a phase of *exploration*. Here, they want to try out how working in the new world might be – but they do not want to give their complete endorsement until they have tested things in some way.

- Finally, people reach a stage of *confidence* and commitment to the new world and new ways of working; and hopefully, their performance in this 'end game' will hit the targets that you set when you designed the new supply chain in the first place.

The 'change' curve is a well known pattern of behaviour that people experience when going through any major transition, either personal or work-related.

The responsibility of the leader is to recognize these different phases and provide the appropriate levels of support as individuals go through these different phases. This will happen at a different pace for each individual, depending on the personal impact of the change on them.

Developing effective change leadership skills

Based on the collective evidence around individual attitude to change, cultural differences and organizational culture, it is easy to see why this aspect of leadership is one of the most difficult to execute successfully. So, what makes an effective change leader in the twenty-first century?

- Encourage people to see the change as reducing rather than increasing their current burden.
- Highlight the links between the change and the personal values and beliefs of the individual.
- Discuss the opportunities for personal benefit and development to meet the new challenges ahead.
- Give people the space to air their views and listen to them.
- Encourage individuals to contribute to the changes and the way they will be implemented.
- Help individuals to build up a support network to help them through the transition – colleagues and peers can often provide more support than the leader.

Reflection point

Task: Think about a major change initiative in your organization.

How well do your leaders understand their roles and responsibilities as change leaders?

How well have your leaders demonstrated these skills and attributes during the transition period?

What further skills development do they need?

How well does your current leadership development offer include skills on change leadership?

How can you provide further opportunities for individuals to develop these skills?

Learning and Development Managers need to develop the skills of their leaders to create and lead successful change journeys on an ongoing basis.

To achieve this, leaders need to achieve the following:

- A clear understanding of the different stages of a change initiative
- Clarity on their roles and responsibilities at each stage of the change process
- Knowledge of the personal effect of change on individuals
- Feedback on their change leadership skills
- Ongoing development of their change leadership and interpersonal skills

Many organizations recognize that change leadership is a core competence in itself; and develop training programmes to introduce this challenging subject to their leaders. The benefit of this approach is that they are raising the conscious competence of their leaders in this often-overlooked area.

Again, this development can either be at the individual level through one-to-one coaching or at a team level by designing and delivering workshops to cover this area.

It may be appropriate to design and deliver workshops on the subject of managing change, particularly if the company is involved in a merger-or-acquisition situation. Additionally, it may be appropriate if the organization is failing to follow through on a change journey, either quickly enough or in a way that is carrying the employee workforce along with it.

This is very much a responsibility of senior leaders within an organization and one of the key topics for them to address as a senior leadership team.

An example change leadership workshop

A starting point for a development workshop on leading change may include the following:

- An introduction to set the context and agree to the need for effective change leadership in the organization
- A discussion of what successful change leadership looks like in practice
- An overview of the Kotter Change framework
- A review on how the organization marks itself against each of these eight stages – using the questionnaire
- Overview of the personal change curve and discussion of personal strategies for managing change
- Overview of key competencies of a change leader
- Personal reflection and action planning on individual skills as a change leader
- Group action plan for creating a more effective leadership approach to change

This type of workshop could then be followed up with one-to-one coaching of key leaders to support them in providing more effective change leadership with their own teams.

The role of HR in supporting organizational change

Think of the difference between a Chauffeur and a driving instructor. The Chauffeur does the driving for you and will follow your directions. However, you are constrained by his speed, skills and motivation to reach the destination quickly and safely. The driving instructor passes on the skills to the individual, allowing them to control and drive, using their own strategy, forward. They will then have full autonomy over the pace, and approach, and can decide when to stop, change direction or take a different turn, depending on the conditions they encounter. They can also come back to the driving instructor if they feel that they are getting into bad habits or need advanced skills to take them further. HR need to take off their chauffeur hats and take on the role of a driving instructor, giving direction where needed but focussing on coaching the individuals to become self-motivated and proficient drivers of their own 'change' journeys.

> *remember that change is most successful when those who are affected are involved in the planning. Nothing makes people resist new ideas or approaches more adamantly than their belief that change is being imposed on them*
>
> – Bennie 1993 An Invented Life: reflections on leadership and change.

5   The leader as coach

In this chapter, we will look at the following areas:

Coaching – a definition

What is coaching?

The skills of an effective coach

The coaching process

How to choose a coach

Choosing an internal or external coach

Selecting an external coach

The difference between coaching, counselling and mentoring

Developing coaching skills in your leaders

Advanced coaching development

Linking coaching with other forms of leadership development:
A coaching case study

There are many definitions of coaching; at times, it seems that each manager has his own. However, for the purposes of this book, we shall use the following definition:

Coaching – a definition

Coaching is the process of helping someone to identify their own solutions to work issues in order to improve their performance.

Using this definition allows us to see the clear parameters that need to operate when coaching in a one-to-one situation.

The word 'issues' is used deliberately to avoid giving the impression that all coaching is about solving 'problems'. Thus, coaching can involve working on issues such as:

- team dynamics
- gaining greater credibility in board meetings
- influencing colleagues and the boss
- improving communications
- raising profile of the team

- raising expectations of the team
- difficult relationships with colleagues or the boss
- improving sales targets
- developing new business
- how to gain partnership
- networking better
- business strategy

What is coaching?

Coaching is a two-way process. It is not beneficial or even possible to coach someone who does not want to be coached. The communication needs to be two-way, with the coach asking thought-provoking questions and the individual working hard to identify new ways of working that will improve performance.

Coaching is not a cosy chat to make people feel better. It is a challenging conversation between two people, which enables the individual to gain new perspectives and clarity of thought.

Coaching is about asking, stretching and challenging questions. The benefit of asking thought-provoking questions is widely underestimated. Coaches who ask great questions reap many benefits:

- The individual starts to think about the issue in different ways.
- The individual starts to gain a new way of seeing the issue, which creates different potential solutions.
- The individual is doing the thinking, rather than relying on the coach to solve his/her problems.
- The coach is managing the process, leaving the individual to work on the content of the discussion.

Coaching is about finding better ways to do things. It is an improvement process; in the same way that good golfers practise their swing every day, good managers daily practise and refine their game of management.

When leaders are asked what three things keep them awake at night, the answer is usually . . . people – people – people.

Coaching is the means to help people improve their performance and deliver better business results. The time spent on coaching will improve results and create more bottomline profit. If you doubt this last statement, just think about the cost of recruitment, turnover and high attrition in companies that do not invest in coaching and development. Look at the amount of investment that the top FTSE 100 companies make in terms of coaching their people, in order to gain better results.

The skills of an effective coach

A good coach needs to be a skilled one-to-one facilitator, with the ability to manage the process and provide a set of frameworks that will enable the individual

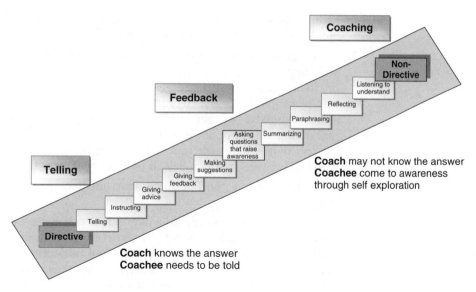

Figure 5.1 The spectrum of communication skills

to reach a clear plan of action. The framework above shows the different styles of intervention we make with other people. The coaching skills are at the right side of the continuum, allowing the individual to take control of the dialogue and come up with his/her own way forward. Most of us have years of practice of telling others what to do; we need far more practice in asking people what they think they could do (Figure 5.1).

What makes a good coach?

In addition, there are several things that differentiate excellent coaches from average coaches.

Excellent coaches can be recognized for their ABC skills:

1. Approachable
2. Build rapport
3. Challenge

1. Approachable – Great coaches have an uncanny ability to make people feel comfortable talking to them. They are genuinely interested in other people's views and are able to switch off the 'judgement button' when working with an individual. They make time for people and recognize when people want to talk something through. Good coaching can take either two minutes or two hours. Effective coaches can tell what is needed and make the appropriate time for it.

2. Build rapport – Excellent coaches listen carefully for what is said and also for what is not said. They pick up on the unspoken word as much as the verbal dialogue, reading cues in body language and eye contact. They use authentic mirroring techniques. They build rapport by active listening and they are not afraid of silence, recognizing the value of reflection and thinking time.

Most importantly, they work at the pace of the individual, matching the individual's own speed of thought, reflection and decision-making.

3. Challenge for results – Coaches challenge people to think out of the box and jump out of their comfort zones. They do this by asking deep, thought-provoking questions that address the real issues and barriers, which get in the way of people making a change in their behaviour. 'Challenging' does not mean 'aggressive' or 'abrasive'. Challenging questions are direct questions that do not skirt around the issue. Good coaches spend time looking at the barriers that people will face when trying to make changes and help the individual realize the obstacles, in order to find ways to overcome them.

Coaching is about good business. It is not 'nice to do' if you have done everything else.

Coaches deliver results. This does not mean that they have to find the answers themselves. They deliver results by clarifying the end goal that a person is working towards and helping the individual to develop a clear action plan that will enable him/her to reach that goal. They then build in review sessions, if needed, to check progress and work with the individual to remove any blockers or obstacles. Coaches want to see a change in behaviour, not just have a cosy chat that makes someone feel better in the short term but does not result in improved performance.

The coaching process

This ABC of coaching needs to be backed up by a robust process for the coaching conversation. A simple process used with skill and fluency, rather than a complicated process that creates difficulty for the coach and the individual, is far more likely to achieve success.

A simple model that is widely used is known as The GROW Process. This was originally developed by John Whitmore and used in the world of sports coaching.

It is a simple process that relies on a key four-stage approach:

G – Goal
R – Reality
O – Options
W – Will

The key to using this GROW model (see Figure 5.2) is to realize that each step is important and cannot be missed.

The goal

Examples of effective goal questions:

- What is the aim of this discussion?
- What do you want to achieve?
- Explain how you would like things to be in 3/6 months.

Figure 5.2 The GROW model of coaching

- What would success look like to you?
- How will you measure it?
- How important is this to you?

Delegates to coaching workshops often say that the individual starts by talking about the reality of the situation rather than the goal. This is true. However, the skilled coach then takes the individual back to the goal by asking him/her a number of questions as discussed above. Often, individuals give a first view of the goal, which is actually a presenting symptom, rather than the real goal itself. For example:

An individual starts to talk about the problems they have with their team not working well together. They describe their goal, as: 'I want them to work better together.' On further discussion, it emerges that the real issue is that the team members are not taking on enough responsibilities from the manager. This is probably because the manger is not delegating clearly enough or setting out clear enough expectations and objectives for each individual. Sometimes, when working in a team, the team members do not have sufficient clarity about each other's objectives and there has been some overlap of activities, leading to bad feelings. The individual being coached soon realizes that the real goal is as follows:

'To agree on clear objectives and responsibilities with each of the team members, and to ensure that they are shared and understood by everyone.'

This is a much more specific goal which leads the coach to then ask questions about how objectives are currently set and how much everyone buys into them.

Reality

Effective reality questions:

- What is happening now?
- Who is involved?

- When it is good, what is different?
- What have you done so far?
- What results did this produce?
- What would other people say about this situation?
- What is stopping you from moving forward?
- What is helping you move forward?

This phase is about helping the individual to gain a wider perspective on the extent of the issue and to look at it from different angles. In the example above, the coach may want to ask the individual how he thinks the team members feel about the manger's approach to objective setting. The purpose of the reality phase is to gain a deeper understanding of the situation; and this will help open up possibilities for a way forward. One of the main traps that coaches fall into is that they rush through this stage because they are so keen to come up with solutions. In our day-to-day work, we tend to be very results-focussed and this sets up patterns of jumping to solutions before we really understand the exact issue we are trying to address. One of the most effective questions at this stage is, 'What else do I need to know?' This often prompts the individual to provide either more personal or more revealing information, which sheds light on the nature of the issue.

Options

- What options do you have?
- Which options are of interest to you?
- Who can help you?
- What else could you do?
- How can I or others help?

Identifying options is one of the most challenging parts of the coaching process. There is a great tendency for new coaches to rush into giving suggestions, offering solutions and generally taking control of the conversation. They see this as their chance to show how much experience and wisdom they have. The key to the Options stage is to challenge the individual to think broadly about the many different ways in which they can approach an issue. One of the most useful models for identifying options is the CREATE framework by Mick Cope in his book 'The 7 Cs of Coaching'.

Coaching questions from CREATE (Figure 5.3):

Challenge

- What are the criteria for a good solution?
- When do you need them by?
- Is there anything out of bounds?
- How would you know a good solution if you saw it?
- What are the cost limitations?

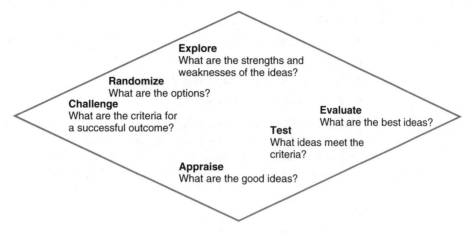

Figure 5.3 The CREATE model

- How much can you spend?
- What are the quality criteria? How perfect does the solution have to be?

Randomize

- What could you do?
- What must you not do? What is the opposite of that?
- What is the most outrageous thing you could do?
- What would the person you most admire do?
- What would the person you least admire do?
- What would the Prime Minister suggest?

Explore

- What are the strengths of each option?
- What are the weaknesses of each one?
- What are the costs of each one?
- What are the consequences of each one?

Appraise

- Which of these seems to be a good idea?
- Intuitively, would you keep it in?

Test

- Does it meet the criteria set in the Challenge stage?
- How can you be sure that it meets the criteria?
- How can you be sure that it does not meet the criteria?

Evaluate

- Which is the best idea?
- How would you rank the others?
- Which is the worst idea? Why?
- Which will you take forward?

This book gives a very structured approach to the coaching process, which will suit many, while others may find it constraining. However, it re-enforces the point that great coaches need to use a clear process, and this will enable them to provide the appropriate challenge and questioning approach.

Will

Examples of effective will questions:

- What are you going to do?
- How will this help you to achieve your goal?
- When are you going to do this?
- What challenges are there?
- How will you deal with them?
- How will you get the support you need?
- How committed are you to this action on a scale of 1–10?

The final part of the GROW process is WILL. This means asking the individuals what they will actually do as a result of the coaching conversation you have just had with them. This phase of the coaching is about recognizing what motivation and commitment the individuals have for changing their behaviour and approach. It is about agreeing on clear actions and timescales. If coaches do not cover the WILL phase, they will simply have had what I call a coffee-machine chat. Many of you will recognize situations where you have met someone in the corridor or at the coffee machine and they tell you about a problem they have. You spend some time discussing it and feel that you have helped them come up with a way forward. A couple of weeks later, you meet them again and they are still rattling about the same issue. They have not resolved it and you wonder why at all you bothered to help them. This is where the benefit of the 'WILL' phase comes in. Unless the individual commits to a number of actions with timescales, it is highly unlikely that they will do anything different after the coaching conversation. Great(?) coaches deliver results by ensuring that the individual they are coaching goes away with a real-time plan of action that they are committed to.

In summary: We have looked at the purpose of coaching and the skills of the coach. We have also outlined a simple coaching process that your leaders and managers can use to coach their people.

How to choose a coach

There are a number of elements that need to be taken into consideration here, especially confidentiality and contracting.

Confidentiality and contracting

An effective coaching relationship has to be based on trust. If an individual is going to be honest about the situation, he/she needs to be convinced that the conversation will not be revealed to a third party or used against them in any way. Coaching is about development, not assessment. Coaches are often asked by clients to give feedback on a coaching relationship with one of their leaders. The response should always be the same: 'Please, go and talk to the individual.'

Individuals will not be honest with the coach if they feel that the feedback is going to be given to HR, their bosses or used in any way that feels like assessment. As HR professionals, you need to be clear why you are arranging coaching for your people; and trust that they will make the best use of the opportunity you are providing them. It is vital to be clear on the different roles and responsibilities of the people involved in a coaching relationship. Often, there are three parties: the coach, the individual and the individual's line manager. It is advisable to hold a three-way meeting, where the roles and responsibilities of each of the parties are decided on. This includes agreeing on the following points:

- Objectives of the coaching relationship
- Confidentiality
- Number of coaching sessions
- Timing of sessions
- Feedback between the line manager and the coach and the individual
- Success criteria for the coaching

This normally only takes a short time and yet sets up a far more robust process for all concerned.

Choosing an internal or external coach

Personality match and fit

A good coach should be able to coach any individual who wants to be coached. That is the true test of whether the coach has the ABC skills and fluency in the coaching process. A good coach adapts their style to fit in with the needs of the individual in terms of pace, approach, challenge and behavioural preference. A coach does not need to be an expert in the technical or professional details. Often, a lack of knowledge can be helpful in that it ensures that the coach does not start to offer suggestions and solutions which may not be appropriate to the individual.

When to use an external coach?

Coaching is not a cure all. There still seems to be a view that coaching is a remedial activity for people who are not doing what is expected of them. Often, the cause is very simple. They have not been told what is expected of them. Coaches are sometimes invited into organizations to provide coaching to someone who is not performing well. After meeting the individual, it becomes obvious that they are not clear why they have been asked to have some coaching; they are not clear what they are doing well or not doing well and finally, they do not understand what their manager requires from them. This is a good time to stop the coaching session and set up a three-way meeting with the individual and their manager. Too many managers think that coaching is a quick and easy way to sort out those issues which they feel are too uncomfortable to deal with, themselves.

However, when it is clear that a series of formal coaching sessions would help, you then need to decide on whether to use an external or an internal coach.

Benefits of an external coach:

- An objective viewpoint
- Unencumbered by organizational baggage
- No political or personal agenda
- Complete confidentiality
- High degree of challenge
- Proven coaching competence
- Perceived credibility

Benefits of an internal coach:

- Understanding of the organizational culture
- Understanding of the skills and competences required by the organization
- A realistic view of what is possible
- Knowledge of the individual and their behaviour
- On-hand support when needed

Selecting an external coach

Senior leaders tend to be busy people, and the traditional development route does not always fit in with their hectic schedules, or even with their own personal or business needs. The executive coach is an external coach who listens and challenges, and who helps to create thinking space, allowing them to examine key issues and create new ways of working.

Executive coaches challenge current thinking to help individuals make sense of themselves or situations, support them to expand their boundaries and truly innovate, resulting in personal and business growth.

Does the coach need to understand the job of the individual?

Often, the first question that coaches are asked is: 'What experience do you have of working with people in this field?' There is a widely-held belief that to be able to coach someone, you need to know the content of their job or have an in-depth understanding of their professional field of work. In reality, coaches can work with people who work in a wide range of industries such as: construction, investment banking, retail, professional services, marketing and finance. Very simply, it is not necessary to understand the technical details of each individual's role. The skill of the coach is in using a clear process and facilitating a challenging two-way conversation to help the individual solve their own problems. Very often, an in-depth expertise in the chosen area can be an obstacle to the coach, as they are then far more likely to offer suggestions and impose a way forward based on their own experience. This is appropriate when acting as a mentor; it is not so appropriate when working as a coach.

Assuming that you have decided that external coaching is an appropriate approach, you should consider the next stage.

Ways to select an external coach

There are a number of approaches that you can take:

- Talk to your existing leaders and ask who has used a business coach whom they would recommend
- Ask your existing suppliers if they provide this service
- Contact your professional network and ask for referrals

The main point here is to work on the basis of recommendation. There are thousands of individuals operating as business coaches and many of them may be very good. However, there is no regulation or professional code of conduct; and it is an area that is easy to set up, with no training and very little competence. There are now several organizations that are providing coaching qualifications and could put you in touch with a coach; but again, personal recommendation is the safest bet.

Some questions to ask a potential external coach:

What is your definition of coaching?

What is your approach to coaching?

What coaching models or processes do you use?

What training, qualifications and experience have you gained?

To whom can we speak to as a reference for your work?

What results have people gained from the coaching you have provided?

How do you measure the success of the coaching you provide?

What challenges do you face when coaching people – how do you deal with them?

How do you package the coaching you provide in terms of the number of sessions and costs?

Many external companies offer coaching, but it is important to decide on what sort of coaching is appropriate for the individual. There is a whole spectrum from life coaching to focussed business-improvement coaching.

What is life coaching?

Very simply, this is an approach to coaching which considers the whole person rather than just their work-based performance. It is based on a holistic approach to change, suggesting that we are the result of the intertwining of home, personal life and work life. Therefore, any coaching session will necessarily focus on all three areas, depending on the issue being addressed. This leads to coaching sessions often taking a turn from pure business improvement to a more personal counselling approach, looking at family or personal issues and how they affect performance. This may be appropriate, but it needs to be a conscious choice of the company to invest time in this for the benefit of the individual. The difference between coaching or counselling an individual on personal issues is that personal issues tend to be far more deep-seated and take a lot longer to understand and then address.

The difference between coaching, counselling and mentoring

This brings us to the difference between coaching and counselling. Coaching is about helping someone to help themselves improve their performance at work. Counselling is about helping people to manage their personal lives more effectively. This may be in the case of bereavement, divorce or other significant trauma they might have experienced. There are many excellent books on this subject, and it is not proposed to cover this subject here. Suffice to say, business coaching is a far more straightforward process, and can be learnt and applied competently and more easily.

What is the difference between coaching and mentoring?

The following definitions from several different expert writers give an indication of the wide variety of interpretations of mentoring in the workplace.

> *'A mentor is more like an off-line friend, able to offer a valuable second opinion.'*
>
> – Alan Martin (Industrial Society)

> *'Mentoring has its origins in Greek mythology. In the modern business context, mentoring is always at least one stage removed (from direct line management responsibility) and is concerned with the longer-term acquisition and application of skills in a developing career by a form of advising and counselling.'*
>
> – Parsloe (Coaching, Mentoring and Assessing)

> *'Mentoring includes coaching, facilitating, counselling and networking. It is not necessary to dazzle the protégé with knowledge and experience. The mentor just has to provide encouragement by sharing his enthusiasm for his job.'*
>
> – David Clutterbuck (Everyone needs a Mentor)

Good mentors are:

- Good motivators and inspiring to others
- High performers, secure in their own position within the organization and unlikely to feel threatened by, or resentful of the individual's opportunities

- Able to establish a good and professional relationship, be sympathetic, accessible and knowledgeable about the candidate's area of interest
- Sufficiently senior to be in touch with the corporate structure, sharing the company's values and be able to give the individual access to resources and information
- Good teachers, able to advise and instruct without interfering, allowing individuals to explore and pursue ideas even though they may not be optimum pathways
- Available for the long term, providing career advice, experience and wisdom

Mentors are often people who are older, wiser and who have done the job before. They have technical expertise which they are willing to share with the more junior leaders. From the definitions above, it is clearly a very different role from the coach who is there to help people think for themselves and find their own solutions.

Many organizations confuse these two roles; and part of your role as HR Manager is to clarify what your leaders need. A mentor is often useful for:

- Graduate trainees
- New managers
- New recruits to the business
- Individuals who want to look at their long-term career development

A coach is often useful for:

- Experienced managers
- Newly-promoted senior leaders
- Individuals with a specific performance issue they want to address

So far, we have focussed on formal one-to-one coaching situations. However, part of the skill set of any leader is their ability to coach their managers on a day-to-day basis, whenever needed. The ability to have a 10-minute coaching conversation or a one-hour coaching session is a key part of the leader's responsibility. So, how do we develop leaders in this area?

Once the coaches have mastered a simple grow-type approach, you may wish to develop more advanced coaching skills using different verbal and non-verbal communication techniques.

These following four techniques are based on NLP (Neuro Linguistic Programming) and have a useful part to play in the skills set of any good coach:

(1) Building rapport
(2) Using precise questions
(3) Setting clear outcomes
(4) Using different perceptual positions

Neuro Linguistic Programming is a study of how thinking, language and behaviour can be used to gain successful outcomes. Simply, this means that there is a clear link between how we are thinking, the language we use and the behaviour that we demonstrate. Developing the ability to align our thinking, language and behaviour can result in highly effective communication skills.

We all recognize when someone is saying one thing, but they do not appear to be backing that up with their body language and attitude. This is known as incongruent behaviour. NLP develops our ability to behave congruently, matching our verbal and non-verbal communication.

The following four NLP techniques are particularly useful in a coaching situation. These techniques do not always have to be used; they are simply part of the skills set that one can draw upon when needed.

Building rapport

Reflection point

Think of someone you know who builds excellent rapport.

What language do they use?

What non-verbal behaviour do they demonstrate?

How do they look and behave?

How do you feel when they are talking with you?

We recognize these people because they demonstrate some or all of the following attributes:

- Good eye contact
- Active listening
- Nodding and encouraging
- Active attention
- Using similar language
- Matching your body language
- Speaking at a similar speed and tone

Effective coaches build excellent rapport by matching their body language to the person they are coaching. They intuitively slow down their speed of delivery when talking with someone who has a slower pace. They turn up or down the tone of their voice to match the other person. They match their body language and gestures in order to gain almost a symmetry with the other person.

Why do this?

This may sound very pre-meditated and unnatural. However, if you look at young couples sitting on a park bench or outside a café, you will notice that they mirror each other's behaviour very closely, sitting in a similar position, facing each other and talking together in such a manner that they are completely unaware of the outside world. This is rapport at its best.

Effective coaches build up trusting relationships with the individuals they coach. These rapport-building skills are key to helping the individual feel at ease and be able to talk openly and honestly to their coach.

Reflection point

Choose someone you want to build better rapport with.

Posture – match your posture to theirs.

Eye contact – make clear and regular eye contact.

Voice tone – match the volume and tone to that of the other person.

Voice pace – slow down or speed up your pace to match theirs.

Breathing – watch their breathing (look at their shoulders to see the rise and fall) and start to breathe in a similar rhythm.

This ability to match style and behaviour is a very powerful way of gaining rapport with someone. Start to notice people who do this well and learn from what they do. You will also start to recognize people who do not do it well; and you can often learn even more from them.

Asking precise questions

We have already discussed the need for coaches to ask good questions.

If you listen carefully to a lot of the language we use, it is very general and non-specific.

'The trouble is that they never listen to us.'

'No one lets us make decisions here.'

'Everyone is fed up.'

These statements show the degree of generality that are often faced with when coaching someone. The coach then either makes assumptions about what the individuals mean or we work with data that is neither specific nor clear in its meaning.

There are a number of simple techniques to use, to break down these abstract statements into something more specific:

- Universals
- Limiters
- Generalizations
- Drivers
- Blamers

Universals

Include words such as: 'always', 'never', 'no one', 'everyone', 'all', 'nothing'. These words are used by the individual to generalize from one specific incident to an all-encompassing generalization:

'I never get the time to do it'; 'I always come to work on time.'
One response is to simply question the universality of this statement 'Never?' 'Always?'
This then requires the individual to question the validity of what they have just said.

Other ways to test this universal belief would be to ask: 'Has there ever been a time when you did arrive late?' The role of the coach is to help the individual connect with the active reality of what they do, rather than work on a generalized view of reality.

Limiters

'I can't do that.'
'It's impossible, around here.'

Many people enter into a pattern of limiting statements which are probably the result of internal limiting beliefs.

Again, the coach needs to *challenge* these limiting statements:

'What would help you to do it?'
'What would happen if you did do it?'
'If you could do it, what would be the benefits?'

All these questions help the individual to challenge their own view of reality and realize that there are more choices open to them.

Generalizations

This is when people decide to speak in generalizations rather than specifics.

'They don't tell me what is going on.'
'The trouble with customers is . . . '
'People just don't realize . . . '

The coach needs to *challenge* the generalization with simple questions such as:

'Who are they?'
'Which people do you mean in particular?'
'All customers?'

Drivers

'I must do this now.'
'I have to work at weekends.'
'I ought to do this report.'
'I should attend a training course.'

These statements are often made by people who are working to keep someone else happy rather than themselves. They are not taking active, willing responsibility for the action. Rather, they are carrying out actions because they feel that they will let someone down if they do not do them. The feeling of 'I must do this' is very different from 'I want to do this', with more tension and pressure attached to it.

The coach needs to help the individual challenge the truth of these statements:

'What would happen if you didn't complete the report?'
'What would happen if you didn't work at weekends?'
'How important is it to you to go on the training course?'

Blamers

'My manager makes me do it like this.'
'I have to do this because my team members aren't good enough.'

People using statements like this are passing responsibility on to others for how they feel. No one can actually make someone feel something unless they decide to do so. Part of the coach's role is to help the individual face up to their responsibilities on any given situation, using questions such as:

'What does you manager do to make you do it?'
'What do you need to do with your team to help them?'

This type of question moves the individual to a position where they have the power and ability to make decisions rather than be the victim of a circumstance over which they have no control.

Setting clear outcomes

Agreeing on a clear goal is the most important first step in any coaching conversation. We have already covered some initial questions to help assist in this process.

NLP uses a number of techniques to help people to set well-defined goals or outcomes.

First, outcomes need to be expressed in the positive.

'I don't want to have problems with my manager any more' is very different from 'I want an open, honest relationship with my manager'.

Secondly, outcomes need to be expressed in terms of a rich picture of what the final result will look like, feel like and sound like. The details and richness of the description provides a far clearer goal to work towards.

> First, I 'see' the ball where I want it to finish, nice and white and sitting high up on the bright green grass. Then, the scene quickly changes and I see the ball going there: its path, trajectory and shape, even its behaviour as it lands. Then, there is a sort of fade out, and the next scene shows me making the kind of swing that turns the previous images into reality'.
>
> – Jack Nicklaus

A well-formed outcome needs to be positive – practical – possible.

Reflection point

Write down an important personal development goal for yourself for the next year. Phrase it in the positive with as much colour and detail as you imagine

When you have achieved this goal:
What will you see yourself doing?

What will you hear yourself saying?

What will it feel like to be doing this?

P – Is it written in a positive frame?

A – How practical and appropriate is this goal?

C – Is it possible for you to achieve this? What control do you have over the achievement of this goal?

This exercise can easily take a fair amount of time to complete. If you are looking for your coaches to use these approaches as part of their skills set, it is essential that they experience them for themselves and practise them on each other first. This will give them a two-fold benefit. First, they will gain fluency in the approach, and secondly, they will see and feel the benefits of using this structure for gaining clarity on the goals and outcomes.

Perceptual positions

This is a technique that is really powerful both in a coaching conversation and when working with people who are having difficulty understanding each other's perspectives (Figure 5.4).

1st position – is seeing a situation through your own eyes. You describe the situation from your own viewpoint, thinking about your own emotions and views on the situation.

2nd position – is seeing the situation through the eyes of someone else who is involved in the situation. You will describe how they may feel about the situation and what view they have of your role in it. You will put yourself 'in their shoes' and imagine how they see and feel about the issues involved.

3rd position – is seeing the situation from an objective third-party perspective. You will describe the situation objectively, as would an external party or detached observer. You would see the interaction of the different people and give a detached view of what is happening.

What is the benefit of coaching an individual to describe an issue in these three ways? The benefit of this approach is that you are challenging the individual to step outside their own comfort zone in terms of how they see a situation.

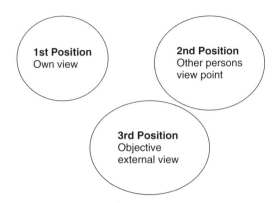

Figure 5.4 Perceptual positions

In the reality phase of GROW, we often work from an internal perspective and forget that there are many different dynamics working together to create a situation. This approach helps the individual to develop a more rounded external perspective about what is happening; and this enables them to develop options that are more likely to address the issue and agree on the will in a way that is helpful for everyone.

Developing coaching skills in your leaders

The theory of coaching is relatively easy. The practice of coaching is far harder. At a basic level, you need to give leaders a clear understanding of the purpose of coaching, a simple coaching process, and lots of time to practise using it.

Depending on the starting point of your managers, you may want to look at a one-day introduction to coaching and follow this up with opportunities for them to practise it with their own managers.

Depending on the size of your organization, you may wish to develop more advanced coaching skills for some of your leaders, so that they can be used as internal coaches to others in the organization. Again, this could start with an introduction day, followed by formal or informal opportunities to practise. The participants can then come back together after a month or so and continue the skills development further. You may also want to consider asking them to complete some assessments, gained from the different people whom they coach. An example is shown below.

Example – introduction to coaching programme

Learning outcomes

At the end of this workshop, participants will be able to:

- Recognize the purpose and benefits of coaching
- Use the GROW process of coaching

- Define the difference between coaching, counselling and mentoring
- Enhance existing skills in coaching team members
- Assess own coaching competence and agree on a coaching action plan

Topics

- Introduction and outcomes
- Coaching exercise to demonstrate the benefits of coaching
- What is coaching – discussion and definitions
- The GROW model – an overview
- Briefing of trios exercise – using the GROW process
- Round one of coaching in trios
- Review of learning
- What does a good coach do?
- Skills of an effective coach
- Coaching demonstration by facilitators
- When to coach and when not to coach
- Rounds two and three of the coaching exercise
- The difference between coaching, counselling and mentoring
- Assessment of own coaching competence
- Action Planning for coaching your team members

The key to success of this Introductory Programme is that delegates have a lot of real-time practice, coaching each other on live issues that they face as leaders or managers within their business organizations. It is probably better not to use pre-written role-plays in order for people to see and feel the benefits of being coached on something that is important to them.

In threes, the groups rotate the roles of:

The coach

The individual being coached

The observer

Participants coach each other for approximately 20–30 minutes on their 'real' business issues, using the coaching process.

The individual then gives feedback on how they felt about the coaching session; and then the observer gives some structured feedback on the use of GROW model and coaching skills, such as listening, questioning, challenge and rapport building during the coaching session.

As with any training and development activity, the opportunity to practise the skills after the event is what counts.

Table 5.1 Evaluation of your coaching session

The coach managed the time well	1	2	3	4	5
The coach allowed me to set the agenda	1	2	3	4	5
The coach helped me identify a clear goal and objective for the coaching session	1	2	3	4	5
They communicated openly and easily with me	1	2	3	4	5
They helped me to identify alternative options	1	2	3	4	5
I have increased self-awareness as a result of the coaching	1	2	3	4	5
I have changed the way I think about the issue	1	2	3	4	5
I will adapt or change my behaviour and actions as a result of the coaching	1	2	3	4	5

Scores:
5 being in total agreement with the statement.
1 being in total disagreement with the statement.

Part of any coaching development programme should include assessment of the coaches' skills by the people they are coaching. Table 5.1 which is a review sheet can be used as a template for ongoing coaching reviews.

Advanced coaching development

Depending on the size of your organization, you may wish to consider developing your own team of internal coaches to provide one-to-one coaching within the company. Again, there are a number of factors to consider:

Competence – consistency – confidentiality

We have discussed the importance of confidentiality, and this needs to be something that is discussed and agreed on by any internal team or external team of coaches. It is important that the coaching approach is consistent in both methodology and operating parameters.

Developing competence

The only way to develop coaching skills is to practise and receive structured feedback on the skills being applied. Obviously, this is difficult, considering the confidential nature of most coaching. This is why it is important to carry out regular coaching training with the internal coaches, where they practise on each other and have an opportunity to extend their skills in questioning and facilitating one-to-one change.

These different skills can be designed into an ongoing Coaching Development Programme that carries on over several months, with a mixture of skills practice, coaching practice, self-assessment, peer assessment and coaching reviews. Leaders need to review the coaching that they have carried out and gain help on some of the issues or barriers that they have encountered.

Linking coaching with other forms of leadership development: A coaching case study

One organization was very committed to developing a strong coaching culture within their company. They were concurrently running two leadership development programme; one for their senior leaders and the other for the next level of managers. Each programme had a one-day workshop on coaching, and all participants on the senior leadership programme received three one-to-one coaching sessions from an external coach as part of the programme.

In order to develop the coaching skills of the senior leaders further, they were given the challenge of providing the one-to-one coaching for the participants on the Management Programme. Each senior leader was matched with one of the management delegates and carried out three coaching sessions over a six-month period.

The benefits were extensive for all parties involved. The senior leaders felt that they were learning a lot by spending focussed time with the managers and were surprised that the coaching issues were not dissimilar to their own. The managers felt that the senior managers had led by example in spending time on coaching and this demonstrated their commitment to developing a coaching culture within the organization. It also created a real momentum within the company and recognition that coaching can deliver real results very quickly. Managers also started to see a difference in the day-to-day behaviour of their senior leaders, in the following ways:

- Asking more questions
- Less telling and orders given
- More involvement in decision-making
- Quicker decision-making
- More delegation

- Greater listening
- Greater acceptance of new and different ideas
- Improved feeling of teamworking

By demonstrating these coaching skills, the senior leaders were freeing themselves up to take on the more strategic elements of their own roles; they were developing their managers to perform better; and finally, the organization benefited as a whole by an enhanced feeling of team work and collaboration.

So, in summary, the benefits of coaching can be far-reaching:

- Greater development of skills
- Greater trust between the manager and the individual
- People feel more involved and recognized
- Enhanced individual capability
- Increased organizational capability
- A more creative organization with more ideas
- Retention of good people
- Development of people for internal succession planning

Reflection point

What coaching do you currently provide for your leaders?

What benefits are you looking to gain?

How consistent is the approach to coaching across the company?

How do you monitor the effectiveness of the coaching?

How do you monitor the effectiveness of the coaches?

What are you doing to develop coaching skills within your organization?

How do you link coaching with other forms of leadership development?

Coaching is about asking great questions, not giving great answers
– R. Adam

6　Assessing leadership behaviour

In this chapter, we shall be looking at assessment of leadership behaviour, with particular focus on the use of competencies to assess and develop this leadership behaviour. We shall cover the following topics:

Background to competency development

Types of competency frameworks

Developing a competency framework

Using the competency framework

Examples of competency frameworks

Benefits of the competency approach

Background to competency development

The use of competencies became popular in the mid-eighties as organizations struggled to clarify what they expected from their managers. Many layers of bureaucracy were disappearing as companies saved money by 'delivering'. This resulted in the need for managers to do more and at a higher level than had previously been expected. In addition, companies were expanding globally, and there was a need to have greater consistency in what was expected at each level of management.

Competencies are, very simply, the behaviours, skills and attributes that need to be demonstrated in order to gain high performance by any given group of managers.

There is much debate about whether competencies should focus purely on inter-personal skills and behaviours or whether they should also encompass technical skills. The majority of competency frameworks focus on behavioural skills; and there are separate means of assessing and measuring professional and technical development. This is owing to the fact that organizations can rely on external standards and qualification routes for technical development. They need to be far more specific in what they need from their employees in terms of behavioural competence, as this depends on the values and culture of each individual company.

Types of competency frameworks

There are three main types of competency frameworks:

(a)　One framework that applies to all employees.

(b) One framework that offers a menu of competency headings from which people choose the ones appropriate to their level and role.

(c) Multi-level frameworks for different levels of managers/leaders with different headings and behavioural indicators.

One framework

The advantages of having one framework is that it is simple to use and to understand. This benefit should not be understated.

Many HR systems and processes are not used because people do not have the time or the inclination to understand how to use complex systems and processes effectively. In addition to simplicity of use, one competency framework has the benefit of being inclusive, by which I mean that it applies to everyone from the MD to the most junior manager. It can then be used as a communication and cultural lever for change by focussing on the core skills and behaviours that need to be demonstrated by everyone within the company. This approach works for companies that do not employ thousands of managers and also for companies that employ professional staff who have clearly defined technical competence and need a simple approach to the behavioural aspect of their leadership role. This may apply in the case of professional services firms such as accountancy firms or law firms.

A typical example of core management headings may be as follows:

- Teamworking
- Communication skills
- People management
- Customer focus
- Results orientation
- Problem solving
- Planning and organizing

These headings are taken from research in 2003 – N. Rankin 'Raising performance through competencies: the Tenth Benchmarking Survey', London IRS 2003.

Under each heading, there should be a number of behavioural indicators giving example behaviours of what this competence looks like in behavioural terms.

Communication skills

- Clearly expresses ideas in a logical manner
- Listens effectively to others' thoughts and views
- Produces written documents that are concise and easy to follow
- Delivers clear and credible presentations

One framework with a menu of different competency headings

This approach is more appropriate to the larger organizations that have several different levels of managers and leaders within a larger workforce. The benefit of keeping the one framework is that it keeps the sense of cohesion for everyone, but the different competency headings also provide 'stretch' for the more senior managers and leaders. An example of this approach would be to cover the following headings:

- Teamworking
- Communication skills
- People management
- Customer focus
- Results orientation
- Problem solving
- Planning and organizing

Plus

- Innovation
- External market focus
- Leadership
- Strategic thinking

Managers would expect to be assessed against the first group of headings and would then select, from the final four, those applicable to their roles.

The benefits of this approach are that it takes away the need for numerous frameworks, each slightly different from the next one. It also ensures that senior managers are still assessed against the core competencies such as teamworking and communications. Also, in addition, it is easier when integrating the competencies into performance appraisals, if everyone is familiar with the majority of the headings. This leads to greater understanding of what these behaviours look like in practice.

Multi-level frameworks

The most complex approach is to have different frameworks for different levels of managers. In using this framework, the more senior managers will demonstrate the behaviours in level 3, as well as in levels 1 and 2.

People management – level 1

- Gives instructions to complete day-to-day tasks and explains why
- Provides feedback on results and task completion
- Provides encouragement and recognition for outstanding performance
- Coaches on a day-to-day basis
- Is open to employee concerns, suggestions and feedback
- Gives development opportunities

People management – level 2

- Sets and agrees on objectives with individuals
- Provides feedback on current performance versus team objectives and takes corrective action
- Provides encouragement and recognition for outstanding performance
- Empowers people to make decisions and voice opinions
- Stimulates employees to find new solutions to overcome problems
- Encourages individuals to learn from mistakes when taking on new and challenging tasks
- Proactively communicates information in a clear and open manner and explains impact on day-to-day activities

People management – level 3

- Translates and implements the company strategy into achievable objectives
- Provides feedback on current performance versus team objectives
- Provides encouragement and recognition for outstanding performance
- Creates a positive and open environment where people can learn from mistakes
- Assesses career aspirations, ensures that everyone has a development plan in place
- Acts as a role model and sets a good example

In addition to having different levels of behaviours under each heading, these frameworks will also have different headings depending on the level of the leader.

The advantage of this approach is that managers are given very specific levels of expected performance, which makes it easier to assess and develop them against the framework. However, there is the likelihood that very few managers can remember all the competencies in a framework such as this. If a leader is unable to recall the behaviours, it is even less likely that they will be working to demonstrate them either consciously or unconsciously.

These frameworks work well in large organizations where there is a lot of resource put into performance management, regular one-to-one review meetings and a clear focus on development. In the worse cases, these frameworks take months of development, are only looked at by HR and then become outdated by the time they have been communicated to the thousands of managers they are designed to support.

Developing a competency framework

There are several ways of creating an organizational competency framework. There are dictionaries of competencies on the web, there are many government-training initiatives that are competency-based, and most HR professional networks have selections of leadership competency frameworks that are available to be adapted and changed. In this book, there are broad selections of competence lists that have been designed for a variety of different organizations.

In order to create a framework specific to the organization, it can be useful to take an 'off the shelf' list (examples are included in this chapter) and then use it as a basis, comparing it with your own organizational data such as:

Company business mission and vision statement
Company business plan
Company values and culture statements
Market and customer data

This would start to give a feel for the key drivers for the business.

Depending on the time and resources available, the approach can then take a number of routes:

- Interviews with sample group of managers from the target audience.
- Interviews with different levels of managers/leaders.
- Use of focus groups with cross-section of all staff to gain their views on what the important skills and behaviours are in the company.
- Critical incident technique – where individuals self-report on their own behaviours in making decisions.
- Repertory Grid – employees report on the behaviour of colleagues by marking them against lists of behaviours and skills.
- Checklists and on-line questionnaires.

The most important aspect of the design is to gain the involvement of the people who are going to be using the framework for their development. The approach can be a mix of one-to-one interviews, focus groups and liaison with the Learning and Development team to put together a draft framework, which is then signed off with the different stakeholder in the process.

It is important not to under-emphasize the benefits of gaining buy-in at this point. If people are to be reviewed and developed against a set of criteria, the whole process is far more likely to succeed if they buy into the content of the criteria.

Again, it is important that this exercise is not seen to be the preserve of HR. Learning and development are there to facilitate the process for the benefit of the users. If the users do not see the benefit, then the Learning and Development team has not done its job well.

Checklist of example questions to ask during a focus group

What skills and behaviours do you think that leaders need to demonstrate in this company?
What are the most important behaviours and why?
What do you think leaders need to do differently here?
Identify a role model in the company – what characteristics do they demonstrate?
Identify a poor leader in the company (no names!) and what behaviours do they demonstrate?

How do you see the company changing over the next 5 years?

What different skills and behaviours will be needed?

What differentiates you from your competitors?

What skills and behaviours does this require you to demonstrate?

What makes the difference between a level 1/ level 2/ level 3 manager?

What do you want to see your leaders doing differently in the future?

What do your leaders want to see you doing differently in the future?

What would your teams say that they would like to see you doing differently in the future?

The answers to these questions will give you a whole set of data that you need to flipchart and note down during the focus group. Your role is not to filter the information being given. At this stage, you are there purely to gather the data. After the focus groups, you can then work with a selection of line managers to agree what are the key headings and what are the different behaviours that underpin each of the competency headings.

Some consultants will start by giving the group a list of competencies to discuss, although my preferred approach is not to give this initial direction, as there is a tendency to agree with, or work on, what is provided. Starting from scratch ensures that you start to mirror the language used by the company and that you reflect the style and culture of the company. There is also greater buy-in to a process when people have developed the ideas themselves rather than worked on a pre-determined list of behaviours.

Using the competency framework

Once you have developed a competency framework, the next step is to integrate it into the various HR and development systems and processes within the organization.

Recruitment

- Assess what competencies are required by the different roles and jobs for which you are recruiting.
- Create competency-based job specifications.
- Gain more from your external recruitment partners, job agencies by discussing with them, the different skills levels, and behaviours and attributes for which you are looking.
- Develop assessment techniques that will measure the demonstration of these competencies more clearly.
- Train your internal interviewers on competency-based questioning techniques.

Performance review process

Integrate the competencies into your yearly performance review process. The work-based objectives provide '*what*' the individual is expected to achieve. The competencies should assess '*how*' someone is operating in order to achieve their objectives. The performance review should review both the '*what*' and the '*how*'. Many performance reviews focus purely on the job-related objectives and ignore the fact that how someone completes an objective is also of importance. A Sales Account Manager may reach all her targets for sales, but fails to maintain effective working relationships with current customers, acts in a competitive way with other team members and has upset her sales team so much that they decide to leave and work elsewhere. In the short term, she has met her objectives, but in the long term, she is not achieving the level of overall performance expected. Including core competencies within the performance review process elevates their importance and ensures that managers are assessed against the whole picture of performance, rather than against a narrowly focussed financial set of measures.

Development planning

For the purposes of this book, we are focussing primarily on how to use competencies to develop leaders and managers within the organization. For this reason, the competencies need to be:

- Clearly defined and understood
- Relevant to the target audience
- Achievable, but stretching
- In a language that fits in with the culture of the organization
- Memorable and inspiring

The key principle is to include a section on the competencies as part of the performance-review documentation. This then needs to be followed up with a development plan that allows the manager and individual to identify development needs, based on the discussion relating to behaviour and competence.

Examples of competency frameworks

Each organization will have its own style and preference for the type of competence framework that they wish to introduce. The following examples have been chosen to show that different approaches and styles and use of language may be appropriate in different sectors and cultures.

The examples have been taken from work that had been carried out in organizations from 1996 to 2006 and reflect the nature of the different organizational structures. They are included purely to provide a useful starting point for creating or amending an existing framework. The different companies are as follows:

(1) UK Charity
(2) High Street Retailer

(3) Corporate Governance Board

(4) NHS Trust

(5) Manufacturing Company

(6) Public Sector City Council

(7) Technical Consultancy

1. Leadership competence framework – UK Charity

Leading others

'Inspires others to work with you to achieve the required outcome'.

- Influences others to follow a given direction by engaging them in a shared purpose.
- Adapts leadership style depending on the nature of the task, the people and the time available.
- Motivates others to deliver the highest standards.
- Provides consistency of leadership within a constantly changing environment.
- Manages performance of others by agreeing on goals, delegating responsibilities and reviewing progress.
- Openly values and recognizes the contributions of others.

Communication

'Uses effective communications to inspire commitment and motivation to deliver results'.

- Shares the vision through words and behaviour with others to achieve their buy-in.
- Communicates confidently and clearly, both in written and spoken word.
- Listens and responds to feedback given.
- Adapts internal and external presentation styles in order to meet the needs of diverse audiences.
- Shows sensitivity and awareness of the non-verbal communications that they portray to others.
- Delivers organizational messages with integrity and in a way that is constructive and helpful.

Involvement

'Works with and through others to deliver outcomes'.

- Involves people at all levels in order to bring a diversity of views.
- Actively works across divisions in order to achieve greater synergy.
- Networks and works in partnership with external bodies in order to gain leverage.

- Actively develops and enables wide participation.
- Demonstrates a belief in diversity and equality in working relationships and practices.
- Collaborates with others in order to create workable solutions and positive outcomes.

Professional integrity

'Provides a role model to others and acts as an ambassador for the organization'.

- Acts in a way that demonstrates the values of the organization.
- Acts ethically at all times.
- Brings enthusiasm and energy to their working practice with others.
- Respects others through being consistent and honest in the way that they work and interact with all others.
- Shows resilience and persistence in seeing a situation through.
- Can be relied on to do what they promise.

Learning and development

'Builds capacity and capability in order to deliver agreed outcomes'.

- Actively reflects on own behaviour, seeks feedback and adapts behaviour as appropriate.
- Gives regular constructive feedback to others.
- Coaches others to develop their performance and potential.
- Creates learning opportunities for others in order to develop their skills and performance.
- Shares own knowledge and expertise with others for the benefit of the whole organization.
- Promotes rigorous sharing of knowledge across the organization.

Decision-making

'Generating solutions and making decisions'.

- Listens and considers all relevant information, views and opinions of others in order to make an informed decision.
- Responds decisively when the context is ambiguous and uncertain.
- Willingly explains own decisions to others, asserting the reason for their view.
- Makes difficult decisions and says 'no' when needed.
- Reaches a conclusion that is satisfactory within an acceptable timescale.
- Is open and adaptable to adjusting decisions if the situation changes.

Delivering results

'Gets the job done within available time, budget and resources'.

- Consults and involves stakeholders in developing plans and goals.
- Continually develops and adapts plans to meet strategic requirements.
- Accepts accountability for delivering results and encourages accountability in others.
- Agrees to clear goals and quality standards.
- Manages financial and other resources required in order to achieve goals within the budget.
- Challenges and confronts difficult situations when needed, in order to deliver results.

Strategic thinking

'Thinks big and can see what we need to achieve'.

- Builds and contributes to a future – focussed vision that will create long-term impact for the organization.
- Thinks creatively about new possibilities and opportunities in own work area.
- Pushes the boundaries and takes considered risks.
- Takes account of the external world and the market in which we operate.
- Initiates and gives direction to changes required to achieve big-picture goals.
- Takes active ownership for turning ideas and concepts into actions.

2. The next example is from a UK retailer who used these competencies for the development of their Head Office staff – including marketing, finance, HR, IT, Facilities, Business Development and Legal.

Customer focus

- Listens to customers, taking time to find out what they need.
- Meets customer expectations at all times by delivering a consistently high-quality service or product.
- Reviews customer satisfaction by regularly asking for feedback and ways to improve the service.
- Is flexible and responsive to changing customer needs, adapting quickly to different business requirements.

Delivering results

- Takes responsibility for turning plans into actions, with a clear focus on achieving results.
- Makes decisions that act in the interests of the whole company.
- Keeps focus on delivering longer-term projects while not ignoring day-to-day issues.
- Keeps promises and is reliable.

Change and innovation

- Actively encourages and builds on new and innovative ideas.
- Praises and rewards those people who develop new solutions and ways of working.
- Uses both analytical and creative thinking to generate solutions and make decisions.
- Makes work fun, taking time to maintain a creative working environment.

Teamworking

- Supports colleagues across the wider team.
- Trusts and respects others to make decisions without needing to get involved in the details.
- Creates and sustains a positive working environment within the team.
- Assesses the abilities of different team members, taking time to consider their different abilities and strengths.
- Willing to challenge others and be challenged by people who have different views.

Personal effectiveness

- Displays a real passion and energy for what they do.
- Manages own time effectively, planning ahead in order to achieve results quickly.
- Shows respect for other people's needs and priorities.
- Actively seeks feedback on own management style and is willing to make changes to own behaviour.

Managing others

- Actively drives individual performance by setting clear objectives and regularly reviewing progress with team members.
- Delegates responsibility to others, trusting them to do a good job.
- Deals with difficult situations and poor performance in a direct and honest manner.
- Provides constructive, regular feedback to team members, attaching real importance to development.
- Praises and recognizes the contributions and efforts of others.

Leadership

- Sets ambitious goals and expectations for self and others, continually raising the standard.
- Is resilient in pursuing business goals even when it is difficult.

- Inspires enthusiasm and motivates others to achieve the best possible performance.
- Coaches and guides others to develop their full potential and performance.
- Adapts leadership style to meet the needs of individuals and the situation.

Strategic thinking

- Takes a broad view of the business, being alert to market and external opportunities.
- Works with others where relevant, to develop longer-term plans that will guide the organization in reaching its vision.
- Develops long-term strategy and plans for their own part of the business.
- Clearly communicates and explains their strategy and the role that their teams play in delivering the business goals.
- Balances long-term plans with short-term demands and the needs of different people when making decisions.

3. The following framework was designed by CR360.com for assessing Board-level competencies. The behaviours rate directly to the responsibilities of Board members and review their ability to operate within a Corporate Governance framework, which is a legal requirement.

Performance and risk review

Directors who consistently, objectively and sensitively review performance and risk lay the groundwork to create a constantly learning and improving organization.

- Presents clearly defined and achievable objectives for the board and the executive.
- Achieves personal and board objectives.
- Sets and adheres to formal, objective and transparent review mechanisms.
- Reviews both process and result in terms of alignment with policy on risk management.
- Reacts appropriately and effectively to problems and crises.
- Analyses causes for problems and crises in order to prevent recurrence where possible.
- Responds in a professional, flexible and positive manner to changing issues.

Corporate Governance

Directors who align the needs of the business with understanding and execution of best practice in Corporate Governance engender the trust and respect of all stakeholders.

- Actively seeks to be informed on best practice and latest development in Corporate Governance.

- Demonstrates, at both personal and board levels, real and practical understanding of the legal and fiduciary responsibilities of a board of directors.
- Separates personal and external opinion when considering the best interests of the company.
- Ensures most appropriate allocation of remit, resources and expertise to committees.
- Develops processes, skills and resources to ensure that the board is composed of the most effective talent to meet current and future requirements.
- Supports the adherence to appropriate best practice in all matters of corporate governance.
- Is supportive in developing the skills and qualities of fellow directors, in order to optimize the effectiveness of the board.

Strategic planning

Directors with strategic planning and risk analysis skills are able to articulate proactively and to monitor the way forward in a complex and challenging environment.

- Takes active responsibility to ensure the development of the current and future direction of the company.
- Formulates and abides by the risk-evaluation processes of the company.
- Provide significant contribution to the critique and development of the company's strategy.
- Considers the best interests of all shareholders, future and present, when considering the direction of the company.
- Successfully and positively integrates previous experience and knowledge into the strategic dialogue.
- Ensures that all board decisions can be clearly seen to align with the company's stated strategy and within the boundaries of risk set by the company.

Board and committee meetings

Directors who plan and prioritize effectively, establish a course of action for themselves and others to accomplish specific goals.

- Actively contributes to agenda, ensuring that appropriate structure, information and resources are allocated and disseminated in advance of the meeting.
- Is always prepared for participation in topics under discussion.
- Is supportive of others to elicit discussion, even when contrary views are held.
- Prioritizes and monitors own-agenda issues in relation to those of other directors, to ensure most effective use of time available.
- Ensures that appropriate time is allocated to enable topics to be thoroughly evaluated.
- Monitors progress, highlighting and managing inconsistencies.

- Uses appropriate expertise within the board appropriately (e.g., company secretary, human resources, financial and other experts).
- Is willing to seek external advice when internal expertise is neither sufficient nor available.

Leadership

Directors with effective leadership skills are able to clearly articulate the company's vision and business goals, inspiring the board to translate them into tangible and workable successes and results.

- Creates and adheres to a clear and easily communicated vision for the company.
- Orchestrates the complex and often-contrary needs of the stakeholders on a continuous basis for the benefit and prosperity of the organization.
- Demonstrates a strong orientation towards achievement and success in self and others.
- Is resilient in pursuing business goals, particularly in difficult circumstances.
- Inspires enthusiasm and energy in others to follow a given direction.
- Demonstrates a confident and assertive approach to taking the lead when needed.
- Delegates effectively, without bias, for the benefit of the company.

Communication

Directors with effective communication skills are able to share ideas and information, presenting ideas using well-developed interpersonal skills to a variety of audiences.

- Communicates confidently and effectively to a wide variety of audiences.
- Is trusted to represent the company to external and internal stakeholders.
- Clearly expresses thoughts and ideas in a logical manner.
- Maintains a precise and constant flow of information.
- Ensures most effective use of external communication mechanisms (AGM, Annual Report etc.).
- Produces written documents that are clear, concise and comprehensible.
- Delivers clear, professional presentations.

Intellectual and moral rigour

Directors displaying intellectual and moral rigour provide the platform for robust critique and thorough evaluation critical to good planning, risk analysis and decision-making.

- Demonstrates a structured and thorough approach towards decision-making.
- Displays flexibility and creativity when appropriate to generate ideas or alternative solutions.

- Probes and tests all assumptions appropriately.

- Solves problems by taking a broad view of the situation, stepping back from the details in order to assess the wider impact of any decision.

- Considers inputs from others – valuing their ideas, opinions and contributions without losing sight of the issue under consideration.

- Makes sound decisions based on consideration of risks, alternatives and practical implications of the outcomes of any decision.

- Makes sound decisions based on consideration of risks, alternatives and practical implications of the outcomes of any decision.

- Effectively and proactively follows up on areas of concern.

Personal commitment and interpersonal skills

Directors with obvious personal commitment and highly developed interpersonal skills can create supportive and open environments in which best practice can flourish. They are also delightful people with whom to work.

- Displays obvious commitment to the company and fellow directors, attending all meetings, devoting time and efforts to understand the company and its business.

- Praises, recognizes and values contributions and efforts from fellow directors.

- Source of good counsel, and is considered trustworthy and discreet by fellow directors.

- Fosters good working relationships with fellow directors.

- Deals with 'difficult' issues in a balanced, direct and honest manner as they arise.

- Adapts personal style to meet the needs of the situation.

- Treats people fairly without undue favouritism.

Personal effectiveness

Directors with a strong focus on personal effectiveness are respected by all members of the board for the value of their contribution.

- Adds significant value in terms of general contribution to board and company.

- Provides particular expertise within the board, or takes responsibility for a specific area of governance (e.g., chair of audit remuneration committees, etc.)

- Respected for offering balanced and well-judged opinion, even when in a minority position.

- Listens carefully, and asks probing questions.

- Reacts professionally and positively when questioned by others.

- Recognizes and manages emotions and emotional situations in a sensitive and appropriate manner.

Company and industry knowledge and awareness

Directors with company and industry knowledge are able to navigate their way within the organization, identifying and enlisting the support of stakeholders for the benefit of the company.

- Demonstrates an awareness of the formal and informal structures and relationships ('politics') that operate within the organization.
- Understands the internal business processes to a sufficient level of detail to enable intelligent and constructive participation in relevant board discussions.
- Works within organizational boundaries for the benefit of the company.
- Networks with key players in order to build strong relationships with both internal and external stakeholders.
- Spends time and energy keeping up-to-date with market data and trends that affect the overall business.

4. NHS Trust behaviours framework

The purpose of this NHS competency framework was to provide a list of the different skills and behaviours that were required by everyone working within this specific NHS Trust. They were designed to ensure that everyone was clear about the expected behaviours and the desired ways of working, in addition to the professional and clinical requirements of their roles.

The framework was designed using the input from focus groups that represented all grades of staff from a cross-section of all departments and care groups.

The following notes were used to introduce the framework to all the staff, which was done through a series of briefing sessions held by the Chief Executive and HR Director. The briefings were held for all staff from the senior manager to the domestic staff on the wards.

- Each category of behaviour is described by a title and a single statement. This describes what is included within the category.
- The examples are intended to suggest the types of each behaviour in practice, rather than a complete list.
- The examples are NOT in any priority order, as they will apply differently to different people.
- Individuals will apply the behaviours at different levels, depending on their job role and different circumstances.
- Behaviours 1–7 are relevant to everyone. Individuals and their line managers discuss and agree on what these behaviours look like in practice, depending on the different job roles that they have.
- Behaviours 8–11 are appropriate for some groups of staff and individuals. Again, the individual and the line manager need to agree as to which of these behaviours are appropriate and what they look like in practice, depending on the job role of the individual.

Communicating information

'Identifies and uses the most effective means of communication appropriate to the situation and the individuals involved'.

- Communicates concisely and clearly in a variety of forms – written, verbal and by phone, depending on the needs of the individual(s).
- Gives attention to others by listening and using positive body language.
- Is aware of what is happening, by reading noticeboards and attending team briefings.
- Responds promptly to communication from other colleagues or staff.
- Helps to set up and contribute to working across different functional/ professional groups as necessary, e.g., handovers with nurse auxiliaries/ occupational therapists.
- Shows energy and enthusiasm in passing accurate messages to staff, colleagues and others, encouraging feedback.
- Plans and delivers clear and concise presentations, and is able to produce reports in a style and language that is appropriate to the individual(s).

Self management

'Manages own behaviour to achieve results, and to develop and maintain effective working relationships with others'.

- Shows tolerance towards others and a calm approach when under pressure.
- Manages time effectively and sets priorities in order to achieve required outcomes.
- Is willing to admit when they are wrong and ask for help from others when needed.
- Takes ownership for problems, wherever possible, and uses initiative to deal with them without waiting to be asked.
- Is continually aware of the impact that their behaviour may have on others.
- Shows perseverance to achieve results within the various constraints.

Teamwork

'Motivated to work together with others and in a variety of different team settings'.

- Able to work across a number of different teams, adapting to different groups and situations as needed, for the benefit of patient care and the overall good of the Trust.
- Gives praise and recognition for the contributions of colleagues and other professionals.
- Is sensitive to the needs of others in the team in terms of both professional and personal circumstances.
- Ensures that other people in the team know what is expected of them and shares information for the good of the team.

Professionalism

'Sets and maintains high personal and professional standards'.

- Treats other people as they would like to be treated themselves, showing both respect and courtesy.
- Dresses appropriately for the working environment, wearing agreed uniform or according to dress protocols.
- Takes active responsibility for the health and safe well-being of self and others.
- Maintains polite and constructive working relationships with others while carrying out their work.
- Respects rules of confidentiality with patients, colleagues and staff.
- Defends the Trust 'in the street' and demonstrates commitment to the NHS in general.
- Refuses to share unfounded gossip and rumours.
- Is willing to confront and handle difficult issues as they arise.

Development and learning

'Willing to learn from experience and continually improve'.

- Shows awareness of own strengths and weaknesses, and willingness to ask for help from others.
- Is willing to ask for and act upon feedback on own behaviour and performance without becoming defensive.
- Takes responsibility for own learning and development, maintaining an active personal development plan, and continually keeps up-to-date with current thinking and knowledge.
- Takes opportunities to help develop the skills of others by sharing learning and experience.
- Sets realistic expectations of self and others in terms of skills, knowledge and behaviour.

Managing tasks (organization skills)

'Ability to plan, organize, prioritize and control work, ensuring effective use of time, money and resources'.

- Sets realistic, personal short-term and longer-term objectives for work activity and reviews progress against them.
- Prioritizes tasks according to importance and urgency.
- Delegates tasks to others where appropriate and supports others in achievement of their tasks when needed.
- Is reliable and honours commitments.
- Carries out routine administration quickly and regularly, in order to make time for priorities.
- Uses problem-solving and objective decision-making techniques when tackling issues.

Innovation and improvement

'Shows creativity and innovation in developing new ways of working'.

- Is willing to be flexible and open to change in the light of the changing organizational environment in which they work.
- Carries out all required quality audits and quality monitoring in an efficient and timely manner, taking the needs of all relevant parties into account.
- Takes action on the findings of quality audits in order to improve working practices, and learns from mistakes on a day-to-day basis.
- Encourages and/or allows others to develop creative ideas which may help to improve the service provided.

Managing meetings

'Facilitates and contributes to meetings effectively, so that the purpose of the meeting can be achieved'.

- Prepares the meetings and makes clear, concise and relevant contributions.
- Listens to and acknowledges the contributions of others in a constructive manner.
- Agrees on decisions and actions using consensus, ensuring that everyone has an opportunity to have their views heard.
- Takes responsibility for completing action points after the meeting and for communicating outcomes to relevant parties within the agreed timescales.
- As leader of meetings, ensures that people are given the start and finish times, so that they understand the reasons for their attendance and the purpose of the meetings in order that they may contribute effectively.

Managing others

'Inspires and motivates teams and individuals to achieve the business objectives'.

- Leads by personal example, matching actions to words – 'practises what they preach'.
- Willing to hear all views and involve others in decision-making, wherever possible.
- Is approachable and accessible, taking time to understand the needs and views of others.
- Prepared to make unpopular decisions to say 'no' when needed, giving appropriate reasons.
- Gives direction and clarity to team members by ensuring that all people in the team have up-to-date job descriptions, clear objectives and the opportunities to discuss their progress as needed.
- Takes active responsibility for the development of others by carrying out appraisals, and providing coaching and support when needed.

- Demonstrates trust in others by delegating responsibility and authority to team members on an agreed basis.
- Sets realistic goals and expectations of others, taking into account existing workloads.

Dealing with the media/PR

'Communicates with the media in order to inform the public of relevant issues, putting the views of the Trust across in a positive and consistent manner'.

- Is always in full command of the facts and has a planned approach before delivering the message.
- Always gives a message that is consistent with agreed views of all team members, and which demonstrates full support for the Trust and individual colleagues.
- Delivers the message in a fair and open manner, using clear, concise language that is non-sensational and reassuring.

Strategic management

'Sets out and evaluates a clear vision and key priorities for the Trust, taking into account both internal and external initiatives and influences'.

- Works with other agencies and stakeholders to create a shared strategy and focus for Island healthcare.
- Develops corporate priorities and objectives for the Trust in order to achieve the shared focus, allocating resources accordingly.
- Communicates the Trusts priorities with energy and enthusiasm so that people understand them and are committed to their achievement.
- Identifies and develops effective working relationships with key stakeholders and partners on an inter-agency basis, reporting back outcomes in a non-judgemental manner.
- Having identified the Trust's strategies, acts as a role model for leading the implementation of those strategies, e.g., use of IT and e-mail, effectively carrying out appraisals.

How was this NHS Framework used?

The framework provided an input at different stages of the performance management system within the Trust. It is used specifically at the following times:

Recruitment of new staff – The behaviours are incorporated in the 'person' specifications and referred to during the selection process.

Development and training – The framework provides the basis for the design of training and development programmes.

Individual coaching – Where appropriate, individuals are given one-to-one coaching and support to develop an individual development plan based on the feedback they receive.

Appraisal – The appraisal process includes discussion about the individual's performance and the performance of their line manager in these areas of behaviour, in addition to reviewing the individual's performance against objectives.

5. The following example was designed for a manufacturing company of 500 staff who wanted to integrate their values into an easy-to-understand set of behaviours that could apply to everyone from the production line to the Board.

Vision and direction

- Clearly communicates the importance of alignment of employees to achieve the company's goals.
- Demonstrates a passion for the business and a determination to succeed.
- Demonstrates a strong grasp of the implications of performance of each function on other functions within the business.
- Effectively articulates the company vision in a clear manner and sees the 'big picture'.
- Takes responsibility for turning plans into actions, with a focus on achieving results.

Best practice and innovation

- Actively increases the company's market knowledge through attending industry forums and sharing learning.
- Benchmarks the company's activities and skills with other companies both within the group and externally.
- Constantly strives to introduce improved ways of working and encourage best practice within their function.
- Keeps up-to-date with market trends and drivers, recognizing changing commercial pressures.

Customer and commercial focus

- Considers the impact on internal and external customers in every decision made.
- Seeks out opportunities and innovative ways of meeting customer requirements while building profitability.
- Takes an overview of the whole business into account when making decisions about their area of the business.
- Understands the financial drivers of the business and communicates them effectively.
- When dealing with the customer, balances the business objectives with the demands of the customer.

Managing change

- Demonstrates a real belief and passion for change.
- Explains the need for change, clearly communicating benefits to the company and impact on the individual.
- Listens to concerns of stakeholders and helps the team to overcome issues/fears when going through any changes.
- Helps others to recognize the need to change and adapt.
- Shows personal flexibility and an ability to adapt quickly to changing business conditions.

Achieving results

- Constructively challenges existing processes and procedures in order to improve output.
- Demonstrates resilience and personal stamina in their drive towards achieving results.
- Overcomes obstacles and is persistent in pursuing solutions.
- Quickly buys into the common agenda of agreed business goals, working for the overall benefit of the business.
- Quickly buys into the common agenda of agreed business goals, working for the overall benefit of the business.
- Regularly reviews progress, actively ensuring that projects stay on track and deliver on time.

People management

- Actively builds relationships across the whole business in order to promote whole teamworking.
- Adapts leadership style, depending on the nature of the task, people and time available.
- Listens and is sensitive to others, taking account of their views and needs.
- Motivates others to deliver the highest standards by giving constructive feedback, praise and recognition.
- Takes time out to coach team members to develop their skills and maximize their contribution.

Professional integrity

- Actively seeks feedback on personal style and works to improve, based on feedback given.
- Can be relied on to do what they say they will do.
- Is self-disciplined, clearly focussed on achieving the best results for the company.
- Maintains a positive 'can do' attitude, controlling own feelings of stress and anxiety when under pressure, to ensure that others are not affected adversely.

This example is taken from a Borough City Council.

Leadership

Influences and facilitates the activity of others, leading by example. Adopts different styles of leadership behaviour to suit the situation or the circumstance.

- Demonstrates a strong focus towards achievement and success in self and others.
- Takes a confident approach to leading the efforts of others.
- Is resilient in pursuing business goals even when the going gets tough.
- Inspires enthusiasm and energy in others to follow a given direction and to deliver outcomes.
- Strives for continual collective performance improvement.
- Delegates effectively by taking into account the potential of the individual and the needs of the job.

Communication and relationships

Consults with others in a way, which encourages open and frank discussion, shows respect and maintains collaborative and productive working relationships.

- Communicates confidently and effectively to diverse audiences, in both spoken and written word.
- Listens effectively to others' ideas and points of view and conducts regular team meetings.
- Adapts personal style to meet the needs of the individual and the situation.
- Maintains a positive attitude, controlling own feelings of stress and anxiety when under pressure, to ensure that others are not affected adversely.
- Demonstrates integrity, fairness and consistency, maintaining confidentiality and honesty in dealings with internal and external customers.
- Demonstrates effective negotiation and influencing skills to achieve 'win–win' outcomes in negotiations.

Problem solving

Use their own and others' experience and knowledge to understand or identify current or potential problems and to look to implement long-lasting solutions for the communities within which we operate.

- Consults widely on the nature of issues, seeking inputs from others in the Council and the wider community.
- Displays flexibility and creativity when generating ideas and options to consider.
- Openly acknowledges the value of other people's ideas and opinions.
- Demonstrates a structured and systematic approach towards decision-making, which involves breaking down complex issues into understandable and manageable elements.

- Makes timely decisions based on consideration of time, cost and quality.
- Challenges established working practices and takes advantage of opportunities to improve council effectiveness and efficiency.

Strategic planning and resourcing

Is able to plan and to prioritize effectively, working towards providing quality services and meeting needs of the community.

- Produces clear business plans that mirror overall Council objectives.
- Manages and monitors resources efficiently in order to maintain consistent performance and quality of services.
- Prioritizes and monitors own work schedules and that of team members, managing issues before they reach a critical stage.
- Takes ownership for turning plans into action.
- Works flexibly, responding readily to the demands of changing priorities and needs.

Learning and development

Adopts an inclusive approach to learning and development, providing equal opportunities. Encourages others to take an active responsibility for their own development.

- Actively builds relationships between team members and departments in a co-operative and effective manner.
- Identifies suitable people for tasks by taking time to assess their capabilities and potential.
- Uses effective delegation to develop others.
- Coaches others to develop to their full potential and to improve their performance.
- Actively seeks feedback on own management style and works to improve performance, based on feedback given.
- Learns from previous experiences of self and others.

Managing performance

Focuses on achieving goals and objectives by creating a culture of continuous performance review.

- Takes active responsibility for the development of others by setting realistic and challenging objectives.
- Actively manages performance by conducting regular appraisals and reviews.
- Praises, recognizes and values everyone's contributions and effort.
- Deals promptly with inappropriate behaviour and performance problems in a direct and honest manner.

- Treats people fairly without favouritism, applying equal opportunities to all.
- Involves staff in creating a shared vision for the service and a sense of collective purpose within the team.

Knowledge and understanding

Employees with knowledge and understanding are able to navigate their way quickly within the Council, in order to influence opinion, motivate others and to deliver efficient services to the community.

- Understands the strategic objectives and environment (within their area of responsibility) to a sufficient level of detail, to successfully manage and plan the activities of their team.
- Networks with contacts in the wider community to identify needs and expectations of the community to help direct and guide council services.
- Spends time and energy keeping up-to-date with organizational, community and technical issues that affect the overall business of the Council.
- Demonstrates ability to manage budgets and resources within Council guidelines.
- Maintains an up-to-date, in-depth knowledge of their own professional discipline and the skills and services available externally.
- Exercises judgement in sharing sensitive information.

6. The following example is taken from a small technical consulting company that specializes in providing highly qualified technical consultants to the oil industry. As consultants, they need to manage projects efficiently. In addition, they need to demonstrate the skills of business development and account management as they become more senior.

Leadership

People with effective leadership skills are able to articulate clearly the group vision and business goals, inspiring their teams to translate them into measureable results.

- Focuses strongly on achievement and success in self and others.
- Inspires enthusiasm and energy in others to follow a given direction.
- Is resilient in pursuing the company's business goals.
- Demonstrates a confident and assertive approach to taking the lead when needed.
- Delegates effectively by taking into account the potential of the individual and the needs of the job.

External focus

People with astute external focus understand the market and how it is changing. This enables them to deliver leading-edge products and services to their clients.

- Keeps up-to-date with market trends and drivers, recognizing changing commercial pressures.
- Listens to customers, seeks to anticipate potential challenges, and creates innovative business solutions.
- Constantly considers the company's overall position with clients, seeking to maximize the value of the contract for both the client and the company.
- Builds effective networks with customers, suppliers and others throughout industry.
- Represents the company with pride, emphasizing its positive attributes with customers and competitors.
- Is flexible and responsive to client's changing needs, optimizing delivery of satisfaction.

Strategic perspective

People with a strategic perspective are able to identify the way forward in a complex and challenging environment.

- Shapes and communicates the current and future direction of the company.
- Translates business goals and objectives into clear operational plans.
- Communicates the role that their 'team' plays in facilitating and achieving the business objectives.
- Balances short- and long-term requirements, ensuring that both are addressed.
- Recognizes and balances the relationships between different business areas to the good of the group.
- Constantly seeks new and better value solutions to business challenges.
- Takes a broad view of situations, with a constant focus on increasing the value of our business.

Communication

People with effective communication skills are able to share ideas and information effectively using well-developed interpersonal skills to a variety of audiences.

- Adapts communication style to needs of different team members, colleagues and clients.
- Freely shares information, ideas and suggestions, keeping others updated and regularly informed.
- Listens effectively to others' ideas and points of view.
- Is willing to challenge constructively and be challenged.
- Shows empathy, taking time to understand other people's views.

Thinking and decision-making

People displaying thinking and decision-making skills analyze information gathered from a variety of sources in order to make sound judgements based both on facts and on personal intuition.

- Collects input from others – valuing their ideas, opinions and contributions.
- Addresses problems using a balance of facts, experience and intuition.
- Displays flexibility and creativity when generating ideas/solutions.
- Assesses priorities swiftly, assigning direction and action to be taken.
- Demonstrates a structured and rational approach towards decision-making.
- Takes appropriate risks in a well-managed way, in order to move the business forward.

Planning and prioritizing: Plan – Do – Review

People who plan and prioritize effectively establish a course of action for themselves and others to accomplish specific goals.

- Produces clear business/project plans that mirror business objectives.
- Ensures that the company's work processes are consistently used and improved.
- Prioritizes and monitors work schedules, managing issues before they reach a critical stage.
- Manages own time effectively, ensuring that priorities are set and dealt with efficiently.
- Demonstrates focus on the objectives and end results by effective timely delivery.
- Manages budgets and resources within projects to ensure maximum profitability within the quality requirements of the job.
- Works flexibly, responding readily to the demands of changing priorities and needs.

Managing and building teams

Employees who build effective teams encourage full participation and effort, building cohesion while maintaining motivation.

- Actively builds relationships between team members and colleagues in a collaborative manner.
- Helps to create solutions with others and welcomes their contributions.
- Demonstrates awareness of the different needs of team members, accepting that people prefer to work in different ways.
- Creates a true team spirit within own team and the wider teams in which they work.
- Resolves conflicts through constructive dialogue to create solutions from which all benefit.
- Establishes clear accountabilities for self and the team.
- Creates an environment to foster development, giving individuals the opportunities to achieve their aims.
- Develops the skills and qualities of team members in order to maximize team and project success.

People and performance

Managers who demonstrate effective People Management Skills ensure that people within their teams maximize their personal contribution and development.

- Takes active responsibility for the development of others by setting achievable but challenging objectives.
- Praises, recognizes and values individuals' contributions and efforts.
- Coaches others to develop to their full potential and to improve their performance.
- Actively manages performance by conducting regular performance reviews.
- Deals promptly with 'difficult' individuals and performance problems in a direct, supportive and honest manner.
- Adapts personal style to meet the needs of the individual and the situation.
- Demonstrates fairness by ensuring consistent application of company policies and procedures.

Personal style

Employees with a strong focus on personal effectiveness show resilience and determination to succeed in the face of pressure and difficulties.

- Demonstrates passion and energy for what they do, showing conviction and enthusiasm for the job.
- Presents a knowledgeable and authoritative presence with clients and colleagues.
- Demonstrates integrity, fairness and consistency, maintaining confidentiality and honesty in dealing with internal and external customers.
- Is self-disciplined and hard working, focused on achieving the best results for the company and client.
- Maintains a positive attitude, controlling own feelings of stress and anxiety when under pressure to ensure that others are not affected adversely.
- Actively seeks feedback on personal style and works to improve, based on feedback given.

All the competency frameworks, as given above, have been designed to meet the particular needs of each company. Although some of them appear to be similar, the language, emphasis and degree of detail are all set within the context of the particular organization.

Benefits of the competency approach

Taking a competency approach has many advantages for the organization.

1. It provides a consistent set of behaviours against which everyone can be assessed and developed.
2. It gives a clear message to all employees about what the organization expects from them.

3. It provides the backbone to any training and development activity within the organization. Any training and development workshop should be related to the different behavioural dimensions of the competency framework.

4. It provides consistency in approach to review of skills and development planning.

5. Depending on the complexity of the framework, it gives clarity about the different levels of competence required at different levels within the organization. This is of help with succession planning and promotion.

A robust competency framework is the backbone of any performance management system. Any leadership development strategy is dependent on a future-proofed competency framework, in order to ensure that the right skills are being developed across the company. Time taken to develop a framework that matches the needs of the business and has buy-in from the employees is time well spent. Once the competency framework has been designed, the company needs to decide on how it will be used in the different stages of the HR cycle – recruitment, development planning, training and performance reviews.

7 360 feedback processes and systems

One of the main uses of a competency framework is for performance review and development planning. This is often done by integrating the competencies into a 360 feedback process. In this chapter we shall look at the following topics:

The purpose of 360 feedback

How 360 feedback works

Developing the 360 feedback questionnaire

Implementing an effective 360 feedback process

Organizational benchmarking using 360 feedback data

The role of HR in 360 feedback

Guidelines for introducing a 360 feedback system

A summary – key guidelines for effective 360 feedback systems

The purpose of 360 feedback

360 feedback is a powerful tool for assessing a person's performance against an agreed set of behaviours. It is a systematic and structured approach to collate both quantitative and qualitative feedback about a person. It involves feeding back the data to the person in a way that helps them clearly to identify their strengths and areas for further development.

Feedback from a number of different perspectives enables the person to compare their self-assessment with the views of others. People learn that their views of themselves can often differ from how others view them. This can have a powerful impact on the person and, in terms of performance review, gives a far more balanced view of their performance than relying simply on self-perception or even the views of the line manager alone.

The key benefit of 360 feedback is (perhaps surprisingly) not in the actual report. It is in how the feedback process is managed and how well the person is then supported in putting together a development plan to work on the different areas highlighted in their feedback. This can include maximizing key strengths as well as working to improve those areas where there are weaknesses.

How 360 feedback works

Case study

Using 360 feedback to develop senior managers

An offshore investment bank decided that they wanted to use 360 feedback to highlight the development needs of their senior managers. In order to gain their buy in, they ran several focus groups with the senior managers to elicit their views on what behaviours were important for the future. Then they ran briefing sessions for each of the people who were going to be involved in the 360 feedback process. These briefing sessions covered the following areas:

The purpose of the 360 feedback process

Confidentiality

Choosing observers

How to use the online system

The role of HR and line managers

Timescales and next steps

After the face-to-face briefing session, which lasted about an hour, the managers were asked to complete a form outlining whom they wished to include as their observers. They were asked to include their line manager, themselves, three colleagues and three direct reports.

They were then given access to the online system and the reports were completed over a one month period.

The bank then followed up the individual feedback reports with a one-to-one coaching session with an external coach, where each manager created a personal development plan for the next six months. The senior leadership team then ran a one-day session where they shared the output of their profiles and discussed the overall strengths and areas for development of the team as a whole. This provided excellent team building as well as reinforcing the learning from the individual feedback. Six months later, a follow-up 360 profile was completed and the company was able to see significant improvements in overall performance of that group. The company now runs a 360 feedback process annually and feeds it into the annual performance review process.

The project was extremely successful and much of the success was owing to the thorough briefing and involvement of all the participants. HR played a key role in managing the briefing process and ensuring that everyone completed a coaching session. They also collated the results for the Board to provide a benchmark of overall performance, which is now reviewed each year.

Developing the 360 feedback questionnaire

A survey in the UK in 1998 by the Chartered Institute of Personnel and Development found that performance appraisal is most effective when it includes 360 feedback as part of the process. In 1997, 11 per cent of the organizations they covered were using it. In 2006, this figure is closer to 35 per cent.

The questionnaire should be based on the key competencies and behaviours required by the organization. These can either be taken directly from an existing competency framework or a generic leadership behaviours framework can be used. There are also several 360 feedback questionnaires available commercially that focus on specific areas such as emotional intelligence or leadership style.

It is generally worth using an external specialist to design the questionnaires in order to ensure that they are well designed with robust questions that will assess the key behaviours as objectively as possible.

Implementing an effective 360 feedback process

Briefing of participants

People need to understand why they are being asked to complete a 360 feedback process. They need to be clear as to the reasons for the exercise, the benefits and the format of the questionnaire and process. For this reason, a face-to-face or online briefing is necessary if the organization wishes people to enter into the exercise with a positive frame of mind. The sample-briefing document explained in Table 7.1 is a document that could be e-mailed to people if face-to-face briefings are not feasible.

Table 7.1 Sample – 360 feedback briefing document

Introduction
The purpose of this briefing note is to outline the 360 programme that is being run for you. We hope it will answer any specific questions that you may have. If you have been asked to be an observer, this will give you some background to the programme and explain your role in it.

360 feedback – an overview
360 feedback is a 'perception-based' performance management tool that offers a participant the opportunity to be reviewed by a wide range of 'observers' – including self, managers, peers and direct reports on the skills and behaviours they possess and demonstrate at work. Participants receive an individual report comprising both numerical ratings and narrative comments on each area of leadership.

The benefits of 360 feedback
360 feedback has benefits for the company and the individual participants.

The initial benefits of the programme for the participants are to be found mainly in the area of 'self-development', where a written feedback profile is produced for each person, which collates the views of their observers. This allows participants to begin to understand how their observers at work perceive them. It is recognized that these perceptions may vary, e.g. managers will generally perceive strengths in particular areas differently from any direct reports. Participants are usually then asked to share their profile with their managers, thus enabling more detailed discussions on perceived strengths and development areas.

(Continued)

Table 7.1 (Continued)

The 360 feedback process can also identify any common development themes for the target audience as a whole. This benchmark data can be used to inform any development and training activities that follow after.

Selecting observers
The feedback is received from a number of observers: Self, 1 line manager, 3 peers and 3 direct reports. Participants should approach those people with whom they work closely and whom they feel will give an honest and constructive perception of their work behaviours. It is better to receive feedback from fewer 'high quality' observers whose feedback is valued than from a wider group of poorer quality observers.

You need to include your manager and then choose three or four colleagues, and three or four people who work for you. If you do not have direct reports or people who work for you, then choose more colleagues.

Choose people whose views you value.
Choose people who have known you for at least six months.
Choose people whom you feel will be both constructive and specific in their feedback.
Do not pick only your best friends.

The role of the observer
The observer's role is to provide an honest and constructive view of how you see the participant, remember that your comments will be put into the report without any editing.

Observer comments and ratings
Feedback reports consist of a summary of the perception of the observers and narrative comments on each of the skill areas. Narrative comments taken directly from the observers' feedback are relevant to the specific person and highlight areas of strength and areas for development in each area. The data in the report is presented in a visually attractive format that is easy to understand and follow. Your comments and ratings will be taken directly from your online questionnaire; they will not be edited in any way. They will appear in the report without any reference to who has made the comment, i.e. non-attributable.

Your role as an observer is to provide constructive comment, which will enable the individual to develop their performance.

Additional questions or concerns

Please contact:

Choosing observers

Most 360 feedback systems allow the participant to nominate several observers. Best practice would suggest the participant themselves, the manager, three to four colleagues and three to four direct reports. In some organizations, it may also be appropriate to ask external customers or suppliers to complete a questionnaire. The number of observers is the key to gain a complete set of perceptions. These observers also need to fulfil certain criteria:

- They need to know the individual well-enough, to be able to comment knowledgeably on their overall performance
- They need to be willing to complete the questionnaire in a way that is constructive and helpful to the individual.

A robust 360 feedback system should enable people to answer the questions only where they have sufficient data. Observers should omit answers to questions where they have insufficient knowledge of the participant.

Participants should be allowed to nominate the observers themselves for several very valid reasons:

- It encourages their buy-in to the process and to the final report.
- Participants will choose a cross-section of people and are in the best place to decide who knows them well enough. The 360 processes should always include the manager and a cross-section of colleagues and direct reports.
- Development is the responsibility of the participant. The 360 feedbacks are for their benefit and, therefore, they should control the process and have the choice over whom they ask for feedback.

Number of questions

Experience shows that people have a very low saturation point once they are asked to complete a similar questionnaire several times. In some organizations, managers may be required to complete 10 or more questionnaires at about the same time, if they manage large numbers of people. For this reason, it is suggested that the maximum number of questions should be around 50, if the questionnaire also includes space for narrative comments. Good practice would be to include a maximum of 10 competency headings with about five questions in each category. (See the previous section for exemplar competency headings.)

Organizational benchmarking using 360 feedback data

The benefit of 360 feedback is that it gives people a personal benchmark of their own performance. Conducting 360 feedback each year is a very powerful way of measuring improvement and progress. In addition, an effective 360 feedback system should be able to provide an overall set of measures for the organization, which can be compared on a group-by-group, or year-by-year, basis for different audiences within the company. Figure 7.1 and Table 7.2 are examples of the sort of data that HR and Development and Training people could use to plan their next year's training programmes and development for their people.

This graph shows the average ratings for a group of middle managers who completed a 360 feedback questionnaire as part of a development programme. Based on the results, the programme was then designed to focus on people management skills and team development skills as these were the areas of most need.

This graph is created to give an overview of the top 10 strengths and the 10 lowest scoring behaviours from the whole population of middle managers in a company. This provides HR with up-to-date data showing which competencies need further development in the organization as a whole. Individual graphs are also provided for each participant in order to assist with personal development planning.

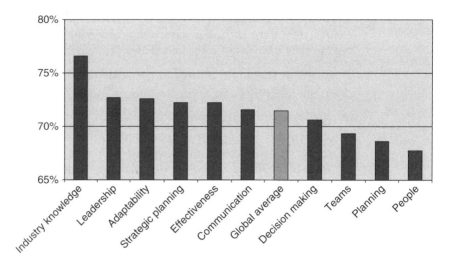

Figure 7.1 Group average ratings (Taken with permission from www.cr360.com).

Providing the feedback after the completion of the 360 profiles

This is the most important part of the process. There are several approaches that can be taken.

One-to-one feedback with a coach

The benefit of a one-to-one session is that the participant can focus on understanding the whole report and identify key themes that come out of the feedback. The coach can then work with them to create a personal development plan to work on with their manager.

Group feedback

The benefit of this approach is that participant is encouraged to share their 360 feedback with others and can compare their feedback with their colleagues. This can be helpful in team building but is less useful on a personal basis. Be aware that people may view this as competitive and feel uneasy about sharing areas in which they were less successful.

The role of HR in 360 feedback

HR needs to act as the process owner of the 360 feedback and ensure that the process runs smoothly, adhering to agreed confidentiality and feedback guidelines. Many HR Directors want to have sight of the 360 reports, but this should be from an organizational development perspective only. The overall data from the 360 feedback process can be enormously helpful in identifying organizational-wide development needs. It can also be useful in creating a benchmark of performance for particular groups.

Table 7.2 Overall scores from sample 360 feedback profile (Taken with permission from www.cr360.com).

	Highest rated behaviours				Lowest rated behaviours			
Rank	Competence	Trait	% Score	Rank	Competence	Trait	% Score	
1	Personal effectiveness	Displays a real passion and energy for what they do	83.2%	1	Personal effectiveness	Actively seeks feedback on own management style and is willing to make changes to own behaviour	61.5%	
2	Delivering results	Takes responsibility for turning plans into actions, with a clear focus on achieving results	81.9%	2	Customer focus	Reviews customer satisfaction by regularly asking for feedback and ways to improve the service	62.9%	
3	Delivering results	Makes decisions that act in the interests of the whole company	80.7%	3	Leadership	Adapts leadership style to meet the needs of individuals and the situation	64.6%	
4	Leadership	Is resilient in pursuing business goals even when the going gets tough?	80.4%	4	Leadership	Coaches and develops others to develop their full potential and performance	66.5%	
5	Strategic thinking	Takes a broad view of the business, being alert to market and external opportunities	76.3%	5	Change and innovation	Makes work fun, taking time to maintain a creative working environment	67.0%	

(*Continued*)

Table 7.2 (Continued)

Highest rated behaviours				Lowest rated behaviours			
Rank	Competence	Trait	% Score	Rank	Competence	Trait	% Score
6	Strategic thinking	Develops long-term strategy and plans for their own part of the business	75.8%	6	Strategic thinking	Clearly communicates and explains their strategy and the role that their teams play in delivering the business goals	68.0%
7	Change and innovation	Uses both analytical and creative thinking to generate solutions and make decisions	75.2%	7	Managing others	Provides constructive, regular feedback to team members, attaching real importance to development	68.1%
8	Managing others	Delegates responsibility to others, trusting them to do a good job	74.2%	8	Change and innovation	Praises and rewards those people who develop new solutions and ways of working	69.4%
9	Delivering results	Walks the talk, keeps promises and can be relied on to do what they say	74.0%	9	Strategic thinking	Balances long-term plans with short-term demands and the needs of different people when making decisions	69.8%
10	Leadership	Sets ambitious goals and expectations for self and others, continually raising the standard	73.8%	10	Leadership	Inspires enthusiasm and motivates others to achieve the best possible performance	69.9%

HR has an important role in ensuring that the 360 feedback is used in the best way possible. They are there to ensure that the follow-up to the 360 profiles is carried out effectively and consistently. They are there to act as a mediator if a participant is unhappy with their feedback and needs to discuss it with a third party. They are also responsible for ensuring that appropriate development activities are planned to meet the needs of the development plans arising from the 360 feedback process.

A key role is to ensure that managers have the required levels of skills to manage the process effectively.

Involvement of the line manager

Participants need to share their feedback with their managers if they are to work together to act on the outcome of the profiles. The managers need to be skilled in running these coaching sessions, as it is not an opportunity for them to give more of their own personal feedback. It is an opportunity for them to coach participants to identify what areas they want to develop within their current work roles and areas of responsibility.

HR needs to ensure that managers are well-briefed on the 360 feedback process and understand how it fits within the overall leadership development strategy. They need to develop managers to be able to run debrief sessions with their own people.

The following template can provide a useful guide for mangers who are involved in running one-to-one feedback sessions with their team.

A process for 360 feedback report debrief

1. Preparation

   - Book protected time in your diary and allow 1–1.5 hours for the feedback debrief.
   - A short time before the feedback debrief (a couple of days), give the person their report. Ask them to read their feedback and make some notes in preparation for your meeting.
   - Prepare for the meeting by reading the feedback, identifying the key themes, etc.

2. Give an overview of key points regarding 360 reports and the feedback session

   - They are purely a set of perceptions, not fact.
   - People will see you differently, therefore the comments may be contradictory.
   - Difference between numerical ratings and narrative. People may be high or low scorers, the value is in the narrative.
   - The narrative is unedited, look at overall themes rather than trying to guess who said what.

- Explain that the importance of feedback is what you do with it. The feedback session provides a process for identifying key themes and making sense of the data.

3. The feedback

   - Talk through the main patterns and trends, higher scoring areas (start with the positives), lower scoring areas and areas of difference between ratings from colleagues/direct reports/manager. What does this tell you?
   - Remember that you are there to ask questions and prompt the discussion. You are not there to give your own personal viewpoint.
   - Comments – get behind them – why do you think they said that?

4. Development actions

   - Gain agreement to specific development actions. What areas is the individual interested in looking at?
   - Focus on three or four areas.
   - If looking for solutions, what could they do differently? Who does this well? What do they do?

5. Sharing the feedback

   - Ask the person to identify with whom they will share the feedback.
   - Discuss the benefits of sharing the data with the team/key colleagues.
   - Discuss the different options, e.g.
     - send out the whole report to all observers.
     - face-to-face discussion with key observers (one-to-one or whole group).
     - share the learning plan with their team.

   The key benefit of sharing the data is in opening a discussion with people whose views you value. The 360 report is the beginning of a process of regular and frequent two-way feedback. It supports a culture of continuing feedback and development.

6. Conclude the session

   - Agree a review date to discuss progress.
   - Agree how they will take the feedback further with their team or colleagues.

Reflection point

Review of your company's 360 programmes:

What benefits are you looking to gain from using 360 feedback?

What briefing do you have in place for the participants and observers?

What is the agreed level of confidentiality for the 360 profiles?

Who sees the individual 360 profiles?

How capable are your managers of debriefing the 360 profiles with their people?

How well do people know how to match the development needs with available development options?

How much follow-up is carried out after the 360 profiles are received?

How do you manage the feedback process after the profiles have been completed?

What benefits have your managers gained from using a 360-feedback process?

How much are you using any organizational data from the 360 processes?

What do you need to do to improve the process and use of the feedback?

Guidelines for introducing a 360 feedback system

360 feedback touches many people within an organization. When communicated properly, as part of a personal development programme, it can provide enormous benefits for both the individual and the organization. Any 360 feedback system will affect many people in an organization and needs to be selected with care in order to suit all those that will be affected by it.

In general, there are three types of persons involved in the 360 feedback process.

The administrator(s)

The administrators of the system are often the internal HR team or learning and development managers. They require a system sufficiently powerful to create questionnaires and reports for perhaps thousands of people, who can still communicate effectively and efficiently with all staff. Even a relatively small project for 25 staff may require feedback from 150 or more people within an organization, and an administrator needs the confidence that the system can track progress and communicate effectively with all those involved without becoming a full time occupation for HR.

Those giving feedback (observers)

It is a rare company that recognizes the time and effort involved in providing quality feedback (we should estimate somewhere around 30 minutes to 45 minutes for questionnaires requesting both numeric and situational feedback). Therefore, people have to find the extra time, often at very short notice, to provide confidential and sometimes sensitive information for their colleagues. If a member of staff is asked to complete feedback for several colleagues, then this can mean trying to find an extra half day's work in a very short period. This is not conducive to provide good quality feedback. Therefore, the 360 system chosen needs to be quick, simple and user-friendly.

Those receiving feedback (participants)

The people who will be receiving a 360 feedback profile need to understand why it is being used, what benefits they will gain from it and whom they should choose as observers. They may also have questions around confidentiality and timescales.

Success criteria for a 360 feedback system

Before deciding on any particular system, it is desirable to conduct a general review of the various criteria that may be required from a system to provide the most effective feedback for an organization.

A standard overall checklist should consider the following criteria.

The purpose of the 360 feedback system, and how success will be monitored
This may sound simple but some consideration needs to be given to what outcomes are expected from the system. Three issues need clarification and weighting in terms of priority: the degree to which the system is intended as a personal development tool for the individual; the degree to which the system is integrated into pay and promotion; and the degree to which the system is a management tool for comparing and contrasting overall performance of individuals and departments. Each of these can cause conflict with the others, but, most importantly, they may well affect the level of 'real' feedback that is given and received. Time taken at the outset to establish a clear and common understanding of how success will be measured may well save much heartache later on.

Number of staff to receive 360 feedback, and how often
questionnaires will be run
This, of course, has a direct correlation with the relative complexity and cost of running a 360 project. However, it also has a more subtle impact on the administration requirements, particularly if a company is considering using internal staff.

Unless the number of staff receiving feedback is sufficiently high and there are multiple projects in the corporate year, it is unlikely that the cost of keeping internal resource trained and competent in the administration of 360s is justifiable. Planning at an early stage the impact of the process on the work schedule of staff, and how best to optimize it, is a very important step that many companies miss.

Confidentiality
How comfortable are people in providing feedback within the company? What will the briefing mechanism be? What measures need to be in place to protect confidentiality? Would employees be more comfortable knowing that their confidential feedback on their colleagues is maintained in-house by other colleagues, or by an independent external third party?

Competency framework
How complex is the competency framework? Is there a single, generic framework for the whole company, or are there core competencies supported by a number of specific competencies across the organization? Is there a competency library? Can the chosen system handle your required level of complexity (nearly every 360 system should be able to offer a single questionnaire based on your competencies, but relatively few currently have the ability to handle complex permutations of competencies).

The generation of the questionnaires from the competency framework is a very important process, but many companies try to save money here by employing an in-house resource, rather than by employing experts, while other companies fail to consider this process at all. In simple terms, the quality of questions has a direct impact on the quality of feedback. This is not so critical when the 360 is used in a personal development context only. However, it is particularly frustrating (and demotivating to those involved) to find companies using the results for 360 feedback as a pay/promotion tool based on global feedback comparisons that have very narrow data distribution curves.

Means of questionnaire distribution and collection
It is usually taken for granted nowadays that all staff have e-mail and internet access, but this is not always the case, and even those who do have internet access may find that it is restricted behind company firewalls. It may be necessary to involve IT in testing systems and configuring firewalls. Some users may have little or intermittent access to computers and, therefore, telephone, personal or postage distribution may be required. Remember, however, that once you move to nonelectronic forms of distribution, issues such as cost, time and control will need to be carefully considered. Even when there is general network and internet availability, the level of general computer expertise needs to be taken into consideration, and any system should be trialled using a sample of people, including the least technically competent (who should not be presumed to be merely the most junior or most unskilled) to check for user friendliness.

What should be in the 360 report?
The array of potential report styles available is bewildering and ranges from the simplest of arithmetical means to complex analysis of data set distribution, including cross tab comparisons of each group of respondents and measurement

against company, industrial or global norms. The final decision needs to be based, of course, on the value that any data set will provide to the individual concerned.

It should also be remembered that the written word is generally much more powerful than any scoring system to the individual (even if not to the company) and that the opportunity to support subjective numeric scoring with individual comment should not be dismissed lightly. Our experience would suggest that people find the narrative comments far more useful than a set of numbers and statistical graphs.

We should suggest the guiding rules:

- Does the numerical analysis add value for the individual?
- Will the individual understand it?
- Is the level of information in line with the original goals?

What management data is required?

In most (although not all) cases, the company will also require some kind of general feedback. At the very least, perhaps to establish forward planning budgets and resources to support those competencies where extra development may be required. Many companies leave this issue until the 360 process has been running for some time and are disappointed to find either that the reports that they would like are not available from the system, or that every report requires an extra cost that is not budgeted for. It is worth agreeing what organizational data is required before starting the process and ensuring that the supplier can provide these services if required.

Security

How strong is password security? How is access to data managed, and how will the data be maintained? Particularly when using third party sources, there is a responsibility to make sure that individual information is managed professionally, at the very least in keeping with the Data Protection laws for the country concerned. Is the third party even registered with the Data Protection Agency of the country in question? If using internet or third party suppliers what back up systems are in place? Specifically, when using internet suppliers, what is the worst case data failure possible, and what data may be lost? (be very sceptical if any supplier tells you 'no data can be lost'.)

Who will administer the process?

The choice here is often driven by pure cost without taking into account the time taken for the internal HR team to manage the process. Many companies will consider it cheaper to manage the administration of the process in-house. Whether this is truly the most cost-effective process will depend on several factors:

- Confidentiality of process
- Training costs and lead in time for administrators of the system
- Administration time required per user
- Frequency of use of system
- Turnover of admin staff

A simple rule of thumb would suggest that somewhere between 15 and 30 minutes per participant be allocated for the process, including set-up, support and final report generation and distribution. It is surprising how many queries will be raised by either the participants or the observers, particularly if the briefing process has not been undertaken very efficiently. This is not perfect and can, of course, be materially changed by other factors including level of user capability, user buy-in to process, corporate culture, etc. However, it may offer a rough guide when considering the pure economics of whether to outsource or keep in-house.

The four cardinal sins of 360

1. Diving in

   Many companies start 360 systems because they have heard either very positive reports from colleagues, or quite simply that everyone is doing it. Thus, 360 systems are often begun without considering the context and impact within the culture of the company. The 360 process is at its best when used as a personal development tool, but if the resource or budget to invest in personal development is not available, or there is no obvious reward for growth from personal development, then the process will founder.

2. Starting in the middle

   Boards and senior management often feel that they are above improving, and that this type of thing is really only for more junior employees. They start in the middle because it is too expensive to start at the bottom. The idea that there will be any credibility for a process where there is a limit on accountability is flawed before it starts and will almost certainly lead to implicit, if not explicit cynicism, about the process.

3. Chinese whispers

   Time and again companies start 360s without understanding the number of people who will be touched by it within an organization. Staff find that they have been 'invited' to provide confidential feedback on colleagues without any idea of the context. If there is no formal and rigorous process to communicate the context and rationale, then people will inevitably form their own conclusions, and these conclusions will travel faster and more effectively than any corporate communication medium.

4. 'It's only a questionnaire – it won't take long…'

   Personal feedback on other colleagues' performance is a serious matter that people need to take seriously. A standard questionnaire should normally take anywhere between 30 and 45 minutes to complete. A standard project, for say 10 people in a department, will require that several members of staff may have to complete many questionnaires perhaps as many as six or eight. The problem can be compounded if several departments are completing 360 processes at the same time. Companies often release 360 projects without any consideration for this fact. Introducing a scheme with little senior buy-in and no briefing as to the benefits and time needed to do it justice will not achieve the best results.

Types of 360 systems

There are hundreds of 360 systems available. A Google search on '360 Feedback software' provides almost 20 000 responses. So where should you start?

Most systems fall into one or more of the following categories:

- Paper-based (either electronic paper or the real thing)
- 'Off the shelf' that can be purchased complete and run in-house
- Third party e-mail based systems
- Internet-based systems
- Personal/telephone interview systems

The main difference between these systems is in the 'front end' user interface, distribution and collection of questionnaires, and associated administration. They should all offer a 'back end' processing system that will provide the final reports and any management data. The quality of the back end system should, in theory, have no correlation with the front end, and will be defined by the sophistication of its data report/graphing and distribution capability.

These systems are not exclusive, and many of the better suppliers should be able to offer a choice of systems to suit individual corporate requirements. In addition, the systems may offer extras such as integration into current HR systems, or additional facilities to manage and integrate the complete personal review cycle.

Table 7.3 gives a brief overview of the strengths and weaknesses of each type of system.

It can be seen from the table that all systems have their strengths and weaknesses, and that there is no single solution for all companies. In fact, most companies will need to consider at least two 'front end' options if they are to service all their needs. In practice, and certainly from the market choice available, it would appear that most companies tend to prefer internet systems, with e-mail as preferred back up. The decision whether or not to use internet or 'off the shelf' packages would appear to be driven primarily by cost of initial acquisition in the first instance. Paper systems tend to be viable only for very small groups of perhaps five or fewer 360 reports.

The elements of a good 360 feedback report

- Created for the recipient audience.
- Take the time to ensure that the content and style of the report is pitched correctly for the intended audience.
- Simple 360 overview.
- The distillation of the numeric results for all competencies onto a single graph (e.g., radar or spider) is a very powerful tool that can provide a wealth of learning for the individual. Keeping the data sets included to the simple rule of three (self, manager and 360) provides clear comparison of perceived performance.
- Easy and logical to follow.

Table 7.3 Overview of the strengths and weaknesses of each type of system

System type	Strengths	Weaknesses
Paper based	Simple to set up Cost-effective for very small groups Excellent for low tech environments	Manual data entry errors Audit difficult to manage Control of process Complexity and cost increase dramatically with numbers Limited confidentiality
Off the shelf	Simple and low cost structure In-house control of process Security is as good as in house systems	Training and admin costs Limited customization beyond package Confidentiality is limited
Third party e-mail	Very accessible No need for internet access Good for low tech environments Confidentiality – all data outsourced	IT issues with data size and file acceptability in bulk e-mails Form compatibility issues Limited tracking capability Possible data entry issues
Internet	Access anywhere with internet facility Fits well with most environments Auditing and tracking User questionnaire management Confidentiality – all data outsourced Simple set up even for large organizations	IT Firewall domain access issues Limited admin control by client
Personal/tele-interview	Low tech solution, very accessible Direct contact with user	Resource intensive (cost and time) May create barriers to confidentiality

- The purpose of each page/section should be clear. Specifically, keep the feedback for each competence within the same section of the report. It is useful to keep to a simple two page rule, so the reader can see and compare at a glance all data for any competence across two folds of an A4 page.
- Summarized strengths and weaknesses.
- Ensure that at the numeric level there is a section that highlights the overall strengths and weaknesses. With a large amount of data, it is important to provide summary pages and a visual portrayal of numerical data.
- Comparison with group norms.
- Once sufficient data has been gathered within an organization, it may be useful to also publish comparison of individual performance against group norms. There are, however, many reasons why this can be inappropriately or incorrectly interpreted, and should always be approached with extreme care and sensitivity. It should be carried out only when there is enough data history for valid norms and an understanding within the company of the benefits of such an approach.

When deciding to introduce a 360 system, think about the following questions:

Reflection point

How many people will participate in the programme?

How often will the 360 feedback process be repeated?

How many different questionnaires will be required for different levels of manager?

How much access do people have to internet and e-mail?

What organizational data will be required from the exercise?

What mix of narrative and numerical data is required in the profiles?

How well is the company IT system able to support this initiative?

What security is needed for individuals and for corporate compliance?

Who will provide the internal administration of the system?

What training do they require?

A summary – key guidelines for effective 360 feedback systems

- Use an expert (either internal or external) to design the system but with the active involvement of the users in deciding the format and content of the 360 questionnaires.
- Use of an external 360 feedback provider in order to retain complete confidentiality of the data and rigour of the process.
- Best practice would suggest a maximum of 50 questions and a questionnaire that takes no longer than 45 minutes to complete.
- A mixture of quantitative and qualitative questions to ensure that people do not rely on numerical statistics alone as a measure of performance.
- Structured briefing and one-to-one feedback with each participant to support them in creating a practical personal development plan after receiving the 360 feedback.

If you would like to review the leadership capability of your own leaders using 360 feedback, then please go to www.cr360.com for a free trial.

All our knowledge has its origins in our perceptions

– Leonardo da Vinci

8 Different approaches to leadership development

This chapter looks at the following areas:

Learning styles

One-to-one coaching

Mentor schemes

Role of HR and development

Buddy pairs

Action learning sets

Work-based projects

The role of HR

Many organizations pride themselves on the breadth and depth of their training courses. They offer courses for every part of the learning curriculum, and many of these training menus are indeed both pitched at the right level and meet a real need within the company. However, there is often a gap in the provision of development activities that do not rely on face-to-face training in a workshop setting.

This chapter looks at the different approaches to develop leaders that can be highly effective either on their own or in conjunction with face-to-face learning experiences.

People do learn in different ways and we often impose our own learning preferences on others. People naturally want to take in information in different ways and effective leadership development requires the providers of development to take this into account and pay attention to the different personality types that we are working with.

Learning styles

Just as people have different personality styles, research has shown that people prefer to learn in different ways. Honey and Mumford developed the model of four different learning styles as follows.

Activists

Activists tend to involve themselves fully and without bias in new experiences. They are often open-minded, not sceptical, and this tends to make them enthusiastic about anything new. Their philosophy is 'I will try anything once'. They tend to act first and consider the consequences afterwards. Their days are filled with activity. They tend to tackle problems by brainstorming. As soon as the excitement from one activity has died down, they are usually busy looking for the next. They tend to thrive on the challenge of new experiences but can get bored with implementation and longer-term consolidation.

Reflectors

Reflectors tend to like to stand back to ponder experiences and observe them from many different perspectives. They generally collect data both first hand and from others, and prefer to think about it thoroughly before coming to any conclusion. The thorough collection and analysis of data about experiences and events is what counts so they tend to postpone reaching definitive conclusions for as long as possible. Their philosophy is to be cautious. They tend to be thoughtful people who like to consider all possible angles and implications before making a move. They might prefer to take a back seat in meetings and discussions. They enjoy observing other people in action. They tend to listen to others and get the drift of the discussion before making their own points. They tend to adopt a low profile and have a slightly distant, tolerant and unruffled air about them. When they act, it is generally part of a wide picture that includes the past as well as the present and others' observations as well as their own.

Theorists

Theorists generally adapt and integrate observations into complex but logically sound theories. They tend to think problems through in a vertical, step-by-step logical way. They assimilate disparate facts into coherent theories. They tend to be perfectionists who will not rest easy until things are tidy and fit into a rational scheme. They generally like to analyse and synthesize. They are keen on basic assumptions, principles, theories, models and systems thinking. Their philosophy prizes rationality and logic. 'If it is logical, it is good'. Questions they frequently ask: 'Does it make sense?' 'How does this fit with that?' 'What are the basic assumptions?' They tend to be detached, analytical and dedicated to rational objectivity rather than anything subjective or ambiguous. Their approach to problems tends to be consistently logical. This is their 'mental set' and they rigidly reject anything that does not fit with it. They are likely to prefer to maximize certainty and feel uncomfortable with subjective judgements, lateral thinking and anything flippant.

Pragmatists

Pragmatists tend to be keen to try out new ideas, theories and techniques to see if they work in practice. They positively search out new ideas and normally take the first opportunity to experiment with applications. They are the sort of people

Table 8.1 Different stages of team development

Training methodology	Learning style
Group discussion/action planning	Pragmatist
Tutor input on theories and models/case studies	Theorist
Group exercises/role plays	Activist
Diagnostic questionnaires/one-to-one coaching	Reflector

who return from management courses brimming with new ideas that they want to try out in practice. They like to get on with things and act quickly and confidently on ideas that attract them. They tend to be impatient with ruminating and open-ended discussions. They are essentially practical, down-to-earth people who like making practical decisions and solving problems. They respond to problems and opportunities 'as a challenge'.

Any development intervention needs to pay attention to all four learning styles (Table 8.1). Face-to-face training often tends more towards a focus on theorist and activist preferences with a mix of tutor input and group exercises. The need for reflection and time to apply the learning to real life situations is often overtaken by an emphasis on high energy 'fun' exercises and a need to cover a challenging number of models and theories from the latest leadership publication.

Taking learning styles into account ensures that people are able to learn in the most effective way possible for them. For this reason, it is important to design leadership development activities that appeal to the different preferences.

One-to-one coaching

In an earlier chapter 'The leader as coach', we covered the process and skills of coaching. In this section, we will look at a practical example of how one-to-one coaching can be used to develop performance.

Coaching can often be a very effective approach to develop leadership skills with more senior leaders who are not prepared or able to attend face-to-face development activities. In order for the coaching to work well, there are a number of steps that need to be taken.

Choosing the coach

We covered earlier the choice between external or internal coaches. In terms of confidentiality and credibility, an external coach is often the preferred choice. If the choice is to use an internal coach, it is good practice to use a coach from another function or department in order to remove the line manager link for this activity. This is not to say that the line manager does not have a coaching role. Obviously, they do play a vital role in coaching and developing their team members. However, one-to-one coaching is often chosen when an individual needs to develop a particular area of their performance and they need an external objective viewpoint and sounding board.

Setting up the coaching contract

One-to-one coaching is often requested by a line manager. HR plays a role in agreeing what the requirements are for the individual and this will help them allocate an appropriate coach. However, these requests for one-to-one coaching can be somewhat vague and ill-defined. The following example shows the importance of clarifying the reasons for the coaching and agreeing rules of engagement and confidentiality.

Case study

Letter from an HR manager to an external coach

'I am hoping that you will do some personal coaching for me with one of our senior sales managers within the business.

He has very low levels of self-awareness and is a difficult individual to work for. The turnover in his team is extremely high with regular comments over the years in exit interviews that he is controlling and does not trust people. We have fed back to him on several occasions (she does not take feedback well) and although there have been some short-term improvements – he has always resorted back to type.

Recently his entire team has left and I took that opportunity to talk to everyone and gather feedback. I am hoping to set up a six month coaching agreement with you to raise his levels of self-awareness and get him to the point where he adapts his management style and behaviours as the cost and disruption to the business of persistent turnover is now unsustainable.

Can we catch up to discuss in more detail?'

The note above is an example of the sort of request that may be received. The coach then needs to ask a number of questions to ascertain what is required. This is the purpose of the contracting meeting between the line manager, the individual and the coach.

When the coach did meet the HR manager and the individual, they discussed the feedback that they had received during the exit interview of the individuals who left this particular manager.

John does not read e-mails and therefore does not keep up to date with changes. Rarely keeps to appointments in diary when in the office. Everything ends up being a rush at the last minute. Rarely makes time for members of the team when he said he would; they often get left feeling frustrated or have got to the point where they just do not bother to try any longer. Several people said that putting time in his schedule is a waste of time as it will not happen.

Lack of delegation and empowerment

Team feel that they are not allowed to make decisions, even sending an e-mail has go past John first. Everything is checked. Get to the point where they know, he will change something and therefore do not put as much effort in as there is no point. Also, as he struggles to make the time to check everything, members of team have to repeatedly ask him to do it – the team felt that things end up being a mad panic at the last minute. Account managers feel that they are not allowed to make decisions on their accounts, and that this undermined their confidence. Slows everything down substantially and often keep customers waiting whilst trying to get a decision made. The team felt that John not being around after 3.30 p.m. has made this even more difficult. Business managers feel that customers know when they visit that they are not allowed to make decisions and that everything has to go back to John – undermines their position.

Performance reviews

Most of the team said that they had very few one-to-one reviews. They felt that he does not read the e-mails they send him. Any desk review ends up being a discussion about work and they walk away with more actions. Rarely if ever talk about personal development, future opportunities, etc. everyone felt that John does not listen.

Several of the members of the team felt that they spent as much time managing their accounts as they did managing their relationship with John.

Ways of working

The team felt that things have to be done John's way. 'Almost impossible to change things'. 'His way or no way'. 'Dictates what and how things get done'.

This had not been fed back to the individual, and the manager involved had avoided having this difficult conversation with the individual.

It was agreed that the manager would share this feedback with the individual before they met with the external coach. This was a very powerful and difficult starting point for the discussion, but the individual agreed that some external coaching may be helpful.

During the coaching contracting meeting, the individual, line manger and coach agreed the following outcomes for the coaching sessions:

To improve personal time management and planning skills.

To give more time to the new team in terms of one-to-one reviews and recognition.

To develop trust in the new team in order to delegate more effectively.

The coach and the individual agreed to meet once in a month for six months to work on these issues and it was agreed that there would be a three way meeting with the line manager after two months to review progress and agree what further actions needed to be taken.

Six months later, the individual had improved in many of the areas and his manager was satisfied with the improvement in his performance.

The coach had used the GROW model for each of the two hour sessions and had also used a number of NLP techniques to help John identify a set of clear outcomes for his development. John was asked to complete a 360 feedback questionnaire at the end of the coaching sessions and this provided recognition for the improvements he had made in addition to some specific current data on areas where he still needed to work on.

In terms of confidentiality, there was no real need for the HR manager to remain involved after the initial meeting. The line manager then took on the coaching role after the initial six sessions and had a meeting with the coach at the end of the six sessions to review progress and gain some tips on further coaching for John.

This example shows the benefit of one-to-one coaching and the need for HR, the line manager and the coach to all have complete clarity on their roles and responsibilities in the process.

Mentor schemes

At times, the use of a mentor scheme may be beneficial for individuals or groups of employees.

The difference between coaching and mentoring is that while coaching is focussed primarily on short-term day-to-day performance improvement, mentoring is often focussed on longer-term career development. Coaching is based on the questioning approach, while mentoring is more an advice giving role from someone who has greater experience and wisdom to impart. Like choosing a coach, the choice of mentor is equally important. Some of the following characteristics may provide a guideline to what is required:

- Does not blame – stays neutral
- Will give honest views and answers
- Not intimidating – easy to approach at any time
- Knows what they are talking about – good at own job
- Enabling, caring, open and facilitative
- Gives constructive and positive feedback
- Provides guidance when needed
- Interested and demonstrates genuine concern
- Willing to debate, argue and discuss

The key responsibilities of the mentor can include the following:

- To provide guidance and help
- To keep rules of confidentiality

- To give feedback
- To share own experience and expertise
- To act as a signpost to other people in the organization
- To use the skills of listening and effective questioning
- To provide challenge and different perspectives
- To make time for the mentor relationship
- To be flexible in making the relationship work

The person being mentored also has responsibilities as follows:

- Being open and honest about own skills and feelings
- Accepting help willingly from others
- Able to reflect on strengths and weaknesses
- Willing to accept feedback
- Turn discussion into action for themselves
- To turn up for meetings
- To give time to preparing for meetings
- To appreciate the time given by the mentor
- To be flexible in making the relationship work

At no time, does the mentor relationship override the normal responsibilities of the line manager. The mentor relationship is an additional development route for the individual; it does not replace the contact or support given by the line manager.

In order to keep the line manager involved, it is important for the individual to tell their line manager that they have a mentor. Some individuals may be happy for their mentor to have a chat with their line manager in order to gain some useful data for the future mentor discussions. Gaining the support of the line manager is vital for everyone to benefit, so time taken to gain the commitment of line managers is vital.

The mentor relationship will cover elements of both current work issues and longer-term career issues. It is important to stay within an agreed boundary of what should be discussed or not. It is not appropriate to discuss personal- or home-based issues unless they come within the overall context of how this affects working life.

In order to identify what the mentor and the mentee want from the relationship, both parties should discuss and agree a learning contract before going any further. The first meeting can run to an agenda like the one below:

Agenda for the first mentor meeting

1. The past
    Discussion of individual's career to date and previous work experience:
       Previous job roles
       Experience in company/other organizations
       Academic/professional qualifications

2. The present
   Discussion of current role and the progress being made by the individual:
   What do you enjoy/not enjoy?
   What do you see as your strengths/skills?
   What skills do you feel you need to develop?
   What challenges do you face in your current role?

3. Future
   Where would you like to be in 1–2 years time? Why? For example:
   New responsibilities
   Better working relationships
   New role
   Greater skills/experience

4. Focus
   What are the three most important issues that you want to focus on in this mentor partnership:
   1.
   2.
   3.

5. Roles and responsibilities
   What support are you looking to gain from me?
   What do you see as my responsibilities?
   What do you see as your responsibilities?
   How are we going to work together?

Role of HR and development

Mentor schemes are often set up formally within organizations in order to provide this longer-term help and guidance to individuals. The key messages for a successful scheme are as follows.

Ask for willing volunteers as mentors. This is a role that will take a certain amount of time and commitment. The best mentors are those people who feel they have something to contribute and enjoy sharing their views and experience.

Provide training in the core skills that every mentor needs:

- Self-awareness
- Listening skills
- Question skills
- Process skills
- Feedback skills

Choose mentors who have specific functional expertise and experience.

Mentors need to have certain specific functional expertise and career expertise that they can pass on to their mentees.

Some individuals may look for a mentor who they see as a role model in terms of the path they have taken career-wise. Others may look for someone who displays the same values and aspirations and has succeeded in areas important to them. Role models can also be picked because of their drive and ambition, attributes that the mentee might be keen to develop. Mentees often choose individuals to be their mentor because they are inspired by what the mentor has achieved. The key is to let the mentee choose who they want to have as their mentor because unlike performance coaching, this is a more personal relationship.

Mentees might value the contribution to their development because of the mentor's networking skills and contacts. The mentor may be able to access other people who can provide support, knowledge, advice or career opportunities.

In addition, the mentor may be able to access information that is useful to the individuals, either through professional memberships or through links to industry networks. Unlike coaching, the mentors knowledge, expertise and functional contacts are all an important part of their role.

Brief both mentors and mentees on the purpose of the mentor programme and the ground rules for how the scheme will work.

This should include:

- Overview of the benefits to the individual, mentor and the business
- Purpose of the mentoring scheme
- Confidentiality
- Allocating mentors
- Frequency of meetings
- Content and format of meetings
- Any concerns and questions

However well the mentor schemes are set up, some of the mentor relationships will fall along the way. This is due to the fact that mentoring is a very difficult relationship to formally introduce. The best mentor partnerships often evolve naturally and informally, without any clear ground rules and meeting structure. People naturally seek out those people they feel can be of help to them.

David Clutterbuck in his article on informal mentoring gives some invaluable advice on how organizations can make the most of both formal and informal mentoring systems:

An online registration and matching system, where people can seek and make their own pairings. The system needs to have very good guidance as to how to go about selecting an appropriate partner and, ideally, a resource, which prospective mentees can go to for personal advice.

Sufficient, visible role models of good mentoring practice to demonstrate what quality mentoring looks and feels like and to provide a voluntary, informal advisory resource for mentors. If top management can be among those role models, it provides a very strong message to the organization.

A mixture of voluntary training resources. These might include a regular open training programme, run in-house or externally with a consortium of other organizations; an e-learning package to run on PC or online and a library of wider reading materials on mentoring and related disciplines. It may also be useful to provide an option for people, who have a strong interest in developing their mentoring skills, to take a certificate or degree course through one of the several providers now available.

An understanding that the quality of mentoring rests to a considerable extent on the amount and relevance of the training of both parties have received. While an informal process cannot insist that mentors and mentees are trained, the desire to have an effective relationship should drive both parties away from matching with someone, who is not sufficiently committed to be trained in the role.

An opportunity for mentors (or developers in general) to meet informally as a mutual support and learning group through an online chat room and/or self-organized gatherings. In this scenario, mentors may request some help from HR in arranging venues and perhaps finding external speakers on specific learning topics, but the impetus has to come from them. Some organizations already run 'lunch and learn' events – in one case monthly – along these lines. Good practice 'snippets' sent monthly to all managers (or indeed all employees), on developmental behaviours, from both the learner and the developer perspectives. This is perhaps the closest to a formal arrangement the organization may go. These short advisory bulletins (no more than a few hundred words each time) would be generated by HR, with the aim of stimulating awareness, discussion and incremental improvements in people's behaviour to mentor and be mentored, coach and be coached and so on.

Source: David Clutterbuck Associates – website article on Informal Mentoring.

Buddy pairs

This is a development activity that can pay huge dividends with little upfront investment.

It is useful for the following individuals:

- New recruits
- Graduate trainees
- Delegates on a modular development programme

The purpose of the buddy system is for two colleagues/peers to provide support and development for each other. It is not a formal mentoring relationship, rather a chance for two people in similar roles to exchange information and share their understanding of how the organization works.

Buddy pairs are frequently used for new recruits and graduate training schemes. Graduates or new individuals are paired with someone of a similar level who has been in the organization for at least a year, so, they understand the organization. It can often be a graduate who has just finished the training period.

The purpose of the buddy relationship is:

- To explain how the organization works
- To help each other understand the internal politics and culture
- To act as a signpost to other individuals
- To share knowledge about key activities and projects
- To answer questions the individual does not want to raise with their manager
- To provide support during the first six months of the induction period

For more established individuals the buddy relationship can play a slightly different role. The buddy relationship is often introduced as part of an ongoing development programme, consisting of face-to-face training and then project work or purely application of learning between each module.

The objectives of this buddy pairing can be as follows:

- To share learning from the face-to-face training
- To share progress and successes from using the learning back at work
- To help each other overcome barriers and challenges back at work
- To provide informal coaching to each other
- To extend the individuals network of colleagues across the business
- To learn from each others work area

Case study

Buddy pairing was used in a company where the participants on a two part leadership development programme came from a number of different operating companies from within the group. Part of the programme included setting up buddy pairs and the pairs met between the two workshops and also visited each others sites. This provided learning about different companies within the organization and also gave the individuals useful benchmark data for how similar factories could be operated in different ways. They also toured the production lines and analysed the management style in place. This learning was then discussed by the whole group on the second workshop and provided useful insight to the whole group. Buddy pair learning was providing development for the wider group as well as individual learning and support for the individuals on the programme.

Again, spending time with the individuals explaining the purpose of the buddy pairs and how they can work together is time well spent and will help the relationships get off to a good start. This can either be done during a development programme or during the first couple of weeks of induction.

A fun exercise that will help the buddies get to know each other is beneficial:

Share one fact about your family that is similar/different.

Share one fact about your home town that is similar/different.

Share one way in which you are similar/different.

Share one fact about your holidays that is similar/different.

This sort of exercise can be adapted to the level and type of individuals involved. It could then be followed up by a pair's discussion on what they would like to achieve from the buddy pairs:

What do you want to gain from this relationship?

How often will we meet and where?

What are our ground rules for working well together?

Action learning sets

What is action learning?

Action learning is a development approach which can be applied to any number of different work-related issues and challenges. In action learning groups or 'sets' individuals meet regularly with others in order to explore solutions to problems and decide on the actions they wish to take. The phases include:

An individual takes his/her turn to focus on an issue of their choice.

They describe the problem as they see it.

They then receive contributions from others in the form of questions, suggestions and feedback.

They reflect on the discussion and decide what actions to take.

In the next meeting, they report back on what progress they have made.

The next individual then takes their turn to discuss their issue using the same structured format.

The basis of action learning is that 'action' takes place after the discussion and learning. It is not merely a talking shop, it is the process by which individuals can develop a tangible action plan for taking an issue forward. It can be likened to group coaching. The skills of the set members will influence the effectiveness of this approach but there is a real benefit in colleagues helping each other as opposed to an external facilitator.

In order to set up an action learning set, it can be useful to have an external facilitator for the first few meetings in order to ensure that a clear process and structure is in place. Generally, the group can then go on to facilitate their own meetings without the need for external support.

Sets are normally used to discuss work-related issues. Members may have a wide ranging agenda or they may work on quite specific issues, like the development of new skills or the progress of a particular project. For development purposes, the issue may be around personal leadership style, team development or personal career development topics. Each set member will have their own issues to discuss and the learning is often improved by the wide diversity of topics.

The group agrees how time will be used; normally each member has a turn every meeting. Each is accountable to the group for taking action and reporting progress. At the start of the action learning set, members establish a series of ground rules, which might include confidentiality, attendance and ground rules for working well together.

Depending on the group size, meetings may be from half-a-day to one-day duration. The life of the group will vary depending on the individuals and the organizational support in place.

Benefits of action learning sets

- Helps people solve their own problems
- Develops skills of listening and effective coaching
- Develops understanding of other peoples' issues in the organization
- Creates stronger working relationships
- Cost-efficient approach for development
- Focuses on action and performance improvement
- Creates stronger cross-functional working within the organization

Again, like buddying, this is an activity that does not require a lot of time and investment from HR and development. If there are a group of like minded individuals who you feel would benefit from this then you can simply bring them together and explain the process to them.

Agree some ground rules about the 'set' will work together.

Agree how many set members will be given time to discuss their issue.

Share the time out, so that everyone gets a turn.

One member 'presents', i.e. briefly describes, a problem they would like to work on.

The set works with that person to explore the problem.

Ensure that the presenter has an action plan.

Spend time after each person's turn and at the end of the meeting to discuss what has been learned.

Depending on the time allowed, a set of six people should be able to cover three issues per meeting. A minimum of an hour should be given to any one issue if the individual is to really focus on the issue and action plan. A review of 10–15 minutes should be allowed between each session to review learning and reflect on how the group worked together.

A simple review should follow each session.

Ask the individual – what was useful/not useful during your session?

Ask the whole set – what do we need to do more of and less of during the next session?

This will bring out the feedback on what individuals need to do to gain the most from the process.

Work-based projects

Work-based projects are another approach for development that fit very well in conjunction with a face-to-face development programme. They are an excellent way of applying theory to the reality of day-to-day operations. They also provide some quick wins for the organization and develop individual skills of working together collaboratively to achieve a common goal that is wider than their own departmental perspective.

Elements of a successful work-based project

They key is only to set up projects that are truly useful and important to the organization. It is demotivating to give a group a project where they feel that the sponsors have limited interest and little action will occur as a result of their findings.

The project needs to have a senior sponsor who can make the decision to go ahead with the recommendations from any given project. The choice of projects can often be made by the senior leadership team or Board and then there is a clear link with business plans and company challenges.

The project team need to be given access to the information they need and to the key stakeholders that are affected by the project. Lack of access to the right information or level of leadership will impede their ability to achieve the project outcomes and also it will affect the level of learning they can gain from this type of development.

Work-based projects work best when the project team members are from a variety of different functions. This provides learning from different perspectives and will broaden each individual view of what the appropriate solution may be to any given problem.

What topics make good work-based projects

Internal staff satisfaction surveys area of useful source of work-based projects as they will be identifying key issues that the organizations needs to address on a cross-functional basis. They also tend to be high profile in terms of senior management attention. In addition, they are often focussing on areas in which there is no one particular business owner.

Company communications

No company is ever completely satisfied with the level and quality of communication within the company. This is often an area that benefits from a wide variety of people assessing the issues and proposing improvements. There is often a wide disparity in the level of communication throughout different parts of a business and this provides a complexity to the issue, which is useful for learning.

162

Innovation

This is another area that often fails to be exploited to the best advantage by an organization. Innovation can be looked at from a number of angles – product innovation is very different from customer service innovation. Innovation in team working will be different from that innovation in terms of business development and company growth. This can provide a challenging work-based project for a more senior group of leaders.

Business strategy

Again, this is a challenging area for a more senior group and can be used to develop their understanding of company-wide strategy. Possible topics may include reviewing existing strategy or putting together a new strategy for a part of the business.

Best practice

Many companies do not spend enough time for benchmarking their performance with other external companies or competitors. This is a useful project for a group of managers at any level. The project may include visits to external companies, analysing market data and coming up with recommendations for business improvements in any given part of the business.

Example work-based project

Project title: Job satisfaction: what is it and how can we maximize it?

Purpose of project

Using the results from the 2005 Employee Survey, we would like you to investigate job satisfaction within the group of companies. What contributes to job satisfaction? What has changed between 2004 and 2005? Please investigate all changes, both positive and negative.

Desired outcomes

We would like you to produce an action plan suggesting how we can improve employees' experiences and perceptions of their day-to-day role. This should be as detailed as possible and if appropriate it should include timings for the various actions recommended. However, it must also be realistic and achievable. It will be possible to measure the success of any initiatives you suggest from the results of next year's staff survey.

Completion/presentation date of project

Please be prepared to present your findings to the Board week commencing 3 April.

Link to company objectives

Forms a part of the 'Employee Survey 'objectives

This is an example taken from a development programme for high-potential managers who progress through a year long modular development programme to broaden their leadership skills and business skills.

As discussed earlier, many traditional training courses do not give sufficient time for individual reflection. Self-reflection and time spent reviewing how the individual operates can be very powerful.

TNT run a worldwide leadership development programme, which incorporates a number of different learning methodologies. Part one of the programme is a week-long leadership skills programme, which covers topics such as:

- Learning styles
- Characteristics of effective teams
- Team development
- Self-awareness
- Personal impact
- Leadership style
- Coaching skills
- Diversity
- Emotional intelligence
- Transactional analysis
- Managing performance

After the first week, delegates are asked to complete an assignment on any of the topics that have been covered. This 'personal business challenge' requires them to take any of the topics covered and explain how they can use these models and techniques to develop their own performance as leaders.

The following excellent example shows the benefit of including a self-reflection and application learning element to any leadership development programme.

Case study

Tessa Koster

TNT Express

Introduction

After following the first module of the Gateway to Leadership Programme, we have been asked to write a business case to show that we are able to implement the learning. This first module focused on learning styles, emotional intelligence, leadership styles, effective teams, coaching and managing high performance.

Scope of my business challenge

I am working at the TNT as a project coordinator.

As at this moment I do not have people reporting to me, I have decided to focus on the following two items:

Self-development

Identifying your points for improvement and make better use of your strengths are, in my opinion, critical to become a good manager. Only when you are aware of your own (in)capabilities, you will be able to recognize and make use of the strengths and improve the weaknesses of your individual team members.

Team development

Optimize working relationship with my manager. I have been working together with my manager for two years.

As our team consists only of my manager and me, it is of the utmost importance that we make efficient use of our strengths and recognize and improve our weaknesses.

Self-development

Overview of test results

During module one, we had been asked to fill in several questionnaires to determine our preferred learning styles, to evaluate our emotional intelligence and to improve our self-understanding. Prior to module one, we had to appoint a number of observers to fill in a 360 feedback questionnaire (Table 8.2) to review the skills and behaviours we possess and demonstrate at work. The results of these tests are as follows:

Learning styles		
Style	**Score**	**Preference**
Activist	5	Low
Reflector	13	Moderate
Theorist	14	Strong
Pragmatist	16	Strong

Emotional intelligence	
Intrapersonal	
Self-awareness	4.92
Managing emotions	4.90
Self-motivation	4.72
Interpersonal	
Relating well/social skills	4.85
Emotional mentoring	4.85
Score determined by adding up individual scores for each question and divide this score by the number of questions	

Table 8.2 360 Feedback questionnaire

	Self	Manager	Colleagues
Strategic awareness	59	68	78
Change management	68	78	78
People management	68	80	78
Communication	82	82	78
Managing results	82	82	83
Delighting customer	58	68	69
Team work	68	82	88
Continuous improvement	68	71	72
Integrity	69	88	91

Conclusions

Learning styles

Preferred learning habits may help me to benefit more from some experiences than from others. It also helps to identify and understand the learning preferences and styles of others, enabling me to be most effective in communication and collaboration.

Looking at my scores I can conclude that I have a good balance between 'Reflector', 'Theorist' and 'Pragmatist'. However, my 'Activist' side could be developed better. Aspects I recognize from my preferred learning styles are intellectually demanding, logic, working at own pace, thinking time, see the link between the subject and the job and acquiring skills I can use now. The characteristics say that an 'Activist' enjoys new experiences, group activities, joining in, leading role and challenges. These are all aspects, which at this moment I feel less comfortable with and can therefore be seen as aspects for development.

Emotional intelligence

Emotional intelligence is the ability to understand and control one's own emotions as well as recognize and deal with emotions of others. The emotional intelligence (EI) is twice as important as IQ or TQ skills in defining excellent performance.

Based on the questionnaire scores and after looking at the specific questions in detail, I have selected the 'EI' competencies self-motivation and relating well/social skills as my areas for development. Specific points I would like to focus on are:

Intrapersonal: Self-motivation

Use internal talk to affect your emotional state

Stop or change ineffective habits

Develop new and more productive patterns of behaviour

Interpersonal: relating well/social skills

Know when you become defensive

Know the impact your behaviour has on others

Show empathy to others

360 feedback

The 360 feedback overview shows the opinions of myself, my manager and the average of all participants (including manager, but not myself).

Looking at the scores I gave myself versus the scores from my manager and colleagues I can conclude that on average I rate myself lower than others do. It is therefore not surprising that the key comments I got from my observers are 'have more confidence in own abilities', 'get yourself empowered' and 'more often try new things'. Besides this the feedback I got was that I should tend to show more patience and try to create win–win situations. Based on this feedback, the two main points which I would like to focus on are 'delighting customers' and 'continuous improvement'.

Key areas for self-development

Based on the above mentioned conclusions I have identified four areas for self-development, which cover the above mentioned aspects I would like to focus on:

Gain self-confidence and get more empowered

New experiences, leading role and challenges

Self-motivation

Continuous improvement

Be more patient and listen to others

Group activities, joining in

Relating well/social skills

Delighting customers

Action plan

As some of the actions mentioned in Table 8.3 are difficult to measure, I will evaluate the above mentioned areas for improvement on a weekly basis. I will define the points I improved on as well as the points, which need further development. I will discuss these findings with my manager and make sure specific actions will be taken when required.

Team development

Current situation

The objective of this exercise is to optimize our working relationship and develop a common approach towards becoming a high performing team $(1 + 1 = 3)$.

Table 8.3 Actions

Gain self-confidence	Get more empowered
Join a business presentation skills course Learn more about the express business Force myself to do things I feel less comfortable with Take a risk sometimes Do not be afraid to make mistakes	Redivide tasks with my manager to get more responsibility Join a project outside my department Define further areas for development and get the appropriate training
Be more patient	Listen to others
Discuss this area for development with my manager and ask him to evaluate this on a day-to-day basis and give feedback	Discuss this area for development with my manager and ask him to evaluate this on a day-to-day basis and give feedback

Looking at the different stages of team development, we can conclude that our team is currently moving from the storming to the norming stage (Figure 8.1).

To become a performing team, we will have to identify our current strengths and weaknesses and agree on a common approach to further develop our team.

Overview of test results
I asked my manager to fill in the preferred learning styles questionnaire as well as the emotional intelligence questionnaire. We have taken these two questionnaires as a starting point to draw up a SWOT analysis. Based on the conclusions from this SWOT analysis, we have created an action plan.

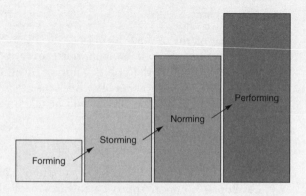

Figure 8.1 Different stages of team development

Preferred learning styles

It appears that we are opposites when it comes to learning styles. My manager has a strong preference for the 'Activist' style, a low preference for the 'Reflector' and 'Pragmatist' style and a very low preference for the 'Theorist' style, while I have a strong preference for the 'Theorist' as well as the 'Pragmatist' learning style and a low preference for the 'Activist' style.

Emotional intelligence

My manager has identified the competencies 'Managing Emotions' and 'Emotional Mentoring' as his key areas for development. As I have selected different competencies (self-motivation and relating well/social skills) we might be able to learn from each other's strengths. To determine the areas which could be a pitfall for our working relationship we identified the questions on which we both scored less than four, these have been included in the SWOT analysis (Table 8.4).

Table 8.4 SWOT analysis

Strengths	Weaknesses
Together we have all aspects needed for an effective team Mutual respect Get on well Mix of experience Open and honest atmosphere Both motivated to do our best	Different learning styles We find it both difficult to: 　calm ourselves when angry 　stop or change ineffective habits 　accurately reflect people's feelings 　back to them 　detect incongruence between 　others' emotions or feelings and 　their behaviours Too much focused on own preferences Don't take enough time to communicate
Opportunities	Threats
Make usage of each others strengths Share experiences Capitalize on broad TNT experience Communicate Improve efficiency Increase job satisfaction	Misunderstanding Frustration Dissatisfaction Don't reach objectives Break up of team

Main conclusions

Strengths versus opportunities

Together, we have all aspects needed for an effective team. We can make usage of each others strengths by sharing experiences thus improving our efficiency and job satisfaction.

Weaknesses versus threats

As we have different learning styles, we are too much focused on our own preferences and do not take enough time to communicate. We not only risk misunderstanding, frustration and dissatisfaction but also risk of not reaching our objectives.

Strengths versus threats

As we get on well, have mutual respect and managed to create an open and honest atmosphere. We can avoid misunderstanding, frustration and dissatisfaction by using our strengths, thus creating an environment where we secure reaching our personal and business objectives.

Weaknesses versus opportunities

Although we have different learning styles and some of the same pitfalls, we have to realize that by communicating and making usage of each other's strengths, we not only improve our efficiency but also increase our job satisfaction.

Action plan

Being different can be a real advantage as we get the opportunity to learn from each other's strengths, share experiences and by doing so improve our efficiency. However, it will be of the utmost important to acknowledge and recognize our differences in order to be able to manage them in a constructive and efficient way and avoid misunderstanding, frustration, underperformance and dissatisfaction. Good communication will therefore be key.

To ensure and secure the transition from the storming to the norming stage we agreed to focus on optimizing our communication by setting weekly meetings.

During these meetings we will:

Resolve discrepancies between expectations and reality

Be open and give feedback

Agree on how we work together

Continue to develop harmony, trust, support and respect

Once we have reached and secured the 'norming' stage our aim will be to create a high performing environment in which we can have full confidence in each other, work together in an efficient way, share leadership and last but not least: retain our job satisfaction and have fun!

Evaluation

Monthly we will monitor our progress and formally in six months time we will revisit the questionnaires and SWOT analysis to determine how successful we have been in implementing the agreed learning outcomes.

In summary, a well focussed self-reflection exercise can provide individuals with a clear plan of how they are going to translate theory into practice. This example shows how the learning from a leadership development programme can be taken back into the workplace and used to tangible develop and support the performance of both the individual and the team. In terms of measuring the cost benefits of training, this case study provides some useful insight into how individuals can assess the benefits for themselves, rather than relying on centrally driven measurement exercises.

Source: Tessa Koster of TNT Express.

The role of HR

As we have discussed, there are a wide number of possible alternatives that can be used to develop leaders at different levels:

- One-to-one coaching
- Mentor programmes
- Buddy pairs
- Action learning sets
- Work-based projects
- Self-reflection and application of learning

Reflection point

Which of these activities do you support in the business?

Which of these activities are working well/not so well?

What benefits is the business gaining from these activities?

What current business projects could be given to particular groups?

When did you last evaluate the effectiveness of your external/internal coaches?

What improvements do you need to make to the coaching that is provided within the business?

How well is your mentor scheme working – how do you measure its effectiveness?

Which individuals would benefit from a self-directed action learning set?

What are you providing for your graduates in the way of personal development activity?

How well are you integrating these different development activities into your existing training and development programmes?

How well are you communicating the availability of these development activities to your people?

Responsibilities for learning

Who takes responsibility for learning – HR or the individual?

One of the key roles that HR and learning and development can play is that of change agent. This role means that they are there as catalysts, to drive change in others and the organization. This can only be done if HR realizes the limits of their responsibility and the respective responsibilities of others. In leadership development, the responsibilities of the individual and the providers of development need to be clearly defined during the different stages of any leadership development strategy.

It is clearly the responsibility of the leadership development team to manage the design of specific learning interventions for individual and teams within the organization. Using their expertise and functional knowledge is how the learning and development team can add real value. They either design programmes themselves or bring in expertise and best practice from external sources.

However, the learning and development team need to make a conscious choice on what role to take in the organization and delivery of development activities. They need to be clear in how they are going to position development and training within the company and what their role in this should be.

Case study

Each year, the training and development manager creates a list of training workshops that are useful for the company. This list is circulated to everyone in the company. People sign up for the courses and the training manager organizes a mix of external and internal providers.

The result
There is low attendance on the courses and people drop out at the last minute. HR sends a note to everyone telling them that they will be charged internally for these courses and people must attend.

People start to attend the courses and the course tutors find that people are not clear why they are there, there is cynicism about the benefit of the training and individuals on the programmes are at many different skill levels and starting points. Some individuals turn up because they are replacing someone from their team who is off sick and the manager does not want to pay for an unused place.

There is no follow-up after the courses. The line managers do not discuss the training with their individuals as they have little idea about the content or purpose of the training.

HR sends out an evaluation two months later. There is minimal return.

This may not seem a realistic scenario, however, it seems to be common practice in many smaller and larger organizations. So what has gone wrong?

The development activities and courses have not been planned in line with an overall business strategy. There is no clear link between the menu of choices and the business plan.

There has been lack of communication between the leadership development team and the Board or key decision makers about what the content or format of the training should be.

There has been no communication to the organization about the purpose of the development and what it is intended to achieve.

Individuals sign up for courses that they think seem interesting. There is no clear link between agreed development plans and choice of development activity.

Lack of briefing of line managers. More senior managers have no overview of the programmes in place and are not clear about their role and responsibilities for pre- and post-briefing and ongoing coaching of their team members.

Lack of discussion between the line manager and the individual as to the purpose of them attending the workshop and what the development objectives are for the individual.

Briefing of course tutors. The tutors have little understanding of how their workshop fits with the overall aims of the development strategy. Tutors are not clear what other training is happening and there is overlap and contradictions between the different courses.

Case study

At a leading investment bank, the approach to development and learning is very structured.

All senior managers attend training to give them the skills of managing high performance. This includes skills training on feedback skills, development planning and coaching skills. This is an integral part of senior management development strategy that takes place on the first six months of taking up a senior role.

All individuals hold six weekly development reviews with their managers to review their development plan and progress against it.

All development activities are linked to the overall competency framework for different level managers within the Firm. For each competency, there are a number of development activities including e-learning, one-to-one coaching, shadowing, CDs, and face-to-face training.

Attendance at development and training events is only permitted if the development need has been identified by the individual with their line manager as part of these reviews.

Individuals complete an online pre-course profile outlining their learning objectives for the workshop. This is passed to the course tutor to give them some further information about the delegates.

Course tutors are assessed by the leadership development team each year. There is a validation form completed by delegates at the end of each workshop, and the ratings are assessed and fed back to the external tutors each year. If there are negative comments, these are picked up by the leadership development team and discussed with the tutors. In addition, the leadership development managers sit in on workshops on an ad-hoc basis.

Individuals can only take up a promotion or job move once they have developed someone else to take over their role. This is a challenging policy that works extremely well. Managers are assessed on how well they perform their job role and also on how well they develop their people to take on a more senior role. This focus on development of others is both unusual and also highly successful in creating an organization that values development and the provision of focussed training to enable people to develop their full potential.

On a coaching skills workshop run within this bank, one of the participants was rehearsing a conversation he needed to have with one of his team. His words to his junior manager were as follows:

...and finally, I would like to thank you for developing your skills to take on my role. It is due to you that I can now move up to my next role........thanks'

The benefit of this approach is that the leadership development team, line managers and individuals are all very clear about their roles and responsibilities in the design and delivery and follow-up of development activities within the company.

Transfer of learning back to the organization

> *Learning is like rowing upstream: not to advance is to drop back.*
> —Chinese Proverb

This is not the responsibility of HR. This responsibility sits clearly with the individual and the line manager. It starts with clear debrief discussion of the content of the training and then should lead to a discussion about specific actions and activities to use this learning back at work. In an organization where individuals take responsibility for their own learning, there is less reliance on the line manager. However, the manager is responsible for ensuring that they provide support and time for this learning to take place.

> *Reflection point*
>
> What pre- and post-briefing guidance do you provide for your leaders and course participants?
>
> How do you assess the benefit of development events after the event?
>
> What skills training are you providing for your leaders to ensure they support the development activities that their team attend?
>
> What materials do you have in place to clarify the purpose and objectives of your different development programmes?

The following examples may provide a useful starting point for designing materials to support the successful transfer of learning from programme to work place.

Sample pre- and post-briefing template:

Pre-briefing meeting between manager and course participant

Workshop   Title   'Managing for results'

The objective of this module is to enable participants to develop their coaching skills in order to help them maximize the potential of their teams for the benefit of the business. They are introduced to the GROW model and the different styles of coaching and learn how and when to use them appropriately.

At the end of this workshop participants will:

be able to explain the benefits of coaching for the individual, the coach and the organization.

be able to apply the GROW model of coaching in practice.

be able to identify different coaching styles and when they should be used.

have developed skills in using the different coaching styles according to the needs of the individual.

have developed a specific coaching action plan to apply back in the workplace.

Please complete this and share with your manager before attending the programme:

What are your current strengths in this area?

What skills do you need to develop in this area?

What are you looking to gain from attending this module?

How will you use these skills after the module?

Signed: Date:

Signed: Date:

Bring this form with you to the workshop.

Postmodule briefing meeting

Please complete and discuss with your manager within a week of this programme.

What did you gain from attending this module?

What will you now do more of?

What will you now do less of?

What will you now do differently?

What benefits are you looking to gain from making these changes?

What can your manager do to support you in this development?

Signed: Date:

Signed: Date:

So, what do HR and the leadership development team need to do differently?

If HR is to successfully support the development of leadership capability within the organization, there are several areas they have to address:

Gain clear agreement and engagement with key stakeholders to the overall development strategy

Provide a regular and clear communication to the organization about the development and how it fits with the overall business plan

Brief and train senior leaders on their role in the development process – creating development plans, pre-briefing, follow-up after workshops and ongoing coaching. Unless senior mangers play their part in the process, the benefits of the development will not be maximized.

Provide briefings and pre-work for training programmes so people arrive at the workshop with a clear understanding of why they are there and what they are aiming to achieve from the training.

At the design phase, include enough reflection time and planning time for people to apply the learning back to their day-to-day work.

Brief course tutors on the overall training plan and how their workshops fit within the overall strategy.

In addition, there are key responsibilities for managers in order to promote transfer of learning back to work.

Responsibilities of line managers

Identify clear development plans for team members that support them to achieve their objectives.

Be creative in how to develop these skills in the team. Attendance at a workshop is not the only solution.

Brief individuals on what you want them to gain from attending any development activity.

Discuss the learning with the individual after their attendance at any workshop and provide ongoing coaching and challenge.

Finally, the individual is the only person who can make it happen!

Responsibilities of the individual

Take responsibility for your own learning.

Take time to reflect on your own performance.

Identify what skills you need to develop and how best to achieve this development.

Identify SMART learning objectives for any development activities you attend.

Plan time in to discuss learning with your manager and an ongoing action plan for transferring the learning back to your day-to-day work.

The following figures are taken from research at the Leadership Research Institute in USA. They show the effect of follow-up meetings on supporting a change in behaviour, one year after a leadership development programme.

- Little to no follow-up with manager: 53 per cent showed an improvement (Figure 8.2a).
- Some follow-up with manager (two meetings): 81 per cent showed an improvement (Figure 8.2b).
- Regular follow-up with manager (more than four meetings): 93 per cent showed an improvement (Figure 8.2c).

These figures show the benefit of post-development action planning and follow-up meetings.

Figure 8.2 The benefit of post-development action planning and follow-up meetings

Reflection point: transfer of learning

How well are senior managers briefing and debriefing the individuals that attend development events

What guidance are you giving managers on pre- and post- briefing?

How much responsibility do individuals take for their own development?

How do you measure this?

What process do you have in place for development planning?

How well briefed are the consultants that deliver the development activities?

How well do you measure their performance?

When did you last review the pre- and post-briefing of your training and development activities?

What does need to change?

Success means doing the best we can with what we have. Success is the doing, not the getting; in the trying, not the triumph. Success is a personal standard, reaching for the highest that is in us, becoming all that we can be.
– Anon

9   Skills of the leadership development specialist

This chapter will cover the following topics:

The role of the leadership development specialist

The skills of the leadership development specialist as an internal consultant

Effective client management – the process

The consulting process

The skills of the internal consultant – process skills

The role of the leadership development specialist

There are three main areas of responsibility for a learning and development specialist:

(1) Functional expertise
Diagnostics and analysis of training needs analysis
Training design skills
Consulting skills
Training delivery skills
Facilitation skills
Coaching skills

(2) Business understanding
Knowledge and understanding of the overall business strategy and plan
Understanding of internal customer operations and working constraints
Knowledge of key business drivers and performance measures

(3) Customer relationships
Knowledge of internal customer objectives and change agenda
Effective working relationships with all customer groups
Understanding customer development requirements and plans

Reflection point **Rate your own effectiveness in these three areas**	
Functional expertise Diagnostics and analysis of training needs analysis Training design skills Consulting skills Training delivery skills Facilitation skills Coaching skills **Business understanding** Knowledge and understanding of the overall business strategy and plan Understanding of internal customer operations and working constraints Knowledge of key business drivers and performance measures **Customer relationships** Knowledge of internal customer objectives and change agenda Effective working relationships with all customer groups Understanding customer development requirements and plans	Rate yourself on a scale of 1 = poor, 3 = satisfactory, 5 = good
What skills do you need to develop further?	
How will you do this?	

The skills of the leadership development specialist as an internal consultant

The three areas of expertise shown above are the keys to enable the development manager to make a valuable contribution to the business. It is not sufficient to have just a good functional experience. The ability effectively with internal customers and within the organizational context is the fundamental to success.

The leadership development manager has an important role as an internal consultant if he/she is to deliver his/her role effectively.

The Institute of Management Consulting defines management consultancy as

> ... the provision to management of objective advice and assistance relating to the strategy, structure, management and operations of an organization in pursuit of its long-term purposes and objectives. Such assistance may include the identification of options with recommendations; the provision of an additional resource and/or the implementation of solutions.

On their website, the Institute of Management Consultants defines the skills of the consultant as in Figure 9.1.

The role of the internal leadership development consultant is different in some ways from that of a general management consultant, but many of the key skills are similar. This template can be a useful starting point for recruitment or development of internal leadership development specialists.

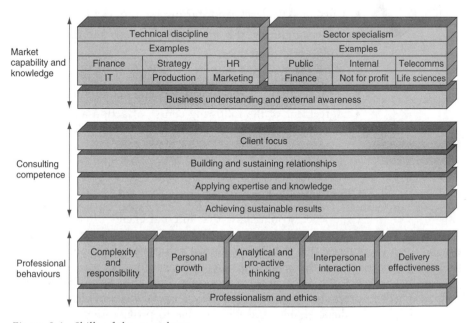

Figure 9.1 Skills of the consultant

In summary, the role of the internal leadership development consultant is to

Demonstrate effective technical and market knowledge.

Demonstrate effective customer-relationship skills.

Provide professional expertise to design interventions that will develop the individuals and organization.

Influence key stakeholders to buy into the proposed recommendations.

Implement and deliver the development activities that have been agreed.

Effective client management – the process

Identifying client needs is the first key step to effective client management. Spending time with the client to understand what they are looking to achieve in terms of the development of their people is important when designing an intervention that will meet their needs. The time for doing this should not be underestimated. Several meetings may be needed to understand the organizational context, the requirements of the users of the development, the background to the needs and the preferred ways of approaching the issues.

When working with a client to identify a training and development requirement, the following questions may provide a good starting point:

- Desired outcomes of the development activity
- Desired benefits for the individuals, the team and the organization
- An overview of the extent and nature of development that has already taken place
- Current skills levels and starting point of the targeted group
- Understanding of the different individuals and their background
- Budget and timescales
- Preferred approach and time commitment to the activity
- Identification of key stakeholders and decision makers
- Agreement of the following course of action and desired involvement in the ongoing development

Client involvement in design

Experience would show that internal clients often want to have a clear say in the proposed design and development of a programme. Good practice would suggest that the client is shown a draft of any proposed development activity and is given the opportunity to put forward his/her ideas and views before it is signed off. Buy-in, at this stage is crucial for the continuing success of a development programme or activity. The client will have a clearer idea of what the target audience is like and will be able to provide the training providers with useful data about what will work or not. In addition, the client is often paying for the work, even in an internal cross-charging set up and, therefore, has the right to know what he/she is buying and what benefits are likely to be gained from his/her investment.

Client involvement in delivery

This is a more difficult area to address. There is no right and wrong to this issue, although the client and providers need to have an open discussion about how much the client wants to be involved in a programme. There is nothing worse than a group of managers attending a development programme and finding that there are three or four observers sitting at the back taking notes. Likewise, the client should be encouraged to take a lead tutor role or facilitator role only if he/she has the requisite skills to do so, because this will damage his/her own credibility if he/she fail to fulfil this role satisfactorily.

There are many benefits to be gained from a client or sponsor attending the inauguration of an event to open the programme and explain the organizational reasons and desired benefits from the programme. Again, the providers need to brief the client carefully and ensure that they are positioning the programme in the right way. At this point, it can often become clear that the client has little idea of the content or approach of the programme. This reinforces the need to hold regular meetings with the client to ensure that he/she is fully engaged with the approach and content of the development activity.

Involving the client in the programme can take many forms. On some leadership programmes, the participants are asked to work on case studies and this is an excellent opportunity for the client to come in to listen to the presentations on a given topic. This involves them in the programme and gives them a detailed view of how the groups are working together as well as an understanding of the content of the programme.

Alternatively, the client may be invited to an evening dinner or end-of-programme review of learning. Again, this needs to be set up carefully in order to gain benefits for all involved.

Client management

Regular communication and feedback is integral to successful client relationship. The internal consultant or HR manager needs to understand that people development is not always at the top of the agenda for senior managers. The use of frequent communication and meetings is a simple way to keep the client involved and feeling comfortable with the progress being made. Asking for feedback from the internal customer has several benefits: it will highlight any areas where the client is unhappy; it will highlight the areas where the client is very satisfied; and, most importantly, it will develop the working relationship and trust between the two parties involved. People like to work with people whom they trust. If learning and development managers are seen as credible and trustworthy colleagues, they will usually be invited to take a stronger role in the development of the business and key organizational initiatives. Managing the relationships with the internal client and the range of stakeholders is vitally important.

Consulting skills case study

The following example shows the importance of stakeholder management and the need to ensure that all parties are brought into a development programme before it starts.

In a large global manufacturing company, the structure of HR was as follows: The Group HR and learning and development function had responsibility for the design and delivery of centrally funded senior leadership development. The management team of each of the countries decided whether to buy into these programmes or to design and deliver their own local programmes. Group HR developed a two-week programme designed to develop the leadership and strategy skills of the senior managers within the business. The programme was run for two separate weeks: one week on leadership skills; then a gap of six weeks before week two which focussed on finance and marketing skills.

The programme was designed with the help of an external provider and business school. The company development manager, the business school and the external providers all worked together to create a programme that was suitable for a worldwide audience.

The company launched the programme in Europe with 10 different countries attending the programme. The programme was delivered by the external provider with the company group learning and development managers acting as facilitators for the group of 30 delegates. The feedback from the first programme was excellent and the different country HR Directors felt they had received good value for their investment, seeing clear development and enhanced performance in those individuals whom they had sent to the programme.

Owing to the excellent feedback, the company management of one of the countries decided that they would like to run the programme for their own division as they had sufficient senior managers to make the programme viable.

The group learning and development team arranged the logistics for the event to be held in the chosen country and sent out the joining instructions and pre-work for the event. When they arrived, they were surprised to find that the country HR Director and two of his managers showed interest to attend the week-long programme. Because this seemed unusual, the group learning and development manager explained that this could inhibit learning on the programme and that, as an alternative, they could meet each evening for a debrief of the day with the course tutors. The country managers were asked to leave after the introductory session and the group learning and development team stayed to work with the external providers as before.

After the first day, the group learning and development manager and the course tutors met with the country HR Director and his team. There ensued a highly charged meeting between all parties as it became evident that the Group HR programme team had no contact with the country team. The country team had little understanding of the details of the programme and they had assumed that they would be attending the programme during the week.

The country team had chosen to use the programme as part of a culture initiative to support the change in leadership behaviour as they went through a transition in their business growth. The HR Director was a colleague of many of the participants and had wanted to use the week to spend time with his colleagues in networking and sharing a common experience. The two country learning and development managers wanted to attend the programme as part of their learning, and also to ensure that they would be able to support the learning after the programme.

Summary of this case study

None of these issues had been raised before the programme and, owing to time pressures and geographical distance, different parties had not thought to raise any of these issues with one another before the programme. The country managers felt that the group had come in like a 'circus into town' with no understanding of the required outcomes of the programme and no understanding of the organizational context in which they were operating.

Likewise, the course tutors, who were external to the company, had run a very successful first event and did not consider the differences in the audience and the organization in this specific business unit.

So whose responsibility was it to clarify the requirements of the programme?

Responsibilities of the country HR director

- To clarify the outcomes of a programme and to ensure that the programme content meets the specific needs of the individuals attending the programme.
- To provide a clear overview of the organization and desired outcomes for the programme.
- To outline what support they want to provide during the programme and the extent of involvement they want during the programme.

Responsibilities of the group learning and development team

- To use their consulting skills to identify the specific needs of the country team and to ensure that they brief the external tutorial team about any changes and additional factors that need to be accounted for.
- To treat the country manager as their 'client', which means developing an effective working relationship with them before the programme commences and ensuring that their needs are being met.

- To be flexible in their approach to programme design, having in mind that the programme should be run in different ways according to the varying client needs.
- To spend time on relationship as well as content.

Responsibilities of the tutorial team

- To understand who their client is. In many situations, there are several clients with different needs. The skill of any external tutorial team is to understand these different needs and to meet them in the best way possible.
- To clarify with their client, the requirements for each programme and to agree changes in style and format.
- To use their consulting skills with their client to ensure that they are delivering what is required and to ask for feedback on the delivery and approach.
- To be flexible enough to work with changing requirements.

Stakeholder management is an area that is often forgotten within large organizations. External consultants are used to working with the different needs of different client groups. Internally, these dynamics can be overlooked for a number of reasons:

Assumptions – Each team assumes that the other teams they are working with have a similar objective and have been brought into the activity that is being planned.

Internal politics – Each team wants to take ownership of an initiative, as it will raise the profile of their department to the rest of the business. For this reason, there is more of a spirit of internal competition rather than of collaboration between teams.

Communication – There may be a lack of focus on clear understanding between teams, and the internal communication can be seen as a time waster and not necessary.

Lack of internal consulting skills – Internal consultants and HR managers need to demonstrate the same skills as they would expect from external providers. There is often a lack of client management skills and an unwillingness to treat colleagues as internal clients. In fact, treating the client as the client will create a far healthier relationship and lead to enhanced respect and team working at all levels. Internal grading structures and job titles seem to take precedence over the working relationship and customer-supplier or partnership relationships that are required.

The consulting process

The internal consultant needs to develop consulting relationships with different people throughout the organization. The content of the projects may be very different but the phases of the consulting relationship remain the same.

Establishment of a relationship with the client and building trust
Identification of the issue to be addressed and the problems to be solved

Exploration of options and possible solutions

Implementation of solutions and interventions

Evaluation of benefits and learning

Establishment of a relationship with the client and building trust

As an internal consultant, the individual is continually creating relationships within the business. This is often cited as one of the benefits of using the internal consultant owing to his/her knowledge of the politics and history of the business, and of the key players. However, this does not negate the need to treat the colleague as a 'new' client when asked to take on a piece of work. Time spent on establishing the relationship is vital. This may involve the following:

- Agreeing confidentiality and ground rules for working together.
- Taking time to understand the structural and organizational context of the client and their team within the organization.
- Understanding their preferred means and frequency of communication. Some clients prefer to work by email and some prefer frequent face-to-face interaction. What works for one individual may not work for the next.

Understanding who the client is

This may seem straightforward but can be the cause of many internal or external consulting failures.

The following definitions may provide a useful starting point.

The decision maker – This may be one person or a number of people who will decide collectively whether to go ahead with a piece of work. This category will include the economic buyer who holds the budget for any given activity.

Decision makers may well take decisions throughout the implementation stage or they may delegate this authority as the project goes on. The skill of the internal consultant is to identify who the decision makers are at each stage of a piece of work and to agree how these decisions will be made throughout the duration of the project. Delay in decision-making is often instrumental in the failure of an initiative to gain momentum and impact.

Influencer – This person, or group of people, will influence how the leadership development activity will be received within the organization. Typical influencers for a leadership development event may be the line managers of attendees, and/or the directors of the work function where the development is taking place. The attitude and behaviour of these influencers can affect the success of a development activity in either a positive or negative manner. The internal consultant needs to identify who these people are and what needs to be done to gain their buy-in.

User – This is the person, or group of people, who will participate in the given development activity. Identifying what they want to gain from an event is obviously important in creating a successful outcome, but is all, too often, ignored by the decision makers or influencers. Senior directors are frequently quite reluctant

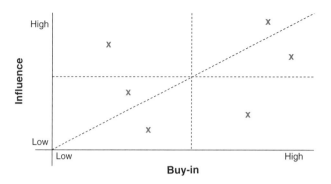

Figure 9.2 Stakeholder analysis

to ask the views of the users about what they think is needed in a development programme, as they are concerned that the objectives will be different from their own. However, this is where the skilled internal consultant is able to mediate between the different parties and to create a programme that will meet the needs of all the different stakeholders.

When undertaking a new assignment, the consultant is well advised to create a simple stakeholder analysis chart as shown in Figure 9.2.

Plot each of the key stakeholders – all the different individuals or client groups – onto the map and then identify what actions are needed either to gain their buy-in or to involve individuals who have high influence more closely.

Time spent on this will ensure that all the different internal parties are clear about the benefits of an intervention, how their needs will be met and what the benefits will be for the individual, team and business.

Ignoring the complexity of client relationships can be disastrous for the internal consultant as well as for the company as a whole.

Identification of the issue to be addressed and the problems to be solved

After the first step of gaining entry, a diagnosis of the situation is required that will help both the consultant and the client to identify what the next steps are.

Mckinsey's 7 'S' framework (Figure 9.3) provides a simple structure to follow when gathering data either with an individual client or with a group of managers. It allows the consultant to look at the implications of making changes in one area and its consequent impact on other parts of the business.

Structure

Reporting structure

Key stakeholders

Spans of control

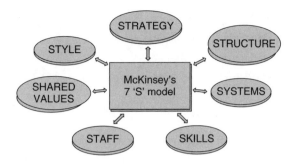

Figure 9.3   McKinsey's 7 'S' framework

Geography
Relationship of different holding companies

Systems

IT systems
HR systems
Processes
Procedures

Skills

Technical
Management
Leadership
Functional
Current skill sets of different levels of staff
Skill gaps

Staff

Number of people in the team/dept
Relationships between them
Diversity of background and experience
Maturity of the team

Style

Norms of behaviour
Formality vs informality of the team
Leadership style

Strategy

Department objectives
Department challenges
Plans for achieving objectives

Shared values

The culture within the department
Agreed ways of doing things

Asking questions to gain information about these different areas is the key to finding out the problems that need to be addressed. These headings provide a useful template for diagnostic meetings with clients designed to create a full understanding of their current situation.

It is only with a clear understanding of their situation, that the consultant can then start to identify what the key issues are and what support and help they require in terms of leadership development.

Other diagnostic skills may include one-to-one interview, focus groups, questionnaires, meetings with customers of the client group and organizational data such as staff satisfaction surveys.

Exploration of options and possible solutions

Once the diagnostics are completed, the key is to present the options in a way that meets the needs and preferences of the sponsor and client group. How this is done will depend on the size and type of the development assignment that is being completed. Many clients prefer an informal discussion of the options so that agreement can be made informally before it is written up into a project scope or project definition. Gaining buy-in at this point is important to gain support for the project during the implementation phase. It is also important to acknowledge any objections or concerns and enter into an honest discussion about how these should be dealt with. At this point, the consultant should clarify what roles that they and the other parties will play in the implementation.

Implementation of solutions and interventions

The role of the internal consultant needs to be clear at this stage of an assignment. Internal consultants are required to play many different roles and it pays to be clear about what is expected in different situations.

Advisor – Takes an expert role as advisor on the implementation of an activity. This could include advising on the suitability of external training providers or educational courses. It may involve advising the client on how they can restructure a department or deliver a message within their own team.

Trainer – Delivers the actual leadership development activities. This may be done in partnership with external providers.

Coach – Provides one-to-one coaching or mentoring to individuals involved in a development programme.

Project leader – Liaises and negotiates with several different stakeholders to ensure that implementation takes place.

Clarity on these different roles is the key to a successful internal consulting relationship. These roles will be different with different clients and on the scale of expertise available in-house. Educating the client about the different roles that can be taken is often useful but sometimes not discussed explicitly enough.

The skills of the internal consultant – process skills

Frequently there is a debate about the role of the consultant: is he/she an expert consultant or is he/she a process consultant? An example of the 'expert consultant' would be a tax advisor who would be brought in for legal and financial expertise. IT consultants may be present in an expert capacity. The role of the internal leadership development consultant is different. It demands both technical skills and process skills. The technical skills will cover the areas such as training design, competency development, and assessment methodology. The process skills focus on the skills of helping people to work together effectively to achieve a common outcome. These are the skills of facilitation and interpersonal effectiveness. The skilled development consultant knows when to be prescriptive and to give expert advice and when to sit back and to act as a catalyst for the group to direct their activities themselves.

At different stages of the consulting process, the leadership development consultant will need to use different styles and approaches.

In his book 'The Complete Facilitator's Handbook', John Heron developed the six Category Intervention model, which looks at the different interventions that may be appropriate during any phase of consulting.

Before making an intervention, it is important to be clear about the result the consultant wishes to achieve. The leadership development manager will meet with people at different levels within the organization. He/she needs to influence them to accept his/her views and thoughts on a number of issues. Often he/she will be facilitating a group of people and will be responsible for gaining a cross-section of views rather than giving their own. On a one-to-one basis, they may need to confront certain behaviours and to challenge the accepted way of going about something. The different styles provide choices in how to intervene:

- Acceptance/support
- Theory /principle
- Catalytic
- Prescriptive
- Confronting
- Cathartic

Each of these intervention styles will be explored in more detail below.

Acceptance/support

As a facilitator you can support a proposal someone has made which might otherwise not be picked up. You can validate somebody's contribution, particularly if they seem to need recognition of their contribution. Or you can simply tell an individual or group how well they are doing, with examples, to reinforce their effectiveness. You are not judging what they say or do, you are simply encouraging them and recognizing their contribution. This will enable people to feel confident to make suggestions or give their views.

Theory/principle

This will be useful if the person/group has lost their place in an agreed process – 'this is where you are and this is what you should do next' (see also prescribing, below). Or you could introduce a model of their behaviour to help them understand what is going on and to depersonalize both the effect and the way out of it. An example would be a team who are working together and achieving the task but who are not paying attention to the dynamics and relationships within the group. You may wish to share a simple model such as what is known to many of us as the 'hamburger' model (Figure 3.1). This simple picture shows the three areas that any leader/manager or team need to pay attention to. Many teams would say that they spend 90 per cent of their time on the task and fail to pay sufficient attention to either the process or to the feelings and relationships within the team.

You may then ask the group to reflect on what they are paying most attention to and what else needs attention. This is an example of using a simple theory to help people to understand themselves better and to work more effectively.

Catalytic

This is used so often that it has become the paradigm of a consultant's intervention. By asking an open question you can create discussion, exploration, problem solving or decision-making. The classic, 'How do you feel?' or 'What do you think you should do next?', are very open questions, but there are plenty of others depending upon the situation and the effect you want to have. It is possible to review the work of a group to date, without having observed any of that work, simply by asking open questions. This style of consulting can be very powerful at the right stage as it gives responsibility to the group to come up with their own solutions. It challenges the group or individual to think for themselves. There will be more buy-in to the solutions if the groups have come up with answers themselves. However, it is important that this does not become the default intervention from the consultant. Much of the 'anti' feeling towards external consultancies in the 1980s came from overuse of this technique. At times, the consultant needs to add value by giving something to the discussion rather than by simply asking the recipients what they think. They are there for their professional expertise and experience as well as for their process skills; therefore, a mix of all styles should be the aim.

Prescriptive

Sometimes it will be necessary to prescribe a process to move the group on. For example, you might prescribe brainstorming, give the rules and run the session. Or you might suggest that the group break into smaller groups to work on a problem, or different aspects of the same problem, and then to report back to each other. Sometimes it might be necessary for the consultant to stop the group where they are, move them to a rest break or onto another task and then to bring them back to where they were earlier. Either way, the consultant needs to manage the energy and climate of the client group, and prescribing a process to work with is often what is needed.

Confronting

This intervention is sometimes directly challenging – 'Chris, you've been dominating the discussion, what impact do you think that's having on the rest of the group?' – or gently challenging – 'Thanks, Chris, those are important points (supportive); what do others think?' Sometimes confrontation could be non-personal, for example, if the group is avoiding an issue because of real or imagined conflict, or just because it is too difficult to address. This is often necessary with a group which is apparently performing well and which has become blind to its own shortcomings and/or ways of working. A useful confronting intervention is to ask the group how well they think they are operating at any given time.

Cathartic

Occasionally, a build up of emotion within a group, on the part of one or more people, will need to be expressed. The emotions might be fear, anger, grief or joy. If they get in the way of achieving the task you may have to help them to find an outlet for these emotions in order to make those people experiencing such emotions to contribute effectively once more. Cathartic interventions are difficult and need careful consideration and support. The leadership development specialist needs to be able to manage his/her own emotions as well as the emotions of the group. Effective development managers keep their own agenda separate from those of their clients and do not get involved in the dynamics and emotions of the group.

The key to using any of these approaches is to understand what is required from each situation. Different people will prefer a different style and the internal leadership development specialist has to be skilful in adapting their style to the needs of the person and of the situation.

Reflection point on your own consulting skills

Review your own skills as an internal consultant. Think about specific pieces of work that you are currently providing for your internal clients.

How often do you use each of the six categories of intervention style?

Which styles could you use more and why?

How well have you identified and managed the different stakeholder requirements?

What types of intervention do your different clients need from you?

How frequently do you review the effectiveness of your client relationships?

What feedback have your internal clients given you in the last three months?

What would your clients like you to do more of/less of?

What three improvements could you make in your internal consulting skills?

10 Training and facilitation skills

This chapter covers the following areas:

Effective questioning techniques

Managing group exercises

Handling difficult training situations

Giving and receiving feedback

Effective listening skills

Using a facilitator

The role of HR in providing training and development

Using internal or external providers

Effective questioning techniques

One of the most important skills a trainer needs is a well-developed questioning technique. There are several reasons for using questions:

- You will stimulate active learning within a group-training session by making use of learners' powers to reason things out for themselves. They will acquire a greater degree of ownership and retention of the knowledge or skill established, and place a higher value on it.

- As a trainer, you need feedback to assess whether your delegates' initial knowledge is correct, whether progress is being made and whether you have met your training objectives.

- As a system of two-way communication, it integrates you into the group and encourages group participation and variety.

- It encourages the practice of clear thinking, both by you, in phrasing your questions, and by your delegates, in phrasing their answers.

- When the trainer highlights the responses on the flipchart, not only does it reinforce the learning, but it can also motivate the delegates by acknowledging their contribution in a positive way.

Types of questions and their uses

Fact-finding

You can use these to establish the level of existing knowledge, and from this decide the scope of the session. They can be used to recap ground, which has previously been covered. They are a means of testing what has been learned. These questions tend to be phrased in a closed way, e.g. 'How many of us have been involved in delivering induction training?'; 'Did you have a structured induction plan to follow?'

Exploring

You may want to build on the facts and find out more information about the details. You may also want to test out opinions and attitudes to gain a better insight into how the group views a particular topic. You can do this by asking your questions in an open way, e.g. 'Why do you think induction training is important?'; 'What areas should an effective induction programme cover on day one?'

Asking questions

Before you ask questions, consider whether the group has sufficient knowledge/information to answer? Take time to consider them and phrase them carefully so that they can be clearly understood, and so that the answer can provide:

- The next logical step in the discussion
- A relevant view or opinion
- The feedback you need for the next section of the session

If you do not get a response to a question, be prepared to rephrase it. On the other hand, it may be that the group members are unable or unwilling to answer. You may need to provide some more information before putting the question again; you may have touched on a sensitive issue with which the group is uncomfortable.

Distribute questions evenly around the group, and name the person whom you wish responds, only if it is relevant to do so. Moving towards a table or giving clear eye contact will encourage people to pay attention, so that there is generally little need to use individual names.

Handling replies

Answers may be correct, partly correct, incomplete or incorrect.

If an answer is correct, check whether the remainder of the group has understood. Does everyone accept it? Is there anything that could be added or could an example be given? If the answer has come very promptly, this is particularly important.

If it is partly correct or incomplete, emphasize your agreement as far as it goes. What about the rest of the answer? You can put it back to the group, but may need to supply additional information or use another question to enable them to complete the answer.

If it is incorrect, you must decide why this is so. Was the question poorly phrased? Has the individual or group insufficient knowledge or understanding? You may need to re-cap, provide additional information, or draw parallels from the known to the unknown. To answer the question yourself is to admit that you have not provided the basic groundwork for it to be a fair question.

Managing group exercises

There are some simple rules associated with running group exercises, which can be broken down into three stages:

(1) Give clear instructions
(2) Monitor group activities
(3) Provide an appropriate summary of learning

Give clear instructions

If you have chosen a good case study or activity, start it off by using a four-stage briefing covering:

- Why? (rationale)
  - Why is it important to do this exercise?
  - How will they benefit?
- What? (task)
  - Exactly what output or discussion are you asking for?
  - Exactly what should the group produce at the end of the exercise?
- How? (context)
  - How long have they got?
  - How big are the groups?
  - How do they access resources to complete the exercise?
- So what? (sharing)
  - What will the outcome of their exercise be?
  - In what form should they report back?

Monitor group activities

During any group exercise or case study, there are several things you need to do:

- Listen for comments from individuals. Are they talking about the task?
- Stay in the room, but out of the way. Make sure you are not disturbing their work, but are still available to answer questions.
- Provide help when they ask for it.

- Watch out for individuals or groups which are clearly not involved. Encourage them to join in.
- Identify groups that are ahead of the others and encourage them to extend the remit of the exercise.
- Identify groups what are behind and encourage them to concentrate on key aspects of the task.

Provide an appropriate summary of learning

The group runs the feedback session

This is the right technique if you have split the main group into smaller groups to do an exercise. But if three groups come back after an exercise and give nearly identical presentations, this is very unlikely to happen. A more useful approach is to ask each group to focus on a different question or to look at a scenario from different perspectives. This will provide a more interesting feedback session and different points will be made by each group.

The trainer runs the feedback session

There are several ways to keep control but still allow groups to say what they have done. You can ask each group for two or three key points each. Alternatively, you may want to ask each group to add points or learning only where they have not already been covered by a previous group. You may want to ask the groups to prepare a flipchart before you run through the points that they have made. The key is to use a variety of techniques to keep the interest and attention of the group.

No feedback session

If people have learnt all that they can in small groups, there may be no need to repeat the learning in a plenary session. This would also apply if people have been discussing confidential issues in small groups.

Handling difficult training situations

There are times when the trainer or facilitator will face situations where the group or individuals are being disruptive or challenging.

Some simple tips for handing difficult situations.

Reading the audience and reacting

In group discussions, individuals can at times demonstrate unhelpful behaviours (Table 10.1).

Table 10.1 Difficult training situations

Behaviours	Why	What to do
Overly talkative	They may be wanting to impress. They may also be exceptionally well informed and anxious to show it, or just be naturally talkative	Slow them down with some more challenging questions. Interrupt with 'That's an interesting point – now let's see what the group thinks of it'. In general, let the group take care of them as much as possible You may need to ask for some other views to be heard
Highly argumentative	They may not have wanted to attend the session and are showing their frustration They have better ideas They may be impatient with the slow pace of the discussion	Keep your own temper in check Acknowledge their point and move on Ask the group what their views are on the particular subject As a last resort, talk to the delegate privately during a break; try to find out what the problem is; see if you can win co-operation Acknowledge that they may be right and change the course of the discussion
Rambler	Has difficulty sticking to the point. May be confused about the topic	Refocus their attention by restating relevant points and move on Thank them for their point and move on to another person in the group Summarize the purpose of the discussion and ask for brief points. Remind the group of the time left for the topic
The wrong answer	They may have misunderstood, be confused or lack knowledge	Say: 'I can see how you feel', or 'That's one way of looking at it' Ask the group for other views and compare views Ensure that the group finds out the correct answer before moving on

(*Continued*)

Table 10.1 (Continued)

Behaviours	Why	What to do
Will not talk	They could be bored, indifferent, shy or nervous, or even disagree fundamentally	Arouse their interest by asking for their opinion
		During a break, try to find out why do they want to contribute
		If a sensitive person is reluctant to talk, compliment them on the first time they do. Be sincere
		Remember that some people prefer to learn by listening and some people prefer to learn by joining in. You may not need to encourage them to join in verbally
Personality clash	Two or more members clash	Ask each to summarize the other's point of view, and then put the argument to the rest of the group. Emphasize points of agreement (if possible). Draw attention to the objective. Cut across with a direct question on the topic
		Stop the discussion and bring the group back to the purpose of the session
Side conversation between participants	They may be interested in one aspect of the subject	Move over to stand by them
		Ask the whole group to give attention
	People who know each other well may chat and may have lost interest in the session	Ask them if they have something to add
		If this fails, ask them to summarize the last person's contribution

Reflection point

Think about the last workshop you attended. What did the facilitator or trainer do well?

The list will be different for different people, e.g.:

- High energy
- Credibility – knew their subject
- Appropriate pace of delivery
- Backed up with relevant handouts and high-impact slides
- Interactive – involving the group
- Reactive to the group energy levels and mood
- Flexible in terms of content and delivery style
- Kept to the agreed agenda and timescales
- Included different sessions to appeal to different learning styles
- Gave time for discussion
- Challenged current thinking
- Gave a different perspective
- Broadened understanding of the topic

Reflection point

Rate yourself against the list that you have drawn up, or the list above:

What are your key strengths as a trainer?

What do you find difficult in running a training session?

How well do you manage the difficult members of a group?

How well do you gain participation and involvement from the group?

When did you last ask for feedback after a training session that you have delivered?

What are your key areas for development?

Giving and receiving feedback

A fundamental role of the trainer or facilitator is to provide feedback to others. This will be either on a one-to-one basis or in a group setting.

Feedback is the mechanism for giving a person (or group) information about how the behaviour of that person or group affects others. Given skilfully, it is a helping, enabling, learning process.

The purpose of feedback

Giving and receiving feedback is a learning process for both giver and receiver. Constructive feedback increases self-awareness, offers options and choices, and encourages personal development. Constructive feedback does not necessarily mean positive feedback; negative feedback, when given skilfully, can be a useful and effective learning tool.

Destructive feedback is essentially that which is given in an unskilled way and, rather than giving the receiver helpful information and options, leaves the receiver feeling dissatisfied with little or nothing to build upon.

Giving skilled feedback

Start with the positive

When offering feedback, it can help the receiver to hear first what you like, appreciate, enjoy or what you found that they had done well.

Our culture sometimes emphasizes the negative, the focus being on mistakes rather than on strengths, and, in the rush to criticize, the positive aspects are overlooked. If the positive is registered first, any negative is more likely to be listened to and acted upon.

Be specific

General comments are not very helpful when it comes to developing skills, because they do not provide sufficient details to be useful sources of learning. Comments such as 'You were great' or 'You were terrible' are unhelpful in terms of learning unless what the person did that led to the use of the labels 'great' and 'terrible' can be pinpointed. It is extremely difficult to act upon general information and comments.

Be descriptive rather than evaluative

Describe your reactions by telling the person what you saw or heard and the effect it had on you. Simply commenting that something was 'good' or 'bad' is not informative, and value judgements are likely to lead to defensiveness.

> *I felt you were really interested and concerned, because of your tone of voice and the way you listened...*

is more likely to be useful and helpful than 'that was good, I enjoyed it'.

Talk about things that can be changed. Giving feedback to a person about something over which they have little or no control or choice is not only unhelpful but pointless, for example

> *'I don't like your appearance' is not offering information about which the person can do very much and it is information likely to antagonize the person and make constructive feedback between you much more difficult.*

> *However, information such as 'It would help me a lot if you smiled more...' provides the person with something that can be worked on.*

Take care with timing

Feedback is most useful when offered as early as possible after the behaviour so that events and feelings are clearly remembered. However, it is important to be as sure as you can that the receiver is ready for the feedback at that time; in some situations, it may be more helpful to reserve the feedback to a later point.

Offer alternatives

In situations where you offer negative feedback, suggesting what could have been done differently, is often more helpful than simply criticizing. Turn the negative feedback into a positive suggestion, e.g.:

> *The fact that you all carried on with the task when Bill joined you seemed unwelcoming. I think if you had stopped for a moment to say 'hello' and to exchange names, he'd have found it much easier to take part in the group.*

Check

Do not immediately assume that the feedback you offer is clearly understood and the message received was the message intended. Check whether the other person understands it. It is also useful, where possible, to test the accuracy of your feedback by checking whether it is one opinion or a view that is shared.

Own the feedback

Offering a universally agreed opinion of the 'you are...' type is an easy trap to fall into when giving feedback. All we can, in fact, offer another person is our own experience of them at a particular time, and it is important that we take responsibility for the feedback we offer. Starting with 'I' or 'In my view' can help to avoid the impression of being a judge.

Do not overdo it

Providing an appropriate amount of feedback is important. When asked for comments and opinions, there is a temptation to say everything and overwhelm the receiver, rather than to select the more appropriate and useful information, and then leaving the receiver to ask for more if they wish.

Leave the receiver with a choice

Feedback, which demands change or is imposed on another person may invite resistance or, in extreme cases, cause relationships to break down. Feedback does not involve telling people how they must be to suit us.

Skilled feedback offers people information about how they affect others in a way that recognizes their rights and leaves them with a choice as to whether or not they act upon it. The feedback should not involve prescribing change, rather it should help people to examine the consequences of any decision to change or not to change.

Questions first

Feedback that is dogmatic can be of a hindrance rather than a help, since it invites the taking up of opposing stances. Helping the receiver to think about where he or she wants to be, by posing reflective questions, is more likely to help than making a statement.

Try to be objective

Objectivity is very difficult to achieve when giving or receiving feedback. Giving facts before opinions and describing observable behaviour can help avoid total subjectivity and can put observations into context.

Think what feedback says about you

Feedback is likely to say a great deal about the giver as well as the receiver. It will certainly be indicative of one's own values and what one focuses on in other people. We can, therefore, learn about ourselves if we listen to the feedback we offer others.

Receiving feedback

As learning and development specialists, there will often be occasions where you will find that there is a need to ask for feedback from others in order to improve performance.

When we receive feedback, we can help ourselves to benefit from it by encouraging the giver to use the skills described above. We can also help ourselves make the most from feedback by:

Listening

Feedback may be uncomfortable to hear, but that may be less of a disadvantage than not knowing what others think and feel. People will have opinions about you as well as perceptions about your behaviour and it can help to be aware of them. However, it is important to remember that you are entitled to your opinion and may chose to ignore information as of little significance, irrelevant, or referring to behaviour you may wish to maintain for other reasons.

Be sure you understand

Make sure you understand what is being said before you respond to it. If you jump to conclusions, become defensive or go on the attack, you may deter people from giving you feedback or you may not be able to make use of it. Check that you have understood the feedback being given; a useful technique can be to paraphrase or repeat it to the giver.

Check with others

Relying on only one source of information can suggest that everyone shares a biased view that you may come to believe. If you check your feedback with other people, you may find that others experience you differently and you may develop a more balanced view of yourself and thus keep the feedback in perspective.

Ask for feedback

If you do not receive feedback at all, you may have to ask for it and indeed help the giver to provide useful feedback to you. Sometimes, you may get feedback restricted to one aspect of behaviour and you may need to ask for feedback you would find useful but do not receive. Do not expect everyone to be able to provide skillful feedback automatically; providing feedback can be uncomfortable and difficult for people unused to the process. They may need help from you.

Do not waste it

We all need to know how other people experience us, to extend our self-awareness; without that knowledge, we have only our own version of ourselves to go by. Feedback can make an important contribution to self-development, provided that it is used.

It is important to assess the value of feedback: to consider the consequences of ignoring it or of using it to influence future behaviour. If we fail to make this assessment, the feedback will have been wasted.

Do not forget to thank the person giving you feedback. You may benefit from it; it may have been very difficult for that person to give; and reinforcing the practice is valuable in any relationship or organization.

Reflection point

Working individually, think of some recent examples of feedback that you have been given and complete the worksheet.

Write your examples in this column. For each example, what was it about the way that the feedback was given that contributed to your response?

(1) An example of negative feedback that you received badly.

(2) An example of praise that you received badly or indifferently.

(3) An example of negative feedback that you received well.

(4) An example of praise that you received well.

In summary, useful feedback is:

Given with care

To be useful, feedback requires the giver to feel concern and to care for the person receiving feedback – to want to help, not hurt the other person.

Given with attention

It is important to pay attention to what you are doing as you give feedback. This helps you to engage in a two-way exchange with some depth of communication.

Invited by the recipient

Feedback is most effective when the receiver has invited the comments. This provides a platform for openness and some guidelines; and it also gives the receiver an opportunity to identify and explore particular areas of concern.

Directly expressed

Good feedback is specific and deals clearly with particular incidents and behaviour. Making vague statements is of little value. The most useful help is direct, open and concrete.

Fully expressed

Effective feedback requires more than a bald statement of facts. Feelings also need to be expressed so that the receiver can judge the full impact of his behaviour.

Well timed

The most useful feedback is given when the receiver is receptive to it and is sufficiently close to the particular event being discussed for it to be fresh in the mind. Storing comments can lead to a build-up of recriminations, and reduces the effectiveness of feedback when it is finally given.

Readily actionable

The most useful feedback centres on behaviour that can be changed by the receiver. Feedback concerning matters outside the control of the receiver is less useful. It is often helpful to suggest alternative ways of behaving, which allow the receiver to think about the new ways of tackling old problems.

Effective listening skills

The trainer or facilitator has a key responsibility to demonstrate effective listening. Listening is a complex activity, which requires a high level of commitment, concentration and genuine concern. It is not, as we tend to think, a passive role just because the speaker is doing most of the obvious input.

An interesting feature of listening is that listening habits are not necessarily the result of training but rather the result of the lack of it. Of the four basic learned communication skills (listening, speaking, reading and writing), listening is probably the most used but least taught. So what is listening? Active listening is more than just hearing. Hearing is the first part of listening – the physical part, when your ears make sense of sound waves. After that, other senses come into play and the thought processes take over.

There are three levels of listening:

Thinking

This is listening to the words used, listening to the more logical, overt sentences or phrases used by the speaker. Transcripts of conversations or speeches mainly convey messages at this level.

Feeling

This is listening at the emotive level, looking for the feelings, which often accompany the spoken words. It requires the listener to focus on voice tones, hesitations etc., together with all aspects of non-verbal communication.

Understanding

This means listening for the 'intent' behind what people say (the subtext). It is the 'real' meaning lying behind the words. The listener should also be able to sense whether the speaker would be prepared to act on what they are saying and what level of real commitment they have.

One approach to listening is to regard it as a skill, which can be developed. As a skill it involves action: it is more than sitting still with an interested look on your face.

The following three skills can help active listening:

- Paraphrasing
- Drawing out
- Suspending judgement

Paraphrasing

Paraphrasing is a process by which the listeners repeat, in their own words, what they think the speaker has just been saying. This can be done at appropriate times – usually when the speaker stops for a moment, or at some other suitable break point.

The main purpose of paraphrasing is that it enables the listeners to check that they have understood the speaker's main points, intentions and feelings. It also serves as a means of letting the speaker know that the listener is indeed listening.

Some guidelines for paraphrasing include:

- If you lose the thread of what the speaker is saying, or do not understand, say so and ask for clarification.
- Pay careful attention to the speaker's basic message which includes looking out for non-verbal messages, listening for the tone of voice and sensing the speaker's intentions and feelings.
- Use your own words when paraphrasing what you think has been said; do not just repeat exactly what was said.
- After paraphrasing, look for some cue or sign from the speaker to tell you if your statement was accurate or not, or ask the speaker directly.

Drawing out

People do not always say what they mean. Sometimes, speakers communicate their ideas unclearly and the listeners can take intended meanings as well as unintended meanings from what is said. It can be useful to 'draw out' a person – that is, to get the speaker to talk about their problems, feeling and ideas.

One way of doing this is by using appropriate questions. In general, open-ended questions will be more effective in drawing out than closed questions.

Some guidelines for asking open-ended drawing out questions:

- Questions such as 'What?', 'How?' tend to be more positive than 'Why?' questions Which may put someone on the defensive.
- If the speaker talks only about fact, ask about feelings.
- If the speaker talks about feelings alone, ask about the facts.
- If the speaker uses generalities, ask for examples.
- Questions that help to draw out needs include: 'What do you want to happen?', 'If everything went well, what would it be like?', 'Imagine the problem has been solved – what has happened?', 'What is the worst that could happen?', 'What is the best that can happen?', 'How would you feel then?', 'What would you do?'
- Questions that help draw out ideas include: 'What are all the relevant facts?', 'How do these facts relate to each other?', 'What alternative courses of action are open?', 'What will be the likely effects of these?'
- Questions that help draw out assumptions and thought processes include 'What makes you say that?', 'What happened to make you feel that way?'

This means, pausing occasionally to reflect back to the listener your understanding of what has been said. This indicates to the listener that you have been listening attentively. It also enables correction of miscommunication and allows the speaker to 're-read' their conversation before moving on.

Suspending judgement

By suspending judgement, a facilitator or coach is able to listen to suggestions and ideas with an open mind, rather than immediately thinking of various reasons why the suggestion is not good or will not work.

Suspending judgement is more difficult than might be imagined. For various reasons (fear of taking a new approach; unwillingness to accept someone else's ideas; fear of uncertainty), refuge can be sought in the instant rejection of an idea, blaming the idea itself on other people, rather than giving it the attention it deserves.

This can have at least two harmful effects. It may lead to rejecting an idea that would, in fact, provide an excellent solution. Even if the objection is valid, rejection can be very demoralizing to the other person.

The act of suspending judgement, on the other hand, involves considering with an open mind. Some guidelines for suspending judgement:

- Listen carefully to what is being said, refusing to allow one's negative reactions to crowd into one's mind. Letting the person finish speaking before you give your view.
- Ask the other person to describe all the advantages and strong points of the idea and listening to the answers.
- Ask about the disadvantages.
- If you think of any disadvantages that have not been mentioned, ask yourself about your motive for raising them. Question whether they are valid, merely acting as substitutes for your own fears.
- If you still consider there are disadvantages that the other person has not thought of, give them in open-ended question form.

Barriers to good listening

'On–off' listening

This unfortunate habit in listening arises from the fact that most people think about four times as fast as the average person speaks. Thus, the listener has three-fourths of a minute of spare thinking time for each listening minute. Sometimes, we use this extra time to think of our own personal affairs, concerns or interests instead of listening.

'Soap box' listening

To most of us, there are particular words or phrases, which can often provoke a negative reaction. When we hear them, we get upset or irritated and stop listening. These terms vary with individuals. However, words like 'should', 'must', 'unfaithful', 'police', discipline', 'school', 'management', 'unions', etc. are common signal words to which there is an automatic response. When this signal comes in, we turn the speaker off.

'Open ears–closed mind' listening

Sometimes, we decide rather quickly that either the subject or the speaker is boring and what is said makes no sense. Often, we jump to conclusions that we can predict what he/she knows or what he/she will say: thus, we conclude, there is no reason to listen because we will hear nothing new.

'Too deep for me' listening

When we are listening to ideas that are complex and complicated, there is a danger that we will not bother to listen.

'Matter over mind' listening

We do not like to have our pet ideas, prejudices and points of view overturned. We do not like to have our opinions and judgements challenged. Consequently, when a speaker says something that clashes with what we think and believe, we may unconsciously stop listening or even become defensive and plan a counter attack.

Being 'subject-centred' instead of 'speaker-centred'

Sometimes, we concentrate on the problem and not the person. Details and facts about an incident can become more important than what the person is saying about themselves.

'Fact' listening

Often, as we listen to people, we try to remember the facts and repeat them over and over again to drive them home. As we do this, the speaker may have moved on to new facts and we lose them in the process.

'Pretend' listening

Sometimes, there are many distractions when we listen – noise, movement or people, or other matters clamouring for our attention. We give non-verbal clues that we are listening such as nodding, but we are actually distracted by other things going on.

Using a facilitator

There are many excellent books on facilitation and this guidebook gives merely an overview of the role and responsibilities of the facilitator within a company. This role is often taken by the learning and development specialists or by people who have been trained to carry out this role. The facilitator needs to clarify their role with any group with which they are working. It is a more challenging role than the training delivery role, as it focuses on process skills rather than content skills.

Definition of facilitation:

A facilitator's role is to help a group to achieve its task by supporting the process and by helping to manage the relationships within the group.

In order to make sure that group facilitation works well, there needs to be some preparation. Malcom Walton from Fairstead Consulting (www.fairstead-development.co.uk) provides the following useful points.

Making the decision to bring an external facilitator into a group meeting or workshop needs to be managed carefully. A team may well feel that they do not need external support in how to work together. They may also feel that they would prefer to manage their business confidentially without a party from another department listening in. Therefore, the context for bringing in a facilitator needs to be explained to the whole team and their buy-in is a requirement to moving forward easily. The learning and development manager or internal consultant needs to think about how they introduce themselves to the group and to agree with the group what role they will be taking.

Some areas to consider:

- What is the history of the group with whom you are working?
- Have they worked with a facilitator before, with what result?
- What is the current situation and how does that fit in with the wider picture?
- What is the group trying to achieve?
- Have the group had any input to their goal?
- Who is the client?
- What is the climate within the group now and what does it need to be in order to be fully effective?

The faciltator's role is to help to create an atmosphere of openness, acceptance, support and clear thinking, in which everyone can contribute fully and confidently. The facilitator has an important leadership role in that they have to model and engender the behaviours that will create this climate.

Fundamentally, a facilitator is someone who helps a group/team/individual to achieve their own outcomes through focussing on *how* the group is working, while the group concern themselves with the *what* they are doing.

It is important that the client group understands the role of the facilitator. A facilitator's role may include, among other things, some, or all of the following:

- Observation of the way the group works and feedback afterwards to the leader and/or the group.
- Intervention, as and when the facilitator judges it to be appropriate.
- Guardian of the process with which the group may be relatively unfamiliar.
- Specific help to solve particular problems within the group.
- Individual coaching based on observation.

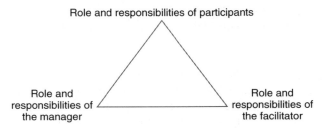

Figure 10.1 Contracting triangle

A facilitator is best having the widest possible brief, but the facilitator should, obviously, work within their capability, and the expectations and the level of trust of the group.

Once the above roles have been discussed and agreed on, the group, the manager and the facilitator are in a position to start the session.

A simple contracting triangle that can be used, adapting the questions as required (Figure 10.1).

The facilitator asks the group to share and agree to their views on each of the three questions. These are generally listed visibly and left as reminders during the meeting or workshop. They can be referred to during the sessions, especially in case of any group conflict or role confusion.

Clear contracting ensures that all parties involved have a heightened level of awareness of expectations and a shared understanding.

Contracting can also operate at three levels:

Procedural, e.g. where and when shall we work?

Professional, e.g. what are the limits of the facilitator's capabilities and agreed scope for action?

Psychological, e.g. what are the attitudes within the group to each other and to facilitation?

It will be necessary for the facilitator to agree that they have permission to address relevant issues or blockages if they get in the way of achieving the task. The process of contracting is an open method of gaining clarity. This is a vital and crucial part of the process. (Lack of clarity at this point often leads to managing different expectations while facilitating.)

Therefore, before the event, the facilitator should be clear about the expectations of all the relevant parties and has helped the group to accept realistic expectations. They will have considered appropriate processes to support the task (e.g. brain storming, creativity sessions, democratic objectives, etc). They will also be aware of the practical, professional and psychological issues related to the group and its organization. The outcomes and guidance will have been agreed with the client. So when the actual facilitation starts there is clarity about the task, and the contract can be reiterated and confirmed with all the delegates.

The following extract is taken from 'The Complete Facilitator's Handbook' by John Heron, 1999, Kogan Page and highlights some of the keys to effective facilitation.

(1) Set the boundaries. You can often prevent problems arising – and it will be much easier to facilitate the process – if you set the ground-rules and create a conducive climate at the outset. It's always best to start by helping the group clarify an outcome that is reasonable to achieve in the time period. Try to reach a consensus on how disagreements or conflicts will be handled and clarify your own role in the process. Make it clear what you're going to do and what you're not going to do.

Once the boundaries have been contracted, you can keep bringing the group back to this agreement to see whether they are on track or not.

(2) Let go of the content. A good facilitator has to let go of the subject matter of the meeting. The challenge is to influence the group but not to dominate. You have to suppress your ideas/solutions and encourage others to talk.

People often fall into the trap of trying to steer the discussion in a particular direction. It is important to restrain this impulse and control any need to express impatience with other people.

(3) Focus on the process. Instead of focussing on the 'content' of the meeting, good facilitators pay most of their attention to the 'process'. This is a level below content and it relates to how people feel about taking part. That is where you get the politics and the interaction between group members.

You need to use your senses, your intuition and your instincts to pick up the atmosphere and the group dynamics. Do people sound enthusiastic, lively, and excited – or not? Are people expressing their feelings or sitting on them?

Keep your finger on what is happening in the group – who is talking? who is not talking? Concentrate on the emotional temperature and try to read the body language and non-verbal behaviour.

(4) Be – do not do. The role of a facilitator is more about 'are' than 'doing'. 'Doing' refers to the techniques you use to help the group move on. 'Being' is more about the energy you bring and your personality.

In order to create a safe environment where people are going to be open and honest, you need an empathic personal presence and the group needs to respect and trust you. They also need to feel confident that you are strong enough to deal with any incidents, which may arise. All this comes as much from your personal style, as from anything you might say.

Where you sit, whether you look in control or flustered, how animated you are – all the non-verbal clues give you a sense of presence, as does your tone of voice.

(5) Intervene when appropriate. As a facilitator, you should be noticing what is going on and making sense of it. Then you can make a decision about what to do about it. You could keep quiet and watch what happens or you could intervene and say something. Your own body language can be a powerful

intervention – with a look, a smile or a nod, you can indicate support or challenge to what is going on.

John Heron, an author and consultant on facilitation, highlights three types of intervention: hierarchical interventions (telling the group what to do), co-operative interventions (making suggestions and asking for group consensus) and autonomous interventions (leaving the group to decide how to proceed). The challenge for a facilitator is to be able to work in all three styles and to know which intervention is appropriate.

(6) Don not shirk difficult situations. Often facilitators feel intimidated about intervening with more senior managers or with people exhibiting disruptive behaviour. But you cannot be effective in the role if you are frightened of making a mistake or of not being popular. You need to develop skills and strategies to overcome these barriers.

If a difficult situation arises, you could suggest taking a break, having a coffee, changing the scenery, working in pairs or brainstorming the particular issue. If it's a disruptive individual, you may choose to confront that person – within the group or in private – and give them feedback on what they are doing and the effect it is having.

If you agreed on your role at the outset – and everyone contracted to that – then you have 'prior permission' to challenge anyone who is breaking a golden rule.

(7) Evaluate afterwards. At the end of the meeting or event, the participants will usually have a sense about where they have ended up and whether or not it was worthwhile. Look at what has been agreed on and how it will now move forward.

Try to get some feedback from the participants and also review your performance against your own assessment criteria. Did you experiment with something new, take any risks, raise the difficult issues? Did you jump on people with two left feet and make things worse? Could you have handled a situation better? Should you have intervened earlier?

The role of HR in providing training and development

The quality and effectiveness of leadership development in an organization can be related to the broader question of how the organization views the role of HR. Figure 10.2, the model of HR, shows the different roles that can be adopted by an HR function. The different roles are:

Strategic partner – helps to execute business strategy successfully and to meet customer needs.

Transactional manager – improve organizational efficiencies.

Staff supporter – maximize employees' motivation and competence.

Change leaders – deliver organizational change and cultural transformation.

Truly effective leadership development depends on the role that HR decides to play in the organization. If the organization demands that HR focuses on

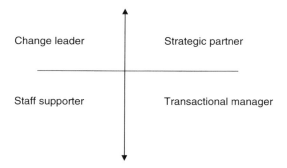

| Change leader | Strategic partner |
| Staff supporter | Transactional manager |

Figure 10.2   Different roles of HR

being transactional managers with little voice in the strategic agenda, then they are not going to be able to deliver transformational leadership development that will help to shape the desired culture. If HR takes on the role of change leader, their approach to development and learning will be accordingly different.

HR as Transactional manager

HR departments that are seen in the role of administrative experts will be likely to run an efficient training department which ensures that people attend for the training courses. They are perhaps less likely to ensure that people gain the appropriate development in order to help the organization to progress. They will be more focussed on the process and policy of training and less focussed on the effectiveness of the development with which people are involved. The menu-driven approach to training is indicative of this approach, and it can be difficult to link the development activity with the strategy of the business. Inevitably, it then becomes difficult to measure the effectiveness of the development activity because there are no clear success measures in place.

HR as staff supporter

In this role, HR works at a strategic level to create the organization that will deliver the customer and shareholder requirements. Leadership development is then seen as one of the key drivers to achieve these outcomes. The implication for leadership development is that it will focus on future skills and competencies with a drive to achieve practical return on investment within a clear time frame. This leads to a more focussed leadership development strategy which is clearly linked to the overall business strategy.

HR as employee champion

This is a more traditional-role focus where HR is seen more in the supportive role of employee welfare and well-being. There will be a strong focus on employee benefits and support services, with less focus on the development of skills and competency to meet the needs of the business. People will be offered development if they want it and often the development may not be directly related to the current needs of the company. Investment in external professional qualifications will be supported as it is seen to be helpful to the individual. Obviously, there is benefit to the organization, but these benefits may not be exploited as well as they could be. This is an HR approach that puts people first with the advantages and disadvantages that go with that approach. Training and development will be given less priority than creating a good working environment with flexible employee reward packages.

HR as change leader

Organizations that see their HR and development people as change leaders will be using them very differently. In these companies, HR will be involved in the first discussions about, and ongoing strategy for, organizational growth and expansion. They will be involved in the highest level talent management and organizational design. They will be expected to help to shape the organization for the future and will do this through a mixture of development activities, organizational design, and individual coaching and influencing. Leadership development will take the form of specifically designed one-off programmes for individuals and teams. Coaching will be individually designed for key individuals and there will be a focus on developing future leaders and succession planning. This is a very future-focussed role which requires the training and development team to deliver and buy-in the best providers of expertise, and work with them in partnership to achieve the transformation they are pursuing.

Action

What role(s) does your HR department take on?

What role(s) do you need to be developing for the future?

How clear are you about the overall business plan and how HR needs to help deliver this plan?

How well does your leadership development activity link to the business strategy?

How much resource in HR is dedicated to development activities versus transactional process improvement?

How efficient is your learning and development department?

How effective is your learning and development department?

What needs to change?

Obviously, the role of HR is different in each company and there is no clear delineation between the different roles. However, this differing focus will have an effect upon the level and quality of the leadership development that is provided.

Using internal or external providers

Choosing providers of your leadership development comes down to a number of factors:

- Budget
- Internal skills levels of leadership development team
- Credibility of internal trainers
- Required expertise for piece of work
- Type of internal audience/population for piece of work

Internal providers of development do differ from external providers in a number of ways. The advantages of the internal provider are as follows:

- They understand the internal politics and agendas.
- They know the key stakeholders and decision-makers.
- They have in-depth experience of working with the teams and the individuals involved.
- They can find their way around the organization quickly and efficiently.
- They know the culture – 'what works around here'.

The advantages of the external provider can be seen as:

- Providing skills not available internally.
- Being objective in their viewpoint.
- Challenging perceptions and asking the obvious questions.
- Bringing external expertise and experience.
- Not being constrained by internal hierarchy and position.
- Being seen to have higher credibility, owing to the fact that they have been hired specifically for the role.
- Being specialists in the particular work area and therefore having functional or sector expertise.

However, there are a number of specific questions that you need to answer before selecting a provider, and the following list may provide some guidance on this.

Checklist for selecting an external provider

- What is the specific piece of work?
- What are the objectives and outcomes for this piece of work?
- What skills and knowledge are required to carry out this piece of work?
- What skills do we have internally to deliver this work or part of this work?
- What is our budget?
- What benefits are we looking to gain by using external providers?
- What sector and functional experience are we looking for?
- What skills and expertise do we want them to bring into the organization?
- What attributes and approach do they need to have to gain engagement from the internal decision-makers and users of the intervention?
- What do we not want from an external provider?
- What references do we want to see/to whom can we talk to about their previous work?
- How much time/resource do we think this piece of work will take?
- Who will manage the project and liaise with the external providers?
- How will we measure their success and effectiveness?
- It is only after answering these questions that you should begin to look for a suitable provider.

Identifying suitable external providers for pieces of work within the leadership development field

People who were interviewed during the research for this book identified the following as reliable or useful sources of information about external providers:

- External providers of professional training can be provided by the appropriate professional organization, e.g: www.lawsociety.org.uk.; The Chartered institute of Personnel and Development www.cipd.co.uk
- Internet-based searches using key words for topics required.
- Local business schools and universities.
- Professional networks and associations.
- Institute of Directors www.iod.com
- Word of mouth.
- Referrals from internal colleagues.
- Referrals from colleagues in similar roles in other organizations.
- HR conferences such as The CIPD conference at Harrogate.
- HR Forums such as Richmond Events Ship based events or the HR Summit.

All of these suggestions are useful avenues to explore. However, the most often-quoted approach by far was personal recommendation and word of mouth.

'People buy people'.

Achieving an effective relationship with external consultants is one of the key skills that leadership development specialists need to develop. The ability to work closely with external providers brings enormous benefits to the business and promotes the credibility of the internal leadership development team as experts in their field who bring in specialist expertise when needed.

The match between the external consultant and the internal leadership manager is of vital importance. The following characteristics all play a part in this relationship:

Trust

Commitment

Respect

Shared goals

Understanding of each other's working style

Confidentiality

Loyalty

Objectivity

Ability to have honest conversations

This is a two-way relationship and the attributes above are attributes that both parties should share. This is not the old-style client and supplier relationship where the client is always right and the supplier always says 'yes'. The secret of good consulting relationships is that the two parties see themselves as equal professionals, each playing a part in delivering what is required by the organization. They have respect for each other's skills and understand that by working well together, they will achieve success both for themselves and for the organization. The ability to be honest and to have challenging conversations with each other can be hugely beneficial. The internal manager needs to give honest feedback about the quality of the work being done. The consultant needs to give honest feedback about what they see as the issues to address and what they need their client to do to support the successful delivery of the work being undertaken.

Reflection point – Using external providers

Think about an existing external provider with whom you are working.

How well would you rate the working relationship between you and the external provider?

How often do you meet to review the effectiveness of what they are providing?

What are they doing well?

What would you like them to do differently?

How well are they perceived by key individuals within the organization?

What else could they be contributing to the organization?

11 Different perspectives on leadership

This chapter looks at the following topics:

Interview with Maarten Putz, TNT Express, Head of HR development

Interview with Bob Reitemeier, Chief Executive of The Children's Society

Interview with Emma Hughes, Director of HR Specsavers

Leadership in law firms

So what do these interviews tell us?

Interview with Frank Dick OBE

Many leadership publications work from the premise that leadership is the same, no matter what the business. Part of the research for this book has shown that this is not the case. A variety of different industry sector Directors have been interviewed as part of this work and this has shown that there are a range of factors that influence the style of leadership and dictate, which approach to leadership development is most likely to lead to success. There is no single successful blue print for a leader. There is equally no single blue print for a successful approach to leadership development.

This chapter will look at four very different businesses and compare the different leadership models, style and approach that work in these different companies. We will assess the different influences on each of these businesses and look at the resulting leadership style and development that is needed in order for them to succeed.

We will also look at the challenges faced by HR and leadership development teams when working in the different environments.

The following questions were used as the basis for these interviews. Each of the interviewees chose which areas to focus on in the discussions.

Questions for leadership interviews:

1. What is your definition of effective leadership in your organization?
2. What skills/attributes are required of the senior/middle leaders in your organization?
3. What makes the difference between leadership in your specific business sector and in other organizations?

4. How would you describe the culture of your business – how does the leadership style reinforce this culture?

5. How does the legal structure of your business influence the type of leadership that is required? For example, partnership, private vs public ownership, etc.

6. What makes your business unique in terms of what you require from leadership development?

7. How do you currently develop your leaders?

8. What do you need to be doing to develop your leaders further?

9. What are the skills you are looking for in your HR and leadership development specialists?

10. What do you look for in external providers of leadership development?

11. What makes an effective consulting relationship for your business?

12. What else is important to you about leadership in your business?

Interview with Maarten Putz, TNT Express, Head of HR development

TNT Express is a global organization of approximately 50 000 employees, active in more than 200 countries with own operations in over 64 countries.

What is your definition of effective leadership in your organization?

Effective leadership in a global company requires an in-depth understanding of different cultures and different approaches. Although we have a global leadership model, there is not a single culture across the organization. The ability for leaders to move away from their own national culture takes effort. Our leaders need to invest more in relationship building across different locations, cultures and teams. There is a strong local culture that builds on company-wide norms and values, but still you would have to understand and learn how to work with the local culture. Our leaders need to be more entrepreneurial in how they meet the different challenges in different regions and work places.

What skills do your senior leaders need to demonstrate?

Many of our top leaders are working with teams who are based across the globe and therefore, they do not have the advantage of close day-to-day working relationships with many of their teams. They need to focus on very visible communication with their teams, so the teams can operate without constant personal presence. They need to give more recognition for effective working, build local heroes and play a smarter game in how they communicate the vision and strategy of the organization. Many individuals might just see their top leader a couple of times per year and this then places a huge challenge on these top leaders to cascade information effectively and to create a culture of high standards and effective working that is self-driven. They need a very strong antenna for what is going on, picking up remote vibes and acting upon them quickly.

The best leaders do this by exploiting existing opportunities to communicate key messages and being creative in how they make the best use of their time with people in different teams and countries. They have an intuitive ability to influence others and be open-minded about different ways of working.

Leaders at middle and senior levels need cultural sensitivity rather than just cultural awareness. This comes from them gaining experience by working in different countries and being immersed in different cultures throughout their career. Many of the successful managers have worked in several countries and are multilingual, which is, again, a key requirement for more senior managers.

How would you describe the culture of TNT Express and how does this impact on leadership?

There is no single, dominant culture in the company although there are a lot of commonalities. In itself this has an impact on leadership. However, there are some key themes that play across the organization in terms of leadership. Due to the nature of the business, which is about customer service and delivery, there is a bias towards action. It is very much a 'do' culture rather than a 'policy and systems' culture. The business demands that people focus on the short term and get the job done quickly to exceed the client's expectation. As a result, there is a bias towards short-term thinking and delivery of quick results. In the leadership programmes we have to balance that with developing a more strategic viewpoint. Part of this is spotting talent relatively early in the career and exposing these individuals to much more long-term strategic thinking via specific projects and assignments. Another way we do this is by development programmes. The results with this approach are quite good.

Another aspect influencing leadership are the differences in maturity and size of the businesses. In some areas of the world – Asia, India, Brazil and Eastern Europe – a very entrepreneurial style is required not like in continental Europe, where the business units are relatively large and established, a style facilitating business excellence is more appropriate. And of course, the cultural differences have an impact on the leadership style. The need for leaders to be flexible in their style and able to challenge the established way of working is a key to success.

The next factor that has a strong impact on leadership development is that each business unit has a separate P&L responsibility. The implication to this is that they are very determined to get things right for their clients. The level of ownership is very high because the line to the client is short. They also carry the responsibility to develop their own leaders. The commitment is very high and we have achieved good results. Consequently, it can be a challenge to get business units to share human resources. We have to do this because some business units are too small to be able to develop their leaders or it takes too long.

This is why, like many other multinationals, we have to take up a central role at divisional level and provide central funding to overcome the barriers and develop the future capabilities of company.

How do you need to develop your leaders in the future?

Currently much of the development is done locally in each business unit. That is, being topped up with central programmes and development activities. We promote development activities such as coaching, shadowing, project work and short-term assignments instead of just training. This is quite a challenging change process to be in as the dominant thinking is that development means formal training.

What do you think is the secret of effective leadership development in your organization?

A central element in the development of leaders is the readiness scorecards. These cards specify the skills, experience and competency levels that you have to achieve to be eligible for the job. As such, they serve as an important guide for people when taking career decisions.

On a global basis, we are starting to design programmes that will benefit leaders across the business rather than purely on a country-wide basis.

We have introduced a group-wide leadership development programmes for senior leaders, which is run in conjunction with a UK Business School over a three month period, which comprises group learning, cross country work groups, individual learning assignments and peer mentoring with a colleague from a different country and business function specialism.

We are also developing an internal graduate development programme to develop talent across the business with approximately 30 individuals taking part each year. This development of a talent pool is a move away from the old style recruitment approach, which was based on a vacancy list approach. This approach will enable us to centrally fund the development of high potential individuals and rotate people around the business over a 2-year period in order to develop their skills as senior leaders for the future.

Project-based development is also being introduced for junior managers, using mentors and work based projects to give these individuals exposure to business-wide issues. We need to create experiences from which they can learn, rather than relying purely on classroom based training.

In addition, we have introduced a company-wide 360 feedback programme that is based on group-wide competencies for each level of leader. Each business unit has access to this and can choose when to use it and how to develop personal development plans with each individual after receiving their 360 feedback.

The 360 degree feedback feeds into the performance management process and the two combined give quite a rigorous feedback that is needed to make current and future leaders reflect on their strengths and weaknesses.

These different projects are part of the challenge to have a consistent approach to leadership development across the business and overcome some of the challenges of the financial and culturally sensitive environment within which these leaders need to operate.

So what you see is that we use the orientation to action and combine it with structured feedback to facilitate leadership development.

What skills do you require of HR and learning and development managers?

It is challenging to gain 'buy-in' to these global development programmes due to certain factors that we have already discussed. Therefore, the role of HR in the different countries is fundamental to developing successful leadership on a local basis. They need to have the ability to create small pools of excellence and work with defined groups or entities that are motivated to develop their skills. The role of HR is to create a process of self-managed learning and to create opportunities for people to gain experience.

They need to spot talent early on and be able to work with individuals and groups to create learning experiences that will develop the skills and capabilities required.

Local units hold substantial budgets and therefore, the HR managers need to have the skills of influencing and persuading, selling the benefits of development and enhanced leadership capability.

Due to the nature of the business, the HR managers need high-level skills of business partnering rather than reactive day-to-day administration skills. They need to demonstrate an in-depth understanding of the business issues and be able to see the bigger system of organizational development. They then need to understand what their internal clients need, how to achieve it and to translate the solution into simple business language with simple processes and user friendly language. The operational managers have little time for 'HR jargon'. They need simple processes that will help them deliver better results; simple but not simplistic. The ability to find the right intervention and to implement it smoothly, in a way that the business welcomes it, is all part of a successful HR consulting approach. The HR managers need to be able to act independently and use their initiative to develop close working relationships with their internal clients and work with them on an equal level, challenging them when needed and providing creative workable solutions that do not waste time.

What do you look for in external providers of HR support and consultancy?

Again, our external providers need to understand the nature of our business. They are working with a quilt of small enterprises rather than a cohesive one culture operation. The ability to adapt and react to different requirements quickly and easily is a key to successful partnering relationships with us. The ability to manage several stakeholders at the same time rather than one main sponsor is the key and, therefore, clear account management and relationship management is very important to us.

We are also aware that we can learn from the external providers' wealth of business experience. We need our providers to support us in the transition from old-school management to the new culture of effective leadership and self-managed learning.

The challenge is to create consistent leadership and processes without losing the entrepreneurship and creativity that contributes to our ongoing success.

Summary of this interview

This case study shows the real impact that the nature of a business has on the leadership style. This business is very day-to-day in approach and focuses on customer service delivery. As a result, the business needs leaders who can be very hands-on and manage the day-to-day operations. The focus on strategic leadership that impacts the long-term planning and development for the future is not always recognized.

In addition, the financial structure of the company puts an additional challenge to the area of leadership development and succession planning. You have to prove that the approach taken adds value. There is no room for 'nice to have' expensive programmes that at the end of the day have very limited value. This has an impact on the overall development of leadership excellence and business process excellence within the company as a whole. Central guidance and coordination, centrally run programmes and initiatives are the key to develop future leaders.

Finally, the cultural challenges of working in an organization made up of over 64 countries is significant. Leaders need to be able to work within a highly diverse culture, with few consistent processes and a high degree of local dominance. Successful leaders need to be highly adaptable, tolerant of differences and have an ability to be open-minded and creative in their personal approach to leadership.

With thanks to Maarten Putz, TNT Express Head of HR Development who kindly gave his time to be interviewed for this book.

Interview with Bob Reitemeier, Chief Executive of The Children's Society

What is your definition of effective leadership in your organization?

We need our leaders to motivate and inspire our staff to follow the strategic direction that we have created. Our leaders have contributed to building this strategy and play a fundamental part in the setting of strategy throughout the organization.

What skills do you look for in your leaders?

We look for people who have expertise in our core operating functions as well as people who can bring in external expertise and knowledge of other industry sectors. We want them to bring in this expertise to help us develop the best ways of working in our environment.

They need to balance their ability to look ahead with the ability to implement the current priorities.

We have a set of leadership competencies, which underpin the different skills that our leaders and managers need to develop. These competencies form the basis of job descriptions for recruitment. They also form part of the annual review process for all managers.

What is different about leadership in your organization?

The key difference in our charity is that we are leading an organization that has multiple stakeholders with very different priorities and needs. We are responsible for raising money from one sector of society and use that money with another sector of society. Mixed with this, we operate within a Christian framework and work closely within the Church context. These different stakeholders have differing needs and the Trustee Board needs to understand these different viewpoints. The effect on leadership style is significant. The need for collaboration and acceptance of differing viewpoints is a key to successful partnership working with our different providers of work for children. Our leaders need to be able to balance the commercial realities of raising more money with the complex task of gaining new work that will benefit our work with children in our four priority areas. The skills of inclusion, collaboration and open-mindedness, linked to a clear understanding of the underpinning Christian values make for a complex leadership challenge.

How would you describe the culture of your business?

A key characteristic of the culture is that we operate a culture of collaborative leadership. This means that all the senior managers meet as a group regularly and work collectively to deliver our 3-year plan. Individuals take responsibility for key processes and work across the different functions to implement the different projects and initiatives. This culture of collaborative working is still developing and it would be wrong to say that we have it all in place. However, people are starting to develop self-confidence in this and to express their authority and expertise when needed.

There is still a high amount of collaboration within the organization, which can have both benefits and disadvantages. The challenge is to retain collaboration while still identifying who is responsible for each activity and knowing when to act and when to consult.

The RACI approach is helping with this balance of collaboration and individual accountability.

R – Who is responsible for a key process or project?
A – Who has overall accountability for delivery?
C – Who needs to be consulted with to gain their view and buy-in?
I – Who needs information about this activity?

Using this approach is helping us to develop a more balanced approach to leadership and move us on from a culture that was probably too consultative and slow to make decisions.

Another characteristic of the culture is that voluntary sector organizations often attract people who want their voice to be heard. The focus of the Children's Society is to enable children's voices to be heard in how they are treated in society and what is needed to make their lives better. In a mirror of this, the individuals who work for such organizations believe in the right to have their voice heard and respected. This influences the culture to be one where there is real respect for different views and an acknowledgement that diversity of view is to be encouraged. The culture is the opposite of the old 'IBM' type culture where people were expected to conform and be very similar in style and approach. The culture is very acceptant of different styles and approaches, respecting of people's individuals' contribution.

In addition, working with hundreds of volunteers brings another dimension to the leadership challenge. It is not possible to treat volunteer workers in the same way as employees. The Retail Division of the Children's Society manages hundreds of nonpaid volunteers who staff the shops and collect money through this activity. This again requires a particular style of leadership that is different in approach.

Finally, the financial basis of the organization has changed significantly in the past few years from an organization that was struggling to break even to an organization that is growing and raising more and more money. Leadership in a cost-cutting environment is very different to leadership in a period of growth and this is an ongoing challenge for us in terms of thinking more broadly, having the space to be more innovative and the challenge of maintaining this growth.

How do you need to develop your leaders further?

Leadership development has not been centrally driven in the organization. There is a lot of independence and autonomy about how to develop leaders in the different pats of the business. As a result, some areas have invested well in developing their teams and others have not made sufficient time for this. There is now a need to provide a more collective approach to leadership and provide development in some of the new skills that our emerging culture requires in order to succeed. This is indicative of the transition towards a more structured approach to accountability and also to the development of individuals. Relying purely on individuals wanting to develop and pursue their own training and learning needs will by nature result in some people not developing in line with where the organization is heading.

What skills and support do you require from HR and learning and development

Like other organizations, we need our people and organizational development team to continue to understand the business and what we are trying to achieve in terms of growing the business and gaining new work. They need to be able to bring in external expertise that will challenge us to review how we operate and give us skills that will equip us for the different environments in which we operate.

An example of this is work we are doing to develop marketing and sales skills in our Children and Young People Division. The senior managers in that division are responsible for developing partnerships with social services, the police and other bodies in order to fund projects related to improvizing the lives of children in particular areas. Bringing in new projects is a key part of their role. To do this they need the skills of marketing, consulting and an understanding of how to build relationships, identify needs, overcome objections and close a financial deal that will fund a project in a particular city or town. Skills development in this area has seen improved results and a realization that individuals need some of the same development that happens in many other commercial organizations.

Development and training activities need to be tailored to the needs of a changing organization and the need to be innovative and challenging also applies to the design and delivery of the development activities designed for the next few years. We have a culture that is by nature very affirmative, which has resulted in a tendency not to have challenging and tough conversations with people. We now recognize that people need to be able to give and take criticism and feedback without becoming defensive. The ability to take feedback and objectively review what has gone well or not so well is part of this transition in our culture. We need to be able to work with both praise and criticism in the same environment. Today, we are in a positive situation and we need to adapt our behaviour to recognize this and maximize the opportunities we have. This is where People and Organizational Development can play a fundamental part in the development of the organization.

Summary of characteristics of this organization

Consensus driven

Collaborative

Acceptant

Affirmative

Flexible

Implications for leadership development

Personal accountability

The organization has said that it needs to retain the benefits of collaboration while introducing a greater sense of individual accountability and expressed authority. Any leadership development activity needs to focus on individual responsibility and leadership qualities of decision making, confidence to make tough decisions and a more pace setting approach to delivering results.

In addition, there is the factor of working with a mix of very different stakeholders. The skills of being able to flex style and approach is key to achieving success with the different partnership working arrangements. Development of these interpersonal skills and relationship skills are vital. In addition, there is a need for leaders to gain more exposure to the external commercial environment, because this is where much of their income comes from. The ability to understand the organizational context of their key stakeholders can only be helpful.

Provision of leadership development
In line with working as a collaborative leadership forum, there may be a need to develop the senior managers more centrally rather than allowing the current amount of autonomy over the amount and type of development takes place.

This case study shows how the culture of an organization can have a great effect on the approach to leadership development. The challenge for HR and people development is not to go native with the prevalent culture. Their role is to remain detached from the current state and be proactive in introducing innovative ways to help the culture move forward. This is often where they need to take a broad view of the organization rather than be drawn into the day-to-day individual development needs. By working at an organizational level, they will add more value to the business and will help develop a leadership capability that will enable the organization to continue to succeed. Close relationship with the key decision makers is important if they are to understand the evolving nature of the organization, and the ability to challenge the status quo is a key skill of any learning and development manager working in such a changing environment as the one that we have detailed above.

With many thanks to Bob Reitemeier, Chief Executive of the Children's Society for allowing us this insight into their organization. If you would like to support the work of the Children's Society, please log onto their website www.childrenssociety.org.uk.

Interview with Emma Hughes, Director of HR Specsavers

Our third interview was conducted with Emma Hughes, Director of HR Specsavers, the retail organization, with 700 stores both in the UK and internationally.

Specsavers is a family owned company with an outstanding record of success over the last 22 years. It is now expanding overseas with stores in Denmark, Holland, Norway and Sweden.

What is your definition of successful leadership for Specsavers?

Within Specsavers, the secret of successful leadership is the ability to make things happen with empathy for the day-to-day demands of each person's role. Successful leaders need to show a down to earth approach rooted in reality with great attention to detail. The leadership team is small enough for everyone to know each other well and they need to work flexibly and get involved in operational implementation as well as long-term strategy and planning. Leaders need to have wide business knowledge as they are expected to contribute across a wide number of disciplines, rather than work in one functional silo. This is due to both the size of the organization and also our team based approach, which comes right from the top.

What influences the style of leadership within the company?

Due to the fact that it is a family owned business with family members on the board, there is a sense of real drive and energy to make things happen as quickly as possible. There is a strong sense of ownership at Board level and also at the senior levels of leadership. They all work closely with the family members to provide the vision and momentum to keep moving ahead of their competitors. The family dynamic creates a sense of belonging within the company and there is a high degree of loyalty to the owners and the company as a whole. This creates an affiliation between people with an associated affiliative style of leadership at all levels. This is matched by a strong pace setting leadership style to deliver results quickly and keep improving processes. The size of the company means that decisions can be made quickly and the decision makers are a small number of individuals who have a very strongly aligned vision for the future.

How would you describe the culture of Specsavers?

As with many retail organizations, there is a fast pace and energy to deliver results. In addition, it is centrally driven from a small highly influential board of Directors. This creates a culture of fast decision making but a lack of challenge from less senior leaders. It is very much a 'Just do it' approach, which gives freedom to act but within very tightly defined parameters.

What do your leaders need to do differently?

As the organization grows from a mainly UK operation to a company that operates internationally, there is a need for leaders to be able to build strong teams quickly and to trust people to get on with the job without day-to-day checking. Leaders need to be able to make tough decisions and yet be able to motivate and support their growing teams on a virtual basis without seeing them every day. The challenge to maintain a shared direction while working at geographical distance is the one that all future leaders in the company need to be aware of. In addition, there is a need to allow decision making to be taken at lower levels in order to free up senior leaders to spend time on longer-term planning and strategy. They need to review the amount of time they are still spending on management activities as opposed to leadership activities.

As in many family owned companies, there is a sense of paternalism. This culture needs to shift if the company is going to start to devolve decision making and trust people to act at a higher level. To move from 'good to great' means that leaders need to empower their teams and act as role models rather than getting involved and protecting individuals who are not delivering.

How does the founder of the company influence the culture?

The founder, Doug Perkins provides an inspirational role model in many ways for his leadership team. He is a self-made man with a very down to earth approach to business. He has huge vision and inspires those around him to consider the big picture while still ensuring the immediate priorities are met. He has no place for complacency and is constantly mindful of the market in which he operates. He lives and breathes the company and expects those around him to do the same. He cares tremendously for the business and has complete passion for what the business is doing. Those around him are hugely influenced by this and understand that he will enjoy a strong debate and yet be prepared to listen. His stretching standards act as the benchmark for everything that is undertaken by teams and individuals. He welcomes ideas from outside and is prepared to bring in external expertise, new ways of thinking and individuals who will challenge the status quo.

What are the challenges for leadership development in this company?

The size and flat structure of the company bring benefits but also challenges. There needs to be a balance between developing new skills and allowing people freedom to put them into practice. There is a move to bring in talented individuals, unchecked; these individuals may find themselves stuck in a role after a short amount of time. This is being eased by the international growth, which is creating opportunities for new roles with broader responsibilities. The different skill base needed to manage internationally is also an area that needs to be addressed. Topics such as cultural diversity, managing remote teams and enhanced cross-functional working are an area for further development.

The company has developed an overall approach to development, which is called the Specsavers Academy. This multi-approach platform provides training and development for the different groups of staff across the company via internally and externally provided development programmes for the different groups of staff. The next challenge is to provide more customized development for key individuals in order to develop their skills and retain their talents within the company.

What do you need from your HR managers?

The company has a good 'can do' attitude and prides itself on flexibility and willingness to adapt processes in order to meet the needs of the stores and end users. This approach needs to be mirrored by the HR team and role modelled in how they work with their internal customers and stakeholders.

They need to:

- Demonstrate high level coaching skills to help managers find their own solutions rather than relying on rules and policies
- Be robust enough to push back when challenged by tough leaders who may want results in unrealistic timeframes
- Demonstrate an in-depth understanding of the wider business issues in order to gain credibility and trust from the leadership team
- Develop a strategic view of the business direction in order to create an HR plan that reflects the real business needs
- Develop excellent internal consulting skills to work in partnership with their customers
- Be proactive not reactive

With sincere thanks to Emma Hughes for her support and willingness to be interviewed for this publication.

Leadership in law firms

The final interview was conducted with Neil May. Neil is an assistant to the managing partner at one of the leading international law firms and has previously worked for a top law firm and for the management consultancy arm of one of the big four global accountancy partnerships.

What is different about leadership in law firms?

Law firms share some common characteristics with other professional service firms, yet they also have some significant idiosyncrasies. It is useful to start by considering common aspects of the professional service firm.

When a client turns to a professional adviser, they are generally seeking expertise they do not possess themselves. Sometimes they must purchase advice even if they do not necessarily want to do so (e.g., in completing tax returns); while at other times they may both need and actively want to take advice.

In some cases clients seek-out 'brain power'. Complex cases (or 'matters' as a lawyer would describe work) involve high client risk. They require a customized service, with an emphasis on needs, diagnosis and creativity, backed up by cutting edge know how and experience. This work therefore has a lower sensitivity to fees.

At the other end of the spectrum there is more procedural work where it is not important for the client to employ a market leader. Such work involves lower client risk and a prime desire is for cost-effective and efficient execution, backed up by standardized know how and templates, automation and workflow. Often there are many more potential suppliers and as a result the work is much more fee sensitive.

The reason this matters for all professional service firms is that *everything* – from type of people hired, to the style of management appropriate for handling them, to economies of scale and investment, to profitability margins – varies significantly depending on what the client is buying and what the firm wants to offer.

Overlaying this situation, clients themselves are always assessing their own costs to get the best value out of the least spend. A good adviser will seek to help clients do this, because long-term relationships are built on trust and clients are more likely to continue to give work to those that look out for them than those advisers who appear more self-interested. Many clients are reducing their panel sizes to make it simple to deal with suppliers; indeed some large businesses have reduced the number of different law firms they use by as much as 95 per cent. For the smaller firms, panel losses can be catastrophic, leading to entire practice areas being closed. Yet at the same time clients may want to use niche specialists and to parcel up 'commodity work'.

This means that the leaders of professional service firms face contradictory challenges. Clients want fewer advisers, and they may want those firms to be able to undertake a broad range of advice. They prefer predetermined rates, yet may also give work to other firms outside their core panel, thus potentially reducing the increase in volume, their core advisers would like in return for entering into fee arrangements. At the same time, they may require their advisers to offer a breadth of services, which means many law firms are unable to restrict themselves solely to the category of premium or commodity work that theoretically they are best structured to provide.

We have seen that law firms operate in a similar way to other professional service firms but also have a few aspects that do differentiate them from other service organizations, so leaders of law firms face some additional challenges.

What other factors affect leadership within a law firm context?

The perceived importance of leadership

- An important factor in a law firm is that for the more complex areas of advice, the more senior the position of the solicitor, the more likely it is that they are required to personally carry out the work for clients. Outside law firms, the more senior leaders spend less time 'doing' and more time on strategy or on developing and supporting the more junior team members. In law firms, it means the amount of time people may be willing to commit to leadership or management is reduced.

- In many companies, people have a clear desire to rise up 'into management'. Many lawyers do not share this ambition and would rather stay being lawyers instead. Traditionally, 'being a good lawyer' is a more praiseworthy skill than any other. Partners are also wary that those who abandon fee earning to take on a leadership or management role can find themselves with no job security when their term of tenure finishes. So, while the quality of leadership will play a major role in determining which firms prosper and which decline, the role itself is played out within a context of individualism, respect for technical excellence, the primacy of personal revenue generation and a client expectation of personal service from many of the more senior individuals. It can make leading lawyers a hugely rewarding – or a hugely frustrating – task.

People issues

- As a 'knowledge business', law firms have to invest heavily in training, motivating and rewarding people. Unfortunately, many of the more senior people who need to push this forward did not grow up in this sort of environment, and this aspect of the generational clash can cause stress. Younger solicitors want to be listened to and to be involved, they want to know how the business is going and how they and their colleagues are performing, they also want life outside work and are quick to voice dissatisfaction. Time spent on teamwork, camaraderie and feedback can matter more to them than it did to their bosses.

This is a common factor affecting all businesses as younger employees expect to be respected and treated equally. But it is only recently that many law firms have woken up to the fact that a high percentage of their trainees became disillusioned and left within the first three or four years – which from an organizational perspective also means their employers have lost money in training and recruiting them and may have made little, if any, net profit on employing them. This has been especially visible in the leading high pressure, long-hour transactional practices where too many employees were concluding that the rewards ceased to make up for the brutal reality of work.

- Mentoring: Another of the generational changes is that when firms were small there was a much closer 'master–apprentice' mindset, where people were being trained as craftsman. Now firms are much larger this has become fractured. In many instances, the need to maintain motivation and to speed up the time in which profit is gained from high cost staff has forced training and developmental processes higher-up the management agenda. Once again this influences the need for senior partners to find ways to address the development of their junior solicitors.

- Partner expectations: In the past, elevation to partnership was often the result of being good technically and looking after close personal clients. Today the process is more formalized and more explicit. As well as generating good revenue, partners now also need to be good at considering the value of their staff, to be more open about staff career opportunities, to empower their lawyers to do more (which also requires higher levels of skill in delegation and supervision), to show a consideration for work–life balance and to be substantially better at communication.

- But as species lawyers often spend much of their formative career shut in offices on their own, their advice is sought out for their ability to stand back to take a logical and technical perspective over all others. And this means that the 'softer' people skills are less at the heart of what a lawyer does and how they think.

These are all increasing expectations on partners, who at the same time need to deliver their chargeable hours. If they do not bring in an appropriate revenue, partners face the threat of losing their job: PWC's 2005 survey of law firms shows a third of the top 100 law firms had reduced the number of equity partners and a primary reason for this was failure to bring in sufficient profitable revenue.

So, for partners the psychological contract has shifted. After the last recession, many recognized that a job was not for life. In general, there was an increasing emphasis by employees on fairness and trust in their dealings with their employers, and that firms would invest in their development and future employability. For partners, the primary expectation coming out of this was one of maintaining collegiate fairness.

Professional services staff earn high salaries compared with others. Law firms also have a high number of nonrevenue generating staff – in fact, they can equate to half the total headcount, most notably due to a high ratio of secretarial staff. So, while the traditional rule of thumb for businesses where staff sell, their expertise may be that each person needs to generate three times their salary in fees, this may be becoming closer to a minimum. This real pressure on 'survival' obviously has a major implication for the time people want to spend on developing their leadership skills and the skills of others.

How does the structure of the law firm influence leadership?

The type of structure created depends upon how many partners want to work as individual practitioners or how many want they work together to build a profitable business. 'Partnership' is a nice word but partnerships, whether within firms or in relation to client ventures, do not always turn out to be as collegiate as the word implies.

Until 1967, all UK partnerships were restricted to 20 partners. Now, with no limit on the number of partners the changes have implications for collegiality and loyalty, which weaken, as firms get substantially bigger and it becomes difficult to know colleagues personally. Partners also share joint and several liabilities with each other and this results in a personal risk for each other's misdemeanours that is different to the situation in a corporation. Investment banks are no longer partnerships while in the UK the Department for Constitutional Affairs is keen to promote new structures for the delivery of legal advice.

There is stronger demand from successful lawyers to move up to partnership (because the pay is much higher), and if they do not get what they want from your firm then they will now move to another firm in order to get it. There are signs, however, that for some lawyers the risks, returns and life style mean, the partnership status is losing its attraction.

As a result, there need to be clearer expectations on what is required to be a partner, which in turn requires clear competence frameworks to show the progression from part qualified to fully qualified to partner. It also means that a suitable position may need to be created for those who wish to have some senior status but stop below partnership.

In conclusion, we can see that the culture of the law firm has not been conducive to time being spent on leadership and development of the talent within. Those who move into management were until recently senior partners moving into a new phase of their career rather than professional managers or leaders. Sometimes, these managers also undertook fee-earning work, sometimes they did not.

- In law firms senior people carry out more client facing work than in some other professional service sectors.
- The more a firm seeks premium city work the harder it is to delegate to the junior people who may deliver a greater profit margin.
- Time spent on development, management or leading may not count as much as time spent earning fees – and if fees are insufficient job security is at stake. End of year profit per partner is a key measure for partners.
- A team approach to client relationships and practice development has to struggle against individualism.
- Partners are technically all self-employed, so leaders often suffer from the silence of support but an onslaught of criticism when an issue threatens autonomy.

So, what are the challenges for HR in developing lawyers?

It will by now be apparent that law firms are perhaps one of the most challenging environments in which to work for HR and development professionals. It is not an environment that naturally recognizes or rewards investment in leadership skills. The culture of the law firm may be understood better when the personality of the successful lawyer is put into this context.

Research has been carried out by Dr Larry Richard, a lawyer–psychologist and former principal with Altman Weil in the USA, into the challenge of providing leadership development for lawyers. It appears there are a number of intrinsic personality traits in lawyers that are significantly different from the general public, which brings specific challenges for managing and developing them.

Personality plays a large part in most big law firms. Partners are expected to develop new business and 'rain makers' who have a certain set of characteristics do this in a very individualistic way. In a study by Caliper and Altman Weil in 1998, they looked at 95 lawyers who were deemed to be 'excellent lawyers' by their peers. Later studies were also conducted on hundreds of lawyers and the following characteristics have been highlighted as differentiating successful lawyers from other members of the public. Lawyers seem to have a higher number of traits that lie on the outskirts of a normal bell-curve than many other professions – they are sometimes described as a slightly different breed to the rest of mankind and this indeed suggests that perhaps they are!

The four key characteristics are as follows.

Scepticism

People who score high on this trait tend to be judgemental, questioning and even cynical about information they are given. People with low scores on this trait tend to trust other people and give others the benefit of the doubt. It is easy to see why this scepticism trait is helpful for lawyers and the studies have shown that lawyers are in the top 90th percentile for this trait.

Urgency

A high score on this is characterized by impatience, a need to get things done and a sense of urgency. Low scorers tend to be patient, reflective and contemplative. On average, the lawyers score 20 per cent above others in this trait. They can be characterized as having a high sense of urgency, seeking efficiency and economy in time spent on activities and as a result can sometimes be less willing to spend time on relationships, preferring to move at their own pace without particularly active listening to others. This need for immediacy is also likely to lead to a need for short-term results from any development activity, with a less strong commitment to long-term benefits.

Sociability

The 'excellent' lawyers in the Caliper/Altman Weil study had an average sociability score of 12.8 per cent compared with an average of 50 per cent for the general public. Sociability is described as the desire to interact with other people and initiate closer relationships. Low scorers on this trait will rely more on family and long lasting friendships rather than take time to develop new relationships. They tend to want to deal with data and information more than people. The law is an area where lawyers are expected to work with high degrees of intellectual rigour and logic. In terms of leadership style, these individuals will be less likely to have a coaching or affiliative style of leadership. They are more likely to be pace setting or authoritative. There will be less awareness of the need for leadership flexibility.

Autonomy

Lawyers in this study came out in the top 89th percentile for this trait suggesting that they resist being managed by others, preferring to work things out for themselves. These people prize independence and freedom to act. In terms of leadership style, there may be a reluctance to take a hands-on approach as this conflicts with a natural preference for autonomy. This can create an environment where the more junior lawyers are not given the coaching and support they may need. In addition, poor performance may not always be addressed as there is a desire to let people do what they want, rather than impose rules on them. There is a tendency to demonstrate individualism rather than actively support corporate initiatives.

So, what are the implications of these characteristics for the development of leadership skills within these organizations?

Factors that affect the approach to leadership development

Cynicism: People with these characteristics are likely to be more cynical than the general public about training and development to improve leadership skills. They will be more likely to question the bottom line benefit and resist the amount of time that people take out of the fee earning mechanism in order to develop their skills. Lawyers are paid to be right and as a result they have a tendency to believe they know best. To achieve partnership in a top tier term is a demonstration of a lawyer's high successful in their careers. People with these characteristics are also more likely to be less self-aware of their own strengths and weaknesses as they spend less time reflecting on their own behaviour.

As a result, these individuals need development that focuses on self-awareness and the impact they have on others. A part of the selection criteria for partnership in most firms focuses not just on business development but also on the ability to manage teams of lawyers and develop their skills for the future.

Credibility of providers: People with a high scepticism score want to work with people who have high credibility and experience of working with people similar to them. So, careful selection of external trainers as delivery partners for this audience is of prime importance.

Length of training workshops: These individuals will not want to spend several days on residential workshops. They need information provided quickly, at a faster pace and in a way that they can easily apply to their own practice. Two to three hour sessions on a regular basis are probably more acceptable as they still allow for a full days work to be maintained.

Learning style: In terms of learning style, there is a high proportion of theorists, so they need to be clear that the content of their leadership development is both academically sound and based on proven theories. Although they show high intellectual rigour, they do not want to stay at the theoretical level because they are pressed for time, so instead seek simple pragmatic steps they can take that will have an impact. This is obviously a challenge where leadership styles may be criticized on the grounds of what works well in one area does not work in another. Lawyers are trained to destroy the other side's arguments. However, using work from the leading business schools and known leadership authors such a Daniel Goleman and John Kotter will be more likely to be accepted.

Self-awareness: Of primary importance to this group is the development of a higher sense of self-awareness. This can be done in a variety of ways, using MBTI, insights or a selection of other diagnostic questionnaires or exercises. 360 feedback can be enormously powerful for these people due to the fact that is data specific and gives them asset of data from which they can easily draw conclusions.

So in conclusion, the development of leadership skills in the legal sector needs to take the following factors into account:

1. High degree of scepticism and low degree of sociability will influence approach to leadership.
2. High independence leads to a natural hands-off style of management. This needs to be compensated during the development of new lawyers coming through the firm. Generally a hands-on approach by the HR and development teams can achieve this.
3. External providers need to be able to demonstrate proven credibility and rigour in both their delivery methodology, the content of any training programme and their previous success in similar environments.
4. Lawyers are less likely to have focussed on their own behaviour than some other professions and therefore any leadership development needs to ensure that this is part of any programme.
5. Training and development activities need to take account of the fact that these individuals will want to work at a naturally faster pace than some others and will want to see tangible gains to the investment of their time. Linked to a natural scepticism, this requires a highly credible delivery team who can be flexible in their approach to the format of training activities and are capable of handling direct challenges to statements and propositions.

It is also important that any development training is seen as both necessary and valued by the leaders of their firms. Some law firms measure performance and remuneration primarily on financial criteria (hours worked, fees billed, profit of their particular practice group, etc.). This will lead to certain kinds of behaviour, which is unlikely to be a helpful environment for the topic of personal or wider development to prosper. Many firms, however, are now moving to a blended list of performance measures – though lawyers remain sceptical as to which measures count more than others.

Development of leadership competence

A case study

Prior to joining his current firm, Neil May worked for a leading litigation specialist law firm in London. During that time he was sponsor of a year long leadership development programme that focussed on the different areas of skills that the firm needed their senior lawyers to develop.

The firm had already made progress in identifying the key competencies that they required at the different levels and together with an external provider; they developed a programme to focus on some of the key areas. One-to-one coaching with the external provider and an active involvement by the management development team was a key to a successful implementation.

The role of HR in law firms varies considerably. Often the HR department does not have the strategic input that would be seen in, for example, a management consultancy or accountancy firm. However, in this firm HR did have more involvement primarily due to the fact that the senior partners were not particularly skilled in feedback, coaching or leadership of their people.

Elevating the skills of this group of senior lawyers and junior partners was seen as part of the long-term succession plan.

The programme took the form of nine three-hour modules as shown in Figure 11.1.

The benefits of this approach were as follows:

- Short time periods for each module maintained focus and a high energy approach.
- Increased networking occurred between the different lawyer teams with opportunities for cross-functional service provision to existing clients.
- Increased awareness of need for effective interpersonal skills with clients.
- Improved business development activity with existing and new clients.
- Increased coaching of more junior colleagues raised skill levels more quickly and allowed higher earning work to be taken on earlier.
- More effective time management and organization skills at senior levels increased fee earning potential and revenue potential.
- Greater self-awareness of strengths and weaknesses created a more collaborative organizational climate.

This programme is now run yearly by Represent Ltd and is seen as part of the criteria for proceeding up to partnership with in the firm.

With thanks to Neil May for his helpful contributions and comments on this subject.

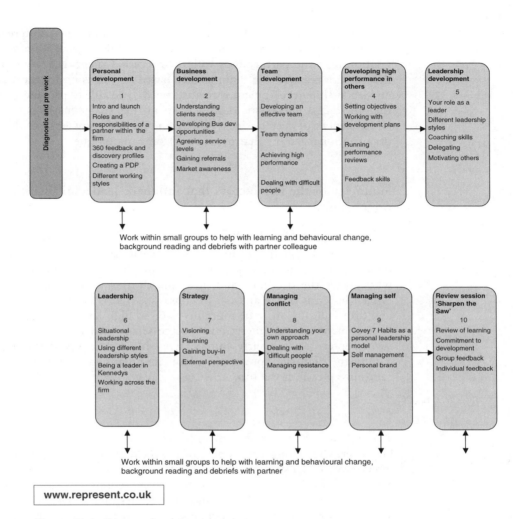

Figure 11.1 Partner development programme

So what do these interviews tell us?

In summary, we can see that there are a number of factors that influence culture and leadership within a company. Different leaders will be successful in different organizations. An effective leader in one company will not necessarily be seen as an effective leader in another. The art is in identifying the culture of the organization and recruiting and developing leaders who are able to operate successfully in that culture. The challenge is to develop leaders who fit with the current culture and yet are able to challenge the status quo. Successful leaders need to work from the starting point of their team members, but be able to inspire them to stretch out of their comfort zone in order to achieve whatever is needed. Leaders need to understand the perspective of others and still retain their independence of thought and action.

Similarly, the role of HR and leadership development is different depending on the nature of the company. The ability of HR to develop effective working relationships and partnerships with their internal clients is a key to their success. Providing a reactive and maintenance based service is no longer acceptable. HR and leadership development specialists need to be able to provide a similar service that their customers would gain from an external consultancy, but with the added benefit of deep business understanding and knowledge of the political and organizational factors that make their company unique.

Summary of the key factors that influence leadership within an organization

Ownership and legal structure

We have highlighted the difference between partnerships, family owners and multinational shareholders. The ownership has a huge influence in terms of who makes the decisions and how quickly they can be made. It also has an impact in terms of the amount of consensus that is needed. Equity partners in a law firm will obviously be more involved in high level decisions about business development and remuneration than the senior leaders within a small privately owned enterprise. Similarly, family ownership creates a powerful dynamic within a company that is not present in a large multinational corporation. This tends to centralize power at the top.

Operating values

This has an almost unspoken influence in the organizations we interviewed. However, the strong values and beliefs held by individuals in the charity we interviewed had a stronger impact on their day-to-day leadership behaviour. This agreed set of values and beliefs seemed less present in the other organizations and there were different pockets of different values and beliefs. There was no clear alignment or desire to align personal values with those of the business. It was more accepted that there may be a mismatch but that was considered acceptable.

Market culture

The culture of the environment within which the company operates plays a fundamental role in influencing leadership within the company. The difference between a fast moving retail culture compared with the client base of a city law firm is evident in the different approach internally to change, flexibility and competitor and business analysis. Leaders seem to be more internally focussed in the legal environment compared to a very externally focussed dimension in the retail company.

Multinational versus UK business model

The challenge for leaders in multinational environments is immense. Their ability to flex their style, work cross functionally and remotely with their teams are all key to successful results. Their willingness to spend time gaining consensus, influencing others and providing strong role model behaviours to people at a distance all add to the challenge. It seemed that some of these skills and behaviours are not given sufficient weight in the development and training that is provided for these individuals. The companies that were starting to expand internationally needed to realize that the skills required of their leaders will be different as they grow to operate in a more decentralized model.

Size

Obviously the size of the organization has an impact on the type of leadership that operates within different companies. Our research highlighted a very clear difference in the speed of decision making and the amount of responsibility people were given. In the smaller companies, decisions were made fluently and almost situationally, whereas the decision making hierarchy of the larger corporations slows the process down. The ability for senior leaders to be able to talk to the owner or chief executive on a daily basis makes for a more open environment. However, the senior leaders in smaller companies have to cope with the fact that they are generally given less autonomy and space to act. The decision making is generally done at the top level and therefore these leaders feel a great sense of responsibility but sometimes a frustrating lack of autonomy.

Maturity of the organization

Each of the companies include in this survey were well-established companies, all of whom who were financially successful. The view would be that maturity and stability of the company would impact on the style of leadership as discussed earlier. The need for pace setting and authoritative leadership would be stronger in a young company or failing company. The benefit enjoyed by the companies in this study is that they have resource and time to commit to development and coaching of their people for the future.

Personality of the managing director or chief executive

This may seem a strange factor to include in such a list. Each of the interviewees spoke about the personality of their leader and how he or she impacts on the leadership demonstrated by others in the organization. This backs up Goleman's work around the influence of senior leaders. The more senior the leader, the more influence they have on others around them. The characteristics of the senior leader were quoted as reasons for why people act as they do. Their behaviour seemed to be the benchmark by which the actions of others were measured. This factor has vital importance in a number of ways:

- Is the senior leader aware of the impact their behaviour has on the organization?
- Are they role modelling the behaviours that are required by the organization?
- Is their behaviour seen as a reason or excuse for inappropriate behaviour by other senior leaders?
- Who provides feedback and development for the senior leader?
- How open is the senior leader to change their behaviour for the benefit of the business?

Interview with Frank Dick OBE

The final interview is with Frank Dick OBE who is renowned as a motivational speaker with many of the top UK and global organizations. As coach to some of the world's highest performing Olympic athletes, he is also the President of the European Athletics Coaches Association.

How do you see the link between sport and business?

The language of sport has become a valuable vehicle in business for understanding how to be more effective in pursuit of achievement in a competitive arena. It creates powerful mental pictures, which facilitate physical, intellectual and emotional buy-in. So we use words like teamwork, teamtalk, league tables, score cards, pulling or punching your weight, results, winning, goals, raising the bar and so on.

All businesses involve teamwork. From leadership teams to front line teams, we know that teamwork matters. When anything to do with team comes into focus, leadership does too. In fact you cannot have one without the other. This has led to embracing both within one concept – Teamship.

Teamship

This concept centres on the tenet that each of us influences the outcome of our collective endeavour by aligning with purpose and principles, commitment to delivering personal excellence and assisting colleagues deliver theirs. In modern sport and business, this is the winning difference.

The winning difference in our competitive arenas exists potentially in every moment we take ownership of, to turn opportunity to personal and team advantage. The moments are all around us. We use them or lose them.

Ownership can be through the number on your shirt; your role in the team; it can be through the badge on your shirt; how you connect with people, be it with colleagues or customer, and how you manage relationships; it can be through you being you in your shirt; the critical edge of difference you bring to the moment because of your personal talents and abilities.

In taking ownership, each of us becomes the winning difference. It is not a shot or play called by someone else. You call it personally. You read the game yourself and for the team at the same time. In that moment you must exercise leadership qualities.

The concept of teamship has each of us delivering as a player or as a leader comes the moment, which calls for being one or the other.

So, the primary function of leadership in sport or business is to prepare and coach our people for such ownership.

The role of the leader

As a coach in sport, this is how I see leadership. The coach cannot own the moment in the arena. The players individually and collectively do that. The coach prepares the players to do so. Leaders in business must do so too – if ownership is to work.

The preparation process is:

1. Select

   Selecting your team, from leadership colleagues to players is the most important decision you make as a leader. Select them on the following criteria:

   - Technical/professional competence
   - Coachability
   - Balance – personally and with team
   - Will to Win – personally and for team
   - Chemistry – The intangibles unique to their personality and character.

2. Develop

   Developing people not only means personal and team training but also getting people to take ownership of their own continuous learning program.

3. Involve

   For people to instinctively deliver quality excellence in what they do and how they do it, they must believe they are part of growing what the team is.

4. Unleash

   If we really mean our people to own the moment, they must enjoy a freedom to be themselves within the framework of shared purpose and principles.

5. Inspire

   This never stops. But be aware that the greatest issue is not motivating people, but avoiding demotivating them.

   The outcome will be a team of players all of whom will demonstrate leadership qualities when the moment demands it. In team sport, you all become player–coaches – one moment being the wind beneath colleagues wings when they need it; the next being supported when a colleague is the wind beneath yours.

   Everyone has the ability to lead; not everyone uses that ability. Within the teamship concept, all can be coached to do so. The process is called player/team centred; coach led.

What differentiates the best leaders?

I believe it is the same thing that differentiates the best coaches in sport.

1. They keep purpose and principles (or vision and values) front and centre. They are visionary and driven to win but never at the expense of principles.

2. They think deeply about holistic development. They ensure a sense of life balance.

3. They are dedicated to life-long professionalism and personal development. As with their message to players, perfection is something you aspire to but never touch. So, there are always ways to be better. Learn them.

4. They are mentally tough. Their resolve to overcome all obstacles and attacks in pursuit of the agreed goal is unshakable.

5. They are meticulous in preparation. They are masters of strategic planning and quality control and their approach to preparation includes anticipation and coping with uncertainty.

6. They have excellent communication skills. They communicate as much through emotions as intellect, making the complex simple and using anecdote and metaphor as much as data and drawing board.

7. They are accomplished relationship managers. They take time to understand each person in their sphere of influence and can address individual needs effectively whilst ensuring that such fit within the team's needs for cohesion and harmony.

8. They are clinically executive in decision making. They are as comfortable with those decisions, which determine the route to achieving long-term goals, as with resolving situations under pressure and at speed, in selecting the right course of action in a crisis.

9. They know themselves. They are strong in self-knowledge and awareness. They never underestimate their leadership role, responsibilities and account-abilities. Yet they may understate their own leadership value. They know they are human, and therefore so fallible. Ninety nine per cent personal performance they consider failure – even when in most people's minds fifty one per cent would win. Achievement for them is only in part reflected in the result. Rather, it is in what they did and how they did it in delivering that leadership/coaching role.

10. They have belief, faith and trust. They radiate self-belief, belief in their people and belief that the agreed goals will be successfully achieved. They have great personal strength of spiritual faith. They have unshakable trust in the irrepressible power of the human spirit to go beyond what others would consider to be the limit.

11. They have persistently infectious passion. They are huge in their passion to seek and overcome challenge. They are driven in this and exude an energy that captures minds and hearts. It is this that gets people to do what they need to do, even when they do not want to do it!

To summarize, leadership is about living teamship; being inspired personally and inspiring others to be the winning difference; and being relentlessly professional in doing so.

With thanks to Frank Dick for his contribution to this publication. Details of his current work on wellbeing in business can be found on www.wellgoal.com.

The interviews with these different leaders in their own fields highlight the multi faceted nature of leadership. Different organizations require different attitudes, skill sets and abilities. Different types of leaders will provide appropriate leadership at different times during the growth and evolution of a company. We can take the characteristics provided by Frank Dick above as a general guideline but these inspirational individuals also need to work within the different contexts of their external market and their internal operating environment. That is what makes a truly successful leader.

Reflection point

What are the top three factors that influence leadership style within your company?
(Think about the legal structure, values, culture, ownership, size, maturity, geographical spread and personality of key individuals)

In what ways do these factors influence leadership style?

How do you assess and review these skills with your leaders?

How well are you currently providing development in these areas for leaders?

What do your HR and Leadership Development team need to do differently in order to develop the future capability of your leadership teams?

Probably the only sustainable competitive advantage we have is the ability to learn faster than the opposition.

– Arie de Geuss

DIFFERENT PERSPECTIVES ON LEADERSHIP

12 Developing self-awareness

This chapter looks at the following topics:

Self-awareness using Johari Window

Development diaries

Feedback exercises

Life journey exercise

The art of positive thinking

Case study

Personal vision setting

Conclusion

It seems appropriate to include this as the last chapter, because self-awareness is the key to develop effective working relationships with others. As leaders or leadership development specialists, everyone surely benefits from developing their own awareness and an understanding of the impact they have on others.

An open mind gains more experience

– Charlotte Ryan, age 13

The following exercises give some ideas on how to increase self-awareness in yourself or for those with whom you are working.

Self-awareness using Johari Window

The first exercise is based purely on self-awareness. The Johari Window framework (Table 12.1) was developed by Joe Luft and Henry Ingham. It is designed to help individuals to understand the difference between how they see themselves and how they are perceived by others. Understanding this can help people to break down the barriers they put up to other people and can help to reduce the misperceptions that occur between people.

The open area

This is the area where our behaviours, attitudes and personality traits are open for everyone to see. We know that we demonstrate these behaviours and attitudes, and we are happy for other people to see them as well.

Table 12.1 The Johari Window framework

	Known to us	*Not known to us*
Known to others	The open area	The blind area
Not known to others	The hidden area	The unknown area

The blind area

This is the area of our behaviour of which we may not be aware, but other people do notice it, i.e. our blind spots.

The hidden area

These are the views and behaviours we have but do not wish to share with others, we keep these views and traits hidden from other people.

The unknown area

This is the area of our potential that has not been developed. We may have traits or behaviours of which we are not aware and no one else has recognized, either. This is often the area for most personal development.

When we first meet people, we are likely to show few of our true feelings and thoughts. Therefore, there will be a large hidden window and a small area of behaviour that is open to everyone around us. As time goes on, we are likely to open up further what we will share with others; the hidden window decreases while the open window increases. This helps people to develop more effective working relationships with each other as they start to understand more about the other person.

The hidden window can be decreased by giving and receiving feedback and self-disclosure.

Part of leadership development is about helping people to develop a wider open window and to decrease the blind window. This can be done by verbal feedback, 360 feedback and involvement in many development activities that have already been described.

For successful communication, people need to be working in the open area. An understanding of how to develop this openness can be beneficial both personally and professionally.

Sharing this framework with groups can be useful in helping people to reflect on which behaviours they have in each of the windows and which areas they wish to change.

Development diaries

For some people, a learning diary (Table 12.2) can be a very powerful development tool. Those people who like to keep a diary are likely to find a development diary equally helpful. This may be as simple as free form writing about the key learning taken from each day at work or may be a more complicated, formalized version that can be used for the duration of a structured development programme.

The learning diary can then be used as a discussion document with a line manager or with an external coach, depending on the situation. For people who have a high reflector preference in their learning style, this can be a very effective tool for their development.

This format can be copied and used at the end of each session during a development programme or at the end of each day of a longer programme

Table 12.3 is taken from a development programme on leadership. This format was used by the participants who had just completed one of the first sessions, which had focussed on learning styles.

Table 12.2 Example development programme learning diary

Session title:	Date:
Notes for self-learning (insights, key issues, points to remember)	*Implications for self/team (What do I need to do more/less of change)*
Planned actions + timescales 1. 2. 3.	*Date for review* 1. 2. 3.

Table 12.3 Example development programme learning log

Session title: A one-hour session on learning styles	Date:
Notes for self-learning (insights, key issues, points to remember) Realized that I spend very little time reflecting on what I have done. Much prefer to learn by doing, rather than reading how to do something. Other people learn in different ways!	*Implications for self/team (What do I need to do more/less of, change, stop)* Need to think about my team members and colleagues and work out how they like to take in new things. Should stop thinking my way is the only right way of learning. Stop being critical of people taking time to think about things – does not mean they disagree. More reading!
Planned actions + timescales 1. Read book on coaching that I was given last year. 2. Discuss learning styles with my team and use it when doing PDPs with them. 3. Start to use a learning diary like this and read it once a week.	*Date for review* 1. By November 2. October – before reviews 3. Now!

Learning is like rowing upstream: not to advance is to drop back.

– Chinese proverb

Feedback exercises

These exercises provide excellent ways of ending a development programme that may have covered several modules or months in duration.

Feedback circle

Each person takes a *post it* note and writes the name of another person on it. They then write a specific piece of positive feedback for that person, taken from their perceptions of how the person has contributed and been involved in the development programme.

Each person is then given the different *post it* notes from their colleagues and takes them home to read them at the end of the programme.

This exercise can either be done anonymously or on a named basis. If the level of trust is high in the group by this point, there is obviously benefit in signing the feedback as this will mean more to the recipient.

Feedback carpark

This exercise can be used to improve open working in a group that may be part-way through a development programme and whose members need to work more effectively together. The exercise allows people the opportunity to give feedback to people on a one-to-one basis for any number of given subjects.

All the participants start in the main room (which acts as the carpark) and can pick each other to go out and spend a maximum of five minutes sharing feedback. They then come back to the main room and wait until asked by someone else to go out for a feedback conversation. This allows freedom for people to choose with whom they work and with whom they need to share feedback.

Possible questions to discuss could be:

- How well do we currently work together?
- What could we do to develop our working relationship?
- What do we do that frustrates each other?
- What do we do well in working together?

The questions can be chosen depending on the issues in the room. This exercise can also be framed in a positive way to ask people to pair up and share positive feedback with each other at the end of a programme.

Development circle

This is another version of the feedback carpark. Everyone sits in a circle. The facilitator then asks each personal to prepare a piece of feedback for the person sitting on their left. The feedback can be a simple 'what does this person do well/not so well in the group?' or can be future-focused on, e.g. 'one area to work on after this programme'. The key is to establish the circle first, so people do not choose to whom they want to give feedback. Several circles can be formed to create a more extended feedback exercise.

Life journey exercise

This is an exercise that can be used with senior managers to help them to identify how they became the leaders they are. It is a method of looking back to identify what events and experiences they have had that have influenced their behaviour and actions over the years (Figures 12.1 and 12.2).

The individual is encouraged to draw a chart with two axes – time and high/low points.

After they have highlighted the high points and low points, they are encouraged to add any significant details and to start to identify themes and points of interest. They may want to focus purely on career history or to also include personal and family history.

Each person is then asked to analyse their life journey and to describe the characteristics they have that have helped them to be successful. This will lead them

Step 1

- Plot a graph of your past
  (high points and low points)
  - Significant events
  - Rich detail and pictures
- Title or theme the different stages of your life

Step 2

- Agree and write down the characteristics you have
  that have helped you achieve the high points

Figure 12.1   The life journey process (www.represent.co.uk)

Step 3

- Chart your life journey going forward: 1 – 3 years ahead
  - Work
  - Personal
  - Friends and family
  - Community and spiritual
  - Health and wealth

Figure 12.2   Life journey – goals for success (www.represent.co.uk)

to identify their true values and beliefs about what is important for them in the future. The benefit of this exercise is that many people have rarely reflected on what has made them into the people they are today. People often realize that their parents had a high impact; their education has influenced how they think; and their childhood experiences in general have been far more influential than previously realized. Understanding why we behave as we do can often be the key to changing future behaviour. Understanding what we see as our achievements in life highlights the things we value most. For example, one person may regard gaining their degree as a high point, while another may regard their first bonus as a high point. Both of these signify somewhat different values in life.

One person completed her life journey picture and identified that the high points were around learning new skills and having time for enjoyment and relaxation. She started to understand why she had left corporate life to start up as a free lance consultant and recognized the enjoyment she gained from managing her own time and developing new skills as she took on new assignments. This helped her to plan what sort of work she wanted to do in the future and revealed the importance to her of having enough leisure time to enjoy her family life and her continuing professional learning and development.

As a next step to this exercise, people can then be asked to plan the next stage of their life journey. This can be done as purely as a career and job planning exercise or can be extended to cover the different areas of life that are important to them.

This can be done either as a picture or as a wheel of life type exercise where the headings are divided into different segments to represent the important areas for the person (Table 12.4).

Table 12.4 Personal goals

Career	Health	Wealth
Family	Friends	Children
Spiritual	Leisure	Community

The person is then asked to identify a key goal for each of the areas as chosen. Different timescales and milestones can be added depending on the nature of the development programme and the needs of the individual.

This life journey exercise can be used in a variety of ways. It can be employed on a one-to-one coaching basis, using the life journey exercise to identify what areas of business or life on which that the person wants to work.

It can also be used as a part of a group development programme where people are given time to complete the exercise individually and then share the pictures with each other. This discussion both helps the individual to reflect further on their life journey and also opens up areas for discussion with the partner. Obviously, the ground rules of confidentiality are particularly important in this type of exercise.

The art of positive thinking

> *Your drive to perform better will make you a one and only. But then again, you always are. You are the best in the world at being you. Don't ever try to be someone else, just be better at being you.*
>
> – Frank Dick OBE

Some people seem to have an in-built reservoir of self-esteem. Others need to work harder to keep it at a healthy level. The ability to think positively is a key driver for enjoying life. People who enjoy life are more likely to do well in life because they create virtuous circles of behaviour and action.

Case study

Several years ago, we were skiing in Italy with our close friends. The morning dawned with heavy clouds and flurries of snow. The weather was closing in and the world was looking very white outside. We set off with a sense of anticipation and one of the party started to voice doubts about the conditions. His wife and I went on ahead and called him to hurry up at the first lift. Once at the top, Peter decided that he was not going to be able to ski well in those conditions and started to worry about getting down the mountain. As he was one of the most skilled skiers, we took no notice and started to descend. Peter was still talking about the fact that he could not see but then sped off ahead of us. The next moment we heard a shout as he went down on the snow ahead of us. He had proved his point and gained a broken shoulder while doing so. Talking to him afterwards, he reflected that he had talked himself into failure. He was physically more than able to ski in those conditions but his attitude had not kept up with his aptitude.

'Confidence is contagious. So is lack of confidence'.

– Vince Lombardi

The mind's ability to influence behaviour is evident in many of us. Understanding that our attitude is what makes the difference is the key to unlocking our potential in life. In sport, we see some incredible world record beating performances. World class athletes have world class mental attitude. If we want to be world class leaders, we need to develop similar positive states of mind and to practise improving our attitude as well as our skills. Focussing on strengths rather than always looking for the weaknesses is one way to build self-esteem.

In terms of leadership development, too many performance review systems focus on areas for development rather than on areas of strength. Development programmes often ask individuals to identify their weaknesses rather than to highlight their strengths. There is great benefit in working to maximize strengths. Firstly, people feel more confident in developing skills that they are already good at. Secondly, it creates an environment of success and a virtuous circle of behaviour.

Reflection point:

As a leader, what do you do to encourage your people to feel good about themselves?

How often do you praise others for what they bring to the team?

How often do you reflect on your strengths and what you are good at?

How much time do you spend playing to your strengths?

How much time do you spend doing what you enjoy?

Table 12.5 Personal goal planning

Time line	What are your key goals?	What will success look like?
Five years from now		
Three years from now		
One year from now		

Personal vision setting

Research carried out with MBA students several years ago showed that the students who wrote down their career goals while at business school were 50 per cent more likely to have achieved them when reinterviewed five years later than those who did not write them down. The discipline of writing down our goals in life engenders higher levels of commitment and focus. A simple exercise to start this goal planning is shown in Table 12.5.

Encouraging individuals at the end of a development programme to write down their long-term performance goals can be a very effective way of developing motivated individuals who are focussed on achievement. This exercise can be used for long-term career goals or shorter-term performance goals depending on the setting. These goals can then be collected and sent to the individuals in one year time to act as a reminder of what they committed to doing.

Conclusion

The key to successful leadership development is a close working partnership between leaders and the leadership development managers who are employed to develop organizational capability. The topics in this book are designed to provide ideas and possible approaches to leadership development. However, there is no single route map to success. As we can see from the interviews with different business leaders, there are many factors that impact on leadership. My belief is that leaders may be successful only in their particular context and time. A successful leader in one organization can move company and find that their approach is not a recipe for success in another. Successful leaders have a wide repertoire of skills. They are flexible and adaptable in their behaviour. Most importantly, they work within the cultural context rather than in their personal comfort zone.

The role of the HR, learning and development is to develop consistent leadership capability that enables the organization to continually grow and succeed.

'If your actions inspire others to dream more, learn more, do more and become more, you are a leader'.

– John Quincy Adams

Index

INDEX